13.49
x

computer   hnology

Pass New CLAiT

using Microsoft Office 2003

P Evans

PAYNE-GALLWAY

www.payne-gallway.co.uk

Acknowledgements

Published by Payne-Gallway Publishers
Payne-Gallway is an imprint of Harcourt
Education Ltd., Halley Court, Jordan Hill,
Oxford, OX2 8EJ

Copyright © P.M. Heathcote and
R.S.U. Heathcote 2006

First published 2006

10 09 08 07 06

British Library Cataloguing in Publication Data
is available from the British Library on request

10-digit ISBN 1 904467 95 4

13-digit ISBN 978 1 904467 95 3

Cover picture © Katherine Palmers-Needham

Design and Artwork by Direction Marketing
and Communications Ltd

Printed by Everbest Printing Co. Ltd.

Ordering Information

You can order from:

Payne-Gallway,
FREEPOST (OF1771),
PO Box 381, Oxford OX2 8BR

Tel: 01865 888070
Fax: 01865 314029
E-mail: orders@payne-gallway.co.uk
Web: www.payne-gallway.co.uk

**We are grateful to the following organisations for
permission to use copyright material:**

Microsoft, Excel, Powerpoint, FrontPage, Outlook and
Windows are either registered trademarks or trademarks
of Microsoft Corporation in the United States and/or
other countries.

Screenshots from www.besafeonline.org
http://www.besafeonline.org/
http://www.besafeonline.org by permission of
Learning and Teaching Scotland.

Every effort has been made to contact copyright owners
of material published in this book. We would be glad
to hear from unacknowledged sources at the earliest
opportunity.

Photo credits

p.125 Getty Images/Photodisc; p.189 Digital Vision;
p204 Getty Images/Photodisc.

Contents

To pass this unit you must be able to:

- ✓ identify and use a computer workstation and appropriate system software

- ✓ use a computer's system software to create and manage files and folders

- ✓ identify and use word-processing software correctly to enter numbers, text and symbols accurately

- ✓ format basic paragraph and document properties

Before you start this chapter, you or your tutor should download a zipped file called **Resources for Chapter 1** from **www.payne-gallway.co.uk/newclait/student**. It will automatically unzip. Specify that the contents are to be saved in your My Documents folder.

Systems software and applications software

This unit introduces you to the two main types of computer software: **system software** and **application software**. System software controls how the hardware of a computer works and is usually just called the **operating system**. The operating system used in this book is **Microsoft®** **Windows® XP**. The main working area of Microsoft® Windows is called the **Desktop**. The main parts of the desktop when in Windows style are shown below.

Icons – double-click these to run application programs

Double-click My Documents to see the work stored on your computer

Start button – click here to run application programs

An open application icon – click here to return to this application program

The mouse pointer

The Taskbar

Figure 1.1

Applications software carries out a particular type of task for a user. This chapter introduces you to **word-processing software** which is used to **write**, **edit**, **format, check** and **print** text-based documents. The tasks you'll work through in this chapter are based on **Microsoft Word XP** (referred to as **Word**). Word, like most other word-processing software, allows users to enter and rearrange text, change the appearance of text using a wide variety of special formatting features, and check documents for errors using spelling and grammar check facilities. Word normally displays documents in **WYSIWYG** format. This stands for '**What you see is what you get**' and means that what you see on the screen looks exactly the same as the final printout.

The practice tasks that follow cover all the techniques you need to learn in order to pass a New CLAiT Unit 1 FILE MANAGEMENT AND E-DOCUMENT PRODUCTION assignment.

Practice tasks

Task 1   File management

The first part of an assessment task for this unit requires that you use a **login** – also called a **user name** – and/or **password** to gain access to data. Your tutor will give you this information and explain what to do.

During this task you'll need to take screen prints to provide evidence of what you've done. We are going to use Word to display and print out these screen prints.

Starting Word

You can load Word in one of two ways:

 Either double-click the **Word** icon on the **Desktop** in **Windows**,

 or click the **Start** button at the bottom left of the screen, then click **All Programs**, Microsoft **Office**.

Word 2003

Word Icon

Figure 1.2

The main **Word** document window will be displayed – it should look similar to the one in Figure 1.3 with a blank document ready to start work on.

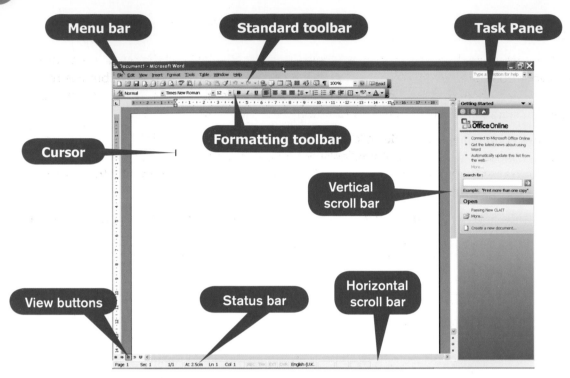

Figure 1.3

You will find out more about the different parts of the document window as you work through the practice tasks.

If there is no blank document:

New button

▶ *Either* click the **New** button on the **Standard** toolbar,

▶ *or* click **Create a new document** in the **Task Pane**.

You now have the option of either working with the current blank document or opening an existing one. The current blank document is fine for this task but we don't need it yet so we'll hide it at the bottom of the screen.

Minimize button

▶ Click the **Minimize** button in the top right corner of the Word window. The window will disappear. If you look at the **Taskbar** at the bottom of the desktop you'll see an icon called something like **Document1 – Microsoft Word**. To get the Word window back you just click this icon. Try this now, then minimise the window again.

TIP

If you want to find out what a toolbar button does just hold the mouse pointer over it for a few seconds. A **ToolTip** will appear with a brief description.

TIP

If you can't see the **Task Pane** or prefer not to work with it on the screen, click **View** in the menu bar and **Task Pane**.

Figure 1.4

6

Files and folders

The rest of this task describes how to organise your **files** and **folders**. All the work you create and save on your computer is stored in **files**. A file can be given any name you like but it is always a good idea to use a name that has something to do with the information that's stored in the file. In New CLAiT assignments you'll often be told exactly what file names to use.

Files are organised by saving them into **folders** that are also given names. Folders often contain **subfolders**. One folder that will be automatically set up on your computer is **My Documents**. This is where Windows expects you to save files and create folders and subfolders to organise them.

To see the contents of your **My Documents** folder double-click the shortcut icon on your desktop.

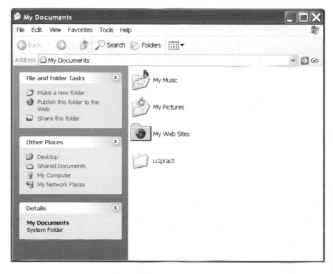

Figure 1.5

> **TIP**
>
> If you don't have a **My Documents** icon on your desktop click **Start** and **My Documents** on the **Start Menu**.
>
> My Documents

The contents of your My Documents folder might not look exactly the same but should contain a folder called **unit1pract**. If you can't see this folder ask your tutor to help you find it. (It needs to be downloaded from the **Student Resources** section of the website **www.payne-gallway.co.uk/newclait** and saved in your **My Documents** folder.)

Renaming files and folders

The first thing we will do is rename the folder called **unit1pract**.

▷ Right-click on the **unit1pract** folder and then click **Rename**.

▷ Type **your name (first name and last name) u1pt**. For example: **chester wheat u1pt**.

▷ Click anywhere in the **My Documents** window. The folder should now be displayed with **your name u1pt**.

Creating a subfolder

Next we will create a subfolder inside this folder.

⊚ Double-click the folder called **your name u1pt**. The contents of the folder will be displayed. You should see a subfolder called **files**, and three files called **breed, info** and **terriers**.

⊚ Right-click in any blank part of the folder window, click **New** and **Folder**, type the name **dogs** for the new subfolder, then click anywhere in the folder window.

Moving, copying and deleting files

Now we're going to move some files between subfolders and delete a subfolder.

First we'll copy the text file called **info** to the subfolder called **dogs**.

⊚ Right-click on the file called **info**. Then click **Copy** on the pop-up menu.

⊚ Right-click on the subfolder called **dogs**. Then click **Paste**.

Now we'll move a file from the **files** subfolder into the **dogs** subfolder.

⊚ Double-click the **files** subfolder. The contents of the folder will be displayed. You should see two files called **temp** and **engterrier**.

⊚ Right-click on the file called **temp**. Then click **Cut** on the pop-up menu.

 ⊚ Click the **Back** button to go back to the **your name u1pt** folder.

Back button

⊚ Right-click on the subfolder called **dogs**. Then click **Paste**.

Now we will delete one of the subfolders.

⊚ Right-click on the subfolder called **files**. Then click **Delete**. Click **Yes** in the **Confirm Folder Delete** window.

Taking screen prints

Next we will take some screen prints of the folders and their contents. The first of these screen prints needs to show the **your name u1pt** folder and its contents.

▶ Click the **Folders** button to get a more detailed view of the folders on your computer.

▶ Click the **Views** button, then the **Icons** button.

Figure 1.6

▶ Click the **your name u1pt** folder in the left pane. The **My Documents** window on your computer should now look something like the one in Figure 1.7.

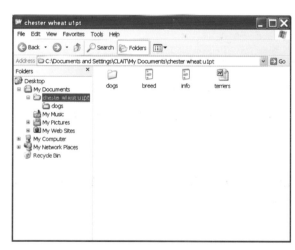

Figure 1.7

▶ Take a screen print of this window by holding down the **Alt** key and then pressing the **Print Scr** key.

▶ Get the **Word** window back by clicking the icon in the Taskbar at the bottom of the desktop.

Figure 1.8

Folders

Folders button

Views button

TIP

The contents of the window showing your folders might not look exactly like the one shown here. It is important your screen prints show the name of the folder along with all of the contents of that folder.

⊙ Click **Edit** on the menu bar, and then click **Paste**. The screen print will appear.

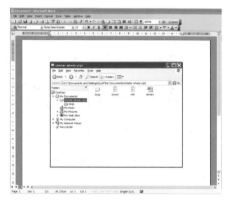

Figure 1.9

Inserting a page break

We will put the next screen print on a new page in the current document. To go to a new page, we need to insert a **page break**.

⊙ Click **Insert** on the menu bar, and then click **Break**. The **Break** dialogue window will appear.

⊙ Click **Page break** in the list of break types if it isn't already selected, then click **OK** and a new blank page will appear.

Now we're ready to take the next screen print. It will show the **dogs** subfolder and its contents.

⊙ Get the **My Documents** window back by clicking the icon at the bottom of the screen.

Figure 1.10

⊙ Click the **dogs** subfolder in the left pane. The **My Documents** window on your computer should now look something like the one below.

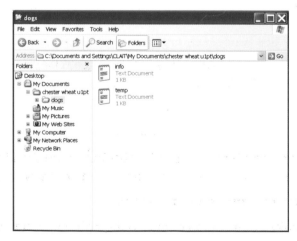

Figure 1.11

⊚ Take a screen print of this window by holding down the **Alt** key and then pressing the **Print Scr** key.

⊚ Bring the **Word** window back again by clicking the icon at the bottom of the screen.

⊚ Click **Edit** on the menu bar and then click **Paste**. The screen print will appear.

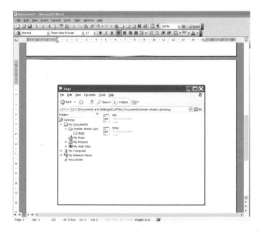

Figure 1.12

Inserting a footer

Before printing this document you are going to insert a **footer** that contains your name and today's date.

⊚ Click **View** on the menu bar and then click **Header and Footer**. The **Header and Footer** toolbar will appear. The cursor will be flashing in the header section.

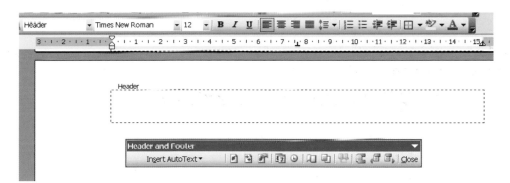

Figure 1.13

⊚ Click the **Switch between Header and Footer** button on the **Header and Footer** toolbar. The cursor will start flashing in the footer section ready for you to enter something.

⊚ Type **your name (first name and last name)**.

⊚ Press the **Tab** key twice to move the cursor to the right-hand side of the footer section.

Switch between
Header and Footer
button

Insert Date button

▶ Click the **Insert Date** button on the **Header and Footer** toolbar. Today's date will be inserted automatically. Your footer section should now look something like the one below.

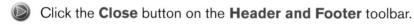

Figure 1.14

Close button

▶ Click the **Close** button on the **Header and Footer** toolbar.

Saving a document

Now we'll save this document in the subfolder called **your name u1pt**:

▶ *Either* click **File** on the menu bar and then click **Save**,

Save button

▶ *or* click the **Save** button on the **Standard** toolbar. The **Save As** dialogue box will appear. The name highlighted in the **File name** box is the default filename which is normally the first line of a document or something like **Doc1**. This can be changed to whatever you like.

▶ Click **My Documents** on the left of the screen to display the contents of your My Documents folder.

▶ Double-click the subfolder called **your name u1pt**, then type the name **screengrabs** and click the **Save** button. The **Save As** dialogue window will disappear. The filename **screengrabs** will be displayed at the top of the screen. This document will now be saved with this name whenever you click the **Save** button on the **Standard** toolbar.

Printing a document

Print button

Now you're ready to **print** the document. You will normally be required to print at least three documents during a Unit 1 assignment.

▶ Click the **Print** button on the **Standard** toolbar.

Closing a document and exiting Word

Finally you need to close this document and close Word. You can perform both these instructions in a single operation:

▶ *Either* click **File** on the menu bar, then click **Exit,**

▶ *or* click **X** in the top right-hand corner of the screen.

TIP

If you want to close a document without closing **Word**, select **File** on the menu bar and then **Close**.

Task 2 Creating and setting up a new document

During a Unit 1 assignment you'll be asked to create one completely new word-processed document from scratch. This task takes you through the steps you'll need to follow to do this.

▶ Load **Word** and create a new blank document.

Setting page orientation and margins

The first thing we need to do is make sure the **page orientation** for the document is set to **portrait**.

▶ Click **File** on the menu bar and then click **Page Setup**. The **Page Setup** dialogue box will be displayed. The **Margins** tab should already be selected – if it isn't just click on it. Your screen should look like this one.

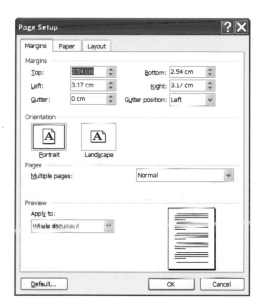

Figure 1.15

▶ Click **Portrait** in the **Orientation** section if it isn't already selected.

Next we'll set the margins for the document. The margin settings for a document determine how much blank space will be left between the text and the page edges. Changing the margin settings is one method that can be used to fit more text on each page of a document.

> **TIP**
>
> During a New CLAiT word-processing assignment you'll be asked to set the margins when you create a new document.

We are going to set the top, bottom, left and right margins for this document to **2.1 cm**.

⊙ Click inside the boxes for the **top**, **bottom**, **left** and **right** margins. Replace each value with **2.1 cm**.

Figure 1.16

Setting line spacing

Line spacing is used to change the amount of space between lines of text. Normal text is single spaced. Common line spacing options include 'single', '5 times', and 'double'.

> **TIP**
>
> During a Unit 1 assignment you'll normally be asked to set the line spacing for a new document and change some of the line spacing in part of an existing document.

We're going to set the line spacing for this document to **Single**.

⊙ Click **Format** on the menu bar, and then click **Paragraph**. The **Paragraph** dialogue box will be displayed.

⊙ Click the arrow next to the **Line spacing** box, and in the drop-down list of options that appears click **Single** if it is not already selected, then click **OK**.

> **TIP**
>
> Single line spacing is the default setting for **Word** documents. If you're asked to use single line spacing it is still a good idea to check the setting. You might be asked to use a different type of line spacing when setting up a document.

Setting font type, size and alignment

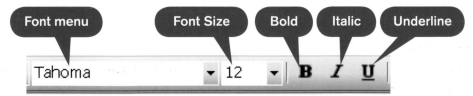

Figure 1.17

Next we'll set the font size and type for this document.

⊙ Click the arrow on the right of the **Font menu** box in the **Formatting** toolbar. You'll see a scroll-down list of available fonts.

Scroll down the list until you see a font called **Tahoma**. Choose this font by clicking its name once with the left mouse button.

 Click the arrow on the right of the **Font Size** box. You'll see a scroll-down list of available sizes.

 Click once on **12** in the list with the left mouse button.

> **TIP**
>
> Always check carefully to make sure you have used the font type and size specified in an assignment. If you've used the wrong font type or font size throughout a document, fix it by clicking **Edit** on the menu bar and **Select All**, then choosing the font type or size again.

Now we'll set the **text alignment** for this document. The alignment buttons on the **Formatting** toolbar provide the quickest way to change the alignment of text in a document.

Text can be **left aligned**, **centred**, **right aligned**, or **fully justified**.

Figure 1.18

We're going to set the text in this document to be **fully justified**.

 Click the **Justify** button on the **Formatting** toolbar.

Justify button

> **TIP**
>
> The alignment of text can be changed at any time by clicking on a line or inside a paragraph, then choosing an alignment option on the **Formatting** toolbar.

Entering text

Now you're ready to enter some text.

 The **cursor** should already be flashing at the top of the blank document – if it isn't, just point at the top of the page and click the left mouse button.

 Enter the heading: **Manchester Toy Terriers**

 Press the **Enter** key twice to leave a blank line and get the cursor into the correct position to start a new paragraph.

Enter the paragraph below. You should press the **Space Bar** once to leave gaps between words, or after commas and full stops.

 TIP

You don't need to press **Enter** at the end of each line of a paragraph – the word-processing software will move down when it is ready using a feature called **word wrap**.

The Manchester Toy Terrier is one of the oldest English breeds. It can be traced back over 400 years to Black and Tan terriers used as ratters. Today's Manchester Toy Terrier is a small, lively, playful and affectionate dog, weighing less than twelve pounds. These little terriers have a smooth, shiny jet black coat with light tan markings. The tan colours probably came about due to crosses with the Italian Greyhound.

TIP

When a New CLAiT assignment tells you to '**insert a paragraph break and clear line space**' it means leave a single blank line between paragraphs. Just press **Enter** twice at the end of a paragraph to do this.

 When you've finished press the **Enter** key twice to leave a blank line and get the cursor into the correct position to start the next paragraph. Your document should now look like the one below.

> Manchester Toy Terriers
>
> The Manchester Toy Terrier is one of the oldest English breeds. It can be traced back over 400 years to Black and Tan terriers used as ratters. Today's Manchester Toy Terrier is a small, lively, playful and affectionate dog, weighing less than twelve pounds. These little terriers have a smooth, shiny jet black coat with light tan markings. The tan colours probably came about due to crosses with the Italian Greyhound.

Figure 1.19

 Check your paragraph and compare it carefully with the one above before you carry on.

 Any mistakes you find must be corrected – this can be done by pointing and clicking to the right of the text you want to change, before deleting it by pressing the **Backspace** key.

TIP

Checking your work carefully during an assignment is very important. Missing words, sentences or punctuation all count as **critical errors** that will cause you to fail a final assessment.

▷ Now enter the second paragraph below in the same manner as the first.

Manchester Toy Terriers are perfect for any size home. They are alert and courageous, making them excellent guard dogs. Their exercise and grooming needs are minimal which makes them a good choice for elderly or disabled owners. They are also good family dogs but aren't a good choice for anyone with other small pet animals such as rats, gerbils or guinea pigs.

▷ Check through this paragraph and correct any errors. Your document should now contain the **heading**, then a **line space**, then the two **paragraphs**, separated by another **line space**.

Next you need to save this document in the subfolder called **dogs** that you created in Task 1.

▷ *Either* click **File** on the menu bar, then click **Save**,

▷ or click the **Save button** on the **Standard** toolbar. The **Save** dialogue box will appear.

Save button

▷ Click **My Documents** on the left of the screen to display the contents of your **My Documents** folder.

▷ Double-click the subfolder called **your name u1pt**.

▷ Double-click the subfolder called **dogs**.

▷ Type the name **toydog**.

| File name: | toydog | ⌄ | Save |
| Save as type: | Word Document | ⌄ | Cancel |

Figure 1.20

▷ Click the **Save** button. The **Save** dialogue window will disappear. The filename **toydog** will displayed at the top of the screen. Your document will now be saved with this name whenever you click the **Save** button on the **Standard** toolbar.

▷ Close the document and close Word.

Task 3   Check spellings

Word, like most other word-processing applications, offers a spelling and grammar checking facility.

A **spell check** uses a built-in dictionary to check the spellings in a document. When a spell checker finds words that are unknown, it will offer possible alternatives from its dictionary and ask if you want to choose a replacement, delete the unknown word completely, keep the word as it is, or enter your own alternative word.

A **grammar checker** uses a built-in set of 'rules' about the grammar of the language that you are using. Grammar checkers don't check spellings they just check that what you've written follows the rules of a language correctly.

This task introduces you to the spelling and grammar check facility in Word. This is a very useful tool for checking your work for the small errors that often cause candidates to fail New CLAiT assignments.

▶ Load **Word**.

To practise using the spell check you need to load a pre-prepared document called **spelling_ errors.doc**. To load this document:

Open button

▶ *Either* click **File** on the menu bar, and then click **Open**,

▶ *or* click the **Open** button on the **Standard** toolbar. The **Open** dialogue box will appear. Your tutor will tell you where to find this document. In the example below the document is inside a folder called **Unit 1**.

▶ Click on the file called **spelling_errors** and then click **Open**. The document will be opened – it should look exactly like the one below.

Transforming yodr home are often much cheaper and more easily done than you might expect. Startling results can be obtained from the simplest of techniques and you don't have to be a 'do it yourself' enthusiast to use them. It's amazing what a bit of emulssion will do for the dowdiest of roms. Home devoration opens up great posibilities for the practical person, for not only is the work easy, profitable and interesting, but there is something concrete to show for the lanour.

Figure 1.21

Spelling and
Grammar button

▶ Click the **Spelling and Grammar** button on the Standard toolbar. The **Spelling and Grammar** dialogue box will appear if errors are present. If the text is OK a 'completed' message appears.

Figure 1.22

The first error highlighted in red is a spelling error and the suggested spelling is correct.

▶ Click the **Change** button to accept and make the correction.

▶ The next error – highlighted in green on line one – is a grammatical error and the suggested change is correct, so click the **Change** button to accept and make the correction.

Now work through the rest of the document yourself. Remember that the spelling and grammar checking facility is not foolproof – sometimes you will need to click the Ignore button when a suggested change is not required. When you've finished, your version of the document should be the same as the one below.

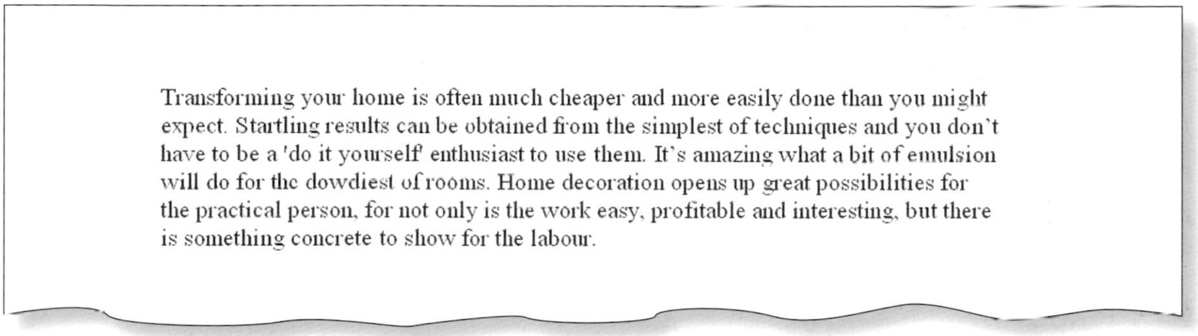

Transforming your home is often much cheaper and more easily done than you might expect. Startling results can be obtained from the simplest of techniques and you don't have to be a 'do it yourself' enthusiast to use them. It's amazing what a bit of emulsion will do for the dowdiest of rooms. Home decoration opens up great possibilities for the practical person, for not only is the work easy, profitable and interesting, but there is something concrete to show for the labour.

Figure 1.23

▶ Click **File**, **Save As** on the menu bar. Save this document in the subfolder called **your name u1pt** with the new filename **spellcheck**.

Next we'll use the spell check facility to check for errors in your new document.

▶ Open the document **toydog**.

▶ Run the spelling and grammar checker and correct any errors.

Inserting a header

Before you save the document again we will insert a header that contains your name and centre number, and a footer that contains the date and a filename.

▷ Click **View** on the menu bar, and then click **Header and Footer**.

▷ Type **your name (first name and last name)** and **centre number** in the header section. You will need to ask your tutor for the correct centre number.

Figure 1.24

Switch between Header and Footer button

▷ Click the **Switch between Header and Footer** button on the **Header and Footer** toolbar.

▷ Click the **Insert Date** button on the **Header and Footer** toolbar.

Insert Date button

▷ Press the **Tab** key twice to move the cursor to the right-hand side of the footer section.

▷ On the **Header and Footer** toolbar, click the **Insert AutoText** button, then click **Filename** from the list of options. Your footer section should now look something like the one below.

Figure 1.25

Close button

▷ Click the **Close** button on the **Header and Footer** toolbar. Now we'll save the file keeping the same name **toydog**.

Save button

▷ Click the **Save** button on the **Standard** toolbar. Close the document and then close **Word.**

Task 4 Formatting text and creating tables

The buttons on the **Formatting** toolbar provide the quickest way to change the appearance of text in a document by formatting it. The formatting tools you might need to use during a Unit 1 assignment are shown below.

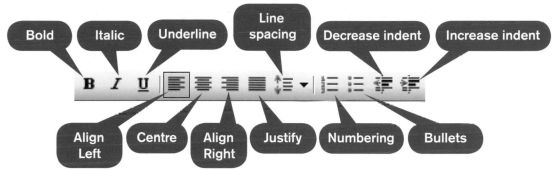

Figure 1.26

Selecting text

Text in a document must be **highlighted** before it can be formatted. Highlighting makes the selected portion of text turn black with the individual characters white.

> Transforming your home is often much cheaper and more easily done than you might expect. **Startling results can be obtained from the simplest of techniques and you don't have to be a 'do it yourself' enthusiast to use them.** It's amazing what a bit of emulsion will do for the dowdiest of rooms. Home decoration opens up great possibilities for

Figure 1.27

There are several ways to select text. Some of the more commonly used techniques are described below. You are going to use the **spellcheck** document from the last task to practise those techniques and apply some formatting.

⊳ Load **Word**, and open the document **spellcheck** – use this document to practise highlighting and formatting text. You won't need to use this document again so don't worry if you make mistakes or the text starts looking a bit strange!

To highlight a single word:

⊳ Position the mouse pointer over the word and double-click the left mouse button.

> Transforming your home is of
> expect. Startling results can be
> have to be a 'do it yourself' en

Figure 1.28

⊳ Now try this a few times anywhere in the document. Click the left mouse button once anywhere in the document to deselect the highlighted word before you try again.

⊳ Once you're happy with this technique, try making some individual words bold, italic or underlined by using the buttons on the **Formatting** toolbar.

To highlight a single line:

- Position the mouse pointer in the **left margin area** next to the line.

- When the pointer changes to a right pointing arrow, single-click the left mouse button.

> Transforming your home is often much cheaper and more easily done than you might
> expect. Startling results can be obtained from the simplest of techniques and you don't
> have to be a 'do it yourself' enthusiast to use them. It's amazing what a bit of emulsion

Figure 1.29

- Try this a few times now anywhere in the document.

- Once you're happy with this technique try making some individual lines **numbered**, **bulleted** or **indented** by using the buttons on the **Formatting** toolbar.

If you accidentally press any key on the keyboard while text is highlighted, it will be deleted. If this happens click the **Undo** button on the **Standard** toolbar.

Undo button

To highlight a single paragraph:

- First of all create a new paragraph to practise on by placing the cursor after the words '**...to use them.**', and pressing **Enter** twice.

- **Triple-click** the left mouse button anywhere in the paragraph. Try this a few times now anywhere in the document.

- Once you're happy with this technique try changing the line spacing of some individual paragraphs – use the **Format**, **Paragraph** option on the menu bar for this.

A commonly used method of highlighting is called **clicking and dragging**. You can click and drag over several words, paragraphs or even a whole document.

To highlight a block of text by clicking and dragging:

- Position the mouse pointer where you want to start, click and hold down the left mouse button, then slowly drag the mouse to where you want to stop highlighting. If you go too far, keep your finger on the left mouse button and drag the mouse in the opposite direction.

- Let go of the left mouse button when the required text is highlighted.

- Try this a few times now in the document. This technique can be quite difficult to master if you're not confident using a mouse, so you might need to practise it for a while.

- Once you're happy with this technique, try out any of the formatting tools on some different blocks of highlighted text, then close the document.

Creating a table

Now we're going to work through the steps needed to create and format a table – we'll use the document you've created to do this.

- Open the document **toydog**.

- Position the cursor at the end of the second paragraph after the text ending **...or guinea pigs.**

- Press the **Enter** key twice. This will leave a blank line between the end of the paragraph and the point where the table will be inserted.

- Click **Table** on the menu bar, then click **Insert**, **Table**. The **Insert Table** dialogue box will appear.

- Type **2** in the **Number of columns** box. You can also use the small arrows on the right of the box to do this if you prefer.

- Press the **Tab** key to move to the **Number of rows** box and enter **5**, then click **OK**. A table will be inserted into your document.

owners. They are also good family dogs but aren't a good choice for anyone with other small pet animals such as rats, gerbils or guinea pigs.

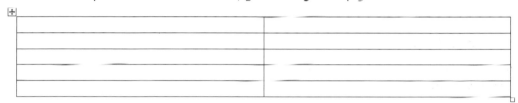

Figure 1.30

- Enter the data shown below in the table:

Group	Toy
Origin	England
Height	25 to 35 cm
Weight	4.5 to 7.5 kg
Life span	12 to 14 years

Now you need to format the table by changing the width of the columns to exactly fit the text inside them. This will make your table look like the one shown above.

Position the pointer over the line separating the two columns and wait for the pointer to change into a **double-headed arrow**.

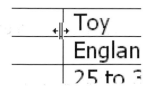

Figure 1.31

 Click the left mouse button twice. The width of the first column will be changed automatically to fit to the widest piece of text in the column.

 Repeat this process, with the pointer positioned over the line on the right side of the second column. Your table should now look very similar to the one in the example.

> **TIP**
>
> You can also click and hold the left mouse button and drag to the right or left to change the width of columns in a table.

Formatting text in a table

We will format the text in the table.

 Highlight the text in the first column.

B
Bold button

 Click the **Bold** button on the **Formatting** toolbar to make all the text bold.

> **TIP**
>
> You can highlight all the text in a column by positioning the pointer above the column until it turns into a down-arrow, then clicking the left mouse button. Triple-clicking in a cell will highlight just the text in that cell

Centre button

 Highlight the first four cells in the second column, click the **Centre** button on the **Formatting** toolbar to centre align the text in these cells, then highlight the last cell in the second column.

I
Italic button

 Click the **Italic** button on the **Formatting** toolbar to make the text in this cell italic. Your table should now look like the one below.

Group	Toy
Origin	England
Height	25 to 35 cm
Weight	4.5 to 7.5 Kg
Life span	*12 to 14 years*

Figure 1.32

Formatting table border lines

Now we need to make the table border lines stand out a little more.

- ▶ Click anywhere inside the table.
- ▶ Click **Table**, **Select** on the menu bar and then click **Table**.

The table will be highlighted.

- ▶ Click **Table** on the menu bar and then click **Table Properties...**.

The **Table Properties** dialogue window will be displayed.

- ▶ Click the **Borders and Shading...** button.
- ▶ Click **All** in the list of settings.
- ▶ Click the down arrow on the right of the **Width** box.

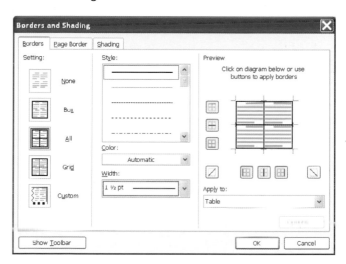

Figure 1.33

- ▶ Click **1½ pt** in the drop-down list of line widths.
- ▶ Click **OK**.

The **Table Properties** dialogue window will reappear.

- ▶ Click **OK**.

The table border lines will be much thicker. Your table should now look like the one below.

Group	Toy
Origin	England
Height	25 to 35 cm
Weight	4.5 to 7.5 kg
Life span	*12 to 14 years*

Save button

Finally, **print** the document and save it, keeping the name **toydog**. To do this:

- Click the **Save** button on the **Standard** toolbar.
- Click the **Print** button on the **Standard** toolbar, close the document then close **Word**.

Print button

Task 5   Editing and reformatting documents

During a Unit 1 assignment you will be required to edit the text in an existing document. You will be asked to add, delete and move text. Some of the text will also need to be reformatted.

- Load **Word**.

- Open your copy of the prepared document called **terriers** – this should be in the folder called **your name u1pt** inside **My Documents**. This document should look exactly like the one below.

> Manchester Toy Terriers were originally known as the Black and Tan Terrier in the 16th century in England and were used as a ratter and a companion dog. Contests between terriers and betting on how long it would take the dogs to kill a number of rats became popular. The toy variety was created by selectively breeding the smallest dogs.
>
> Manchester Toy Terriers make devoted pets that are very faithful to their owners. The breed peaked in popularity during Victorian times. Manchester Toy Terriers are thought to be the oldest English toy breed in existence. The toy variety was created by selectively breeding the smallest dogs. The Italian Greyhound and Whippet are both thought to have contributed to the breed.
>
> Manchester Toy Terriers are a low maintenance dog. The short, fine coat doesn't need regular grooming or bathing. Very small children can often be too rough with this delicate breed. These dogs require just small amounts of exercise; a short walk or a run the garden is normally enough. They don't need a great deal of space which makes them suitable for young families and single people.
>
> Typical breed characteristics:
>
> A long, slender tail
> Almond shaped eyes
> A short, single, fine coat
> Tan markings on the lower legs and sides of the muzzle

Figure 1.34

- The first thing we'll do is save this file with a different name in the **dogs** subfolder you created earlier.

- Click **File** on the menu bar and then click **Save As**. The **Save As** dialogue box will appear.

- Click **My Documents** on the left of the screen to display the contents of your **My Documents** folder.

- Double-click the subfolder called **your name u1pt**, then double-click the subfolder called **dogs**.

- Enter the new file name **terrierinfo** and click **OK.**

Now we'll add, delete and move some text in this document.

Adding text

 Position the mouse pointer in the first paragraph after **...companion dog.**, click the left mouse button and press the **Spacebar** once, then type the following sentence:

In England during the 1800s these terriers were very much in demand due to the large rat population.

Deleting text

 In the first paragraph highlight the text:

The toy variety was created by selectively breeding the smallest dogs.

 Press the **Backspace** or the **Delete** key on the keyboard. The last sentence of the first paragraph should now have disappeared. Check your work carefully and make any corrections before you carry on.

Moving text

 In the third paragraph highlight the sentence:

Very small children can often be too rough with this delicate breed.

Once text is highlighted there are a number of ways to move it. The technique we're going to use is **cut and paste**.

 Click the **Cut** button on the **Standard** toolbar. The sentence will disappear.

Cut button

Point and click after the sentence ending **...single people**.

Paste button

Click the **Paste** button on the **Standard** toolbar and the sentence will reappear. The deleted sentence should now appear at the end of the paragraph be sure to include a space before the moved sentence.

Indenting text

Next we'll reformat some of the text in the document.

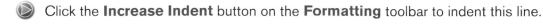 Position the cursor anywhere in the line of text:

Typical breed characteristics:

Click the **Increase Indent** button on the **Formatting** toolbar to indent this line.

Increase Indent button

Adding bullets

 Highlight the four lines of text:

A long, slender tail

Almond shaped eyes

A short, single, fine coat

Tan markings on the lower legs and sides of the muzzle

Bullets button

Increase Indent button

Click the **Bullets** button on the **Formatting** toolbar to bullet these four lines of text. The bullets will appear and the text will stay highlighted – leave it like this.

Click the **Increase Indent** button on the **Formatting** toolbar to indent these lines of text, then click **Format**, **Paragraph** on the menu bar, and set the **line spacing** for this text to **1.5 lines**. This part of your document should now look like the example below.

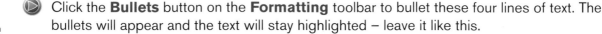

great deal of space which makes them suitable for young families and single people. Very small children can often be too rough with this delicate breed.

Typical breed characteristics:

- A long, slender tail
- Almond shaped eyes
- A short, single, fine coat
- Tan markings on the lower legs and sides of the muzzle

Figure 1.35

Finding and replacing text

We will replace the word **Manchester** with the word **English** wherever it appears in this document. The **Find and Replace** facility in Word allows you look for one word and replace it with another. This can be done **selectively** for just part of a document or **globally**. Selective find and replace will check each time it finds the search word to ask whether or not you want it replacing. Global find and replace finds every occurrence of the search word and replaces it without asking first.

Click **Edit** on the menu bar and then click **Replace...** . The **Find and Replace** dialogue box will appear.

Click in the **Find what** box and type **Manchester**.

Click in the **Replace with** box and type **English**. Click **Replace All** to carry out a global find and replace. In the message box that appears, telling you that **4** replacements have been made, click **OK**.

The next thing you need to do is add some information to the footer of this document.

Click **View** on the menu bar and then click **Header and Footer**.

Switch between Header and Footer button

Click the **Switch between Header and Footer** button on the Header and Footer toolbar, then type in **your name (first name and last name)** and **centre number**.

Insert Date
button

▶ Press the **Tab** key once to move the cursor to the centre of the footer section, then click the **Insert Date** button on the **Header and Footer** toolbar. Today's date will be inserted automatically.

▶ Press the **Tab** key once to move the cursor to the right-side of the footer section. Click the **Insert AutoText** button on the **Header and Footer** toolbar, then select **Filename** from the list of options. Your footer section should now look something like the one below

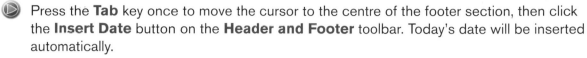

Footer

CHESTER WHEAT 30175   21/10/2006   terrierinfo

Figure 1.36

Close

Close button

Spell Check
button

▶ Click the **Close** button on the **Header and Footer** toolbar, then before you carry on, click the **spell check** button to check your work.

Word count

We will carry out a word count for the number of words in the document and type the figure after the bulleted list.

▶ Click **Tools** on the menu bar and then click **Word Count**. The word count window will appear containing a set of statistics about the document. Make a note of the number of words in the document.

▶ Now click at the end of the last bulleted item, press the **Enter** key twice, and type the figure you have for the number of words.

That finishes everything we need to do to this document – now you can save it and print a copy.

▶ Save the document keeping the filename **terrierinfo**, print one copy, then close the document and shut down **Word.**

That's the end of the practice tasks. Now try the full New CLAiT assignments that follow.

Practice assignment 1

Scenario

You are working as an Education Officer for a company that sells computer control and data-logging equipment to schools. Your job is to prepare resources for pupils and teachers.

Assessment Objectives	TASK 1
1a	1 During this assessment you will need a login and/or password to gain access to data. Your tutor will tell you the password and/or login and when it will be needed.

2a
2b
	2 You need to organise your files and folders.
	    a) Rename the **folder u1pras1** to be **your name (first and last name) u1pa1**.
	    b) In this folder create a new sub-folder called **resources**.

2e	3 Copy the text file provided called **temp** to the folder **resources**.
2d	4 Move the text file provided called **info** from the folder **files** into the folder **resources**.
2c	5 Delete the folder **files** and its contents. a) Take a screen print as evidence of the folder called **your name (first and last name) u1pa1** and the contents of this folder.
1b	b) Take a screen print of the sub-folder called **resources** and the contents of this folder.
1d	c) In the footer of the page(s) displaying the screen prints, enter **your name u1pa1** and **today's date**.
1e	d) Save the screen print(s) within your filing structure.
3g	The file(s) do not need to be displayed in the folder structure on the screen print. e) Print the file(s) containing the screen prints. Make sure that all the contents of the folder and sub-folder are clearly visible on the print(s).
	6 Close any open files.

Assessment Objectives	TASK 2

1   Create a new word-processing document.

2   Set the page orientation to **portrait**.

1b   3   Set the **top**, **left** and **right** page margins to **1.8 cm**.

3a   4   Set the font to an **Arial** font type.

3b   5   Set the font size to **12**.

4a   6   a)   Enter the following text in **single linespacing**.

4b   b)   Make sure that the text is **fully justified**.

3c

Computer control

3d

4h

Computer control is the use of a computer to monitor and control an external process. Input sensors are connected to the computer. These sensors are used by the computer to monitor the various parts of a process that it is controlling. Sensors are used to measure changes in the value of some physical quantity, such as temperature or light.

Input signals are useless to the computer if it does not know how to interpret them or what actions to take as a result. Before any process can be controlled by a computer a control program must be written by a human to tell the computer what to do.

The signals from input sensors are used by the computer to monitor what is going on in the process that it is controlling. Depending upon the value of an input signal from a sensor and the instructions given in its control program, the computer makes a decision about whether an output signal is needed to switch on or off some part of the process's hardware.

7   a)   Check the file for any errors and carry out a spell check.

    b)   In the header, enter **your name u1pa1** and your **centre number**.

    c)   In the footer, insert an **automatic date** and an **automatic filename**.

3g   8   a)   Save the file using the filename **control** in the sub-folder called resources.

    b)   Close the file.

Assessment Objectives	TASK 3

1d

1. Open your saved file called **control**.

2. A table needs to be inserted in the document.

   a) Insert a paragraph break and a clear line space at the end of the first paragraph immediately after the text ending:
   ... temperature or light.

1c
   b) Create a table with 2 columns and 5 rows.

3d
   c) Enter the data below in the table:

3e

3f

Sensor	Used to help control
Light	Street lights
Infrared	Burglar alarms
Temperature	Greenhouses

4d

   d) Make sure all borders will be displayed for the table on the printout as shown above.

   e) Make sure all data in the table is fully displayed.

3. Format the heading **Sensor** to be bold.

4. a) Centre only the text in the second column.

   b) The remaining text must be left-aligned.

5. Save your file keeping the filename **control**.

4c
6. Print one copy of the file **control**.

7. Close the file called **control**.

Assessment Objectives	TASK 4

3c

You will need to make the amendments below in a file that has been provided for you.

1. a) Open the file provided called **data logging** that is in your folder called your name u1pa1 (first and last name).

   b) Save the file using the new filename **loggers** in your folder called **resources**.

1e
2. Go to the paragraph that starts **Data logging is...**

Insert the following text as a new sentence after **... period of time.**

The data which is being logged is measured using sensors or probes.

1c	3	Go to the paragraph that starts **Data is often ...**
		Delete the text/sentence:
		Another way of logging data is to use the input-output port on the computer.
1d	4	In the paragraph that starts **Data logging is ...**
		Move only the text
4e		**Once the data has been collected it can be analysed by the computer.**
		to follow the sentence ending ...**human supervision.**
4g	5	a) Apply a bullet character to the following three lines of text:

scientific data

remote weather data

traffic flow data

4f		b) Apply double line spacing to the bulleted text only.
		c) Indent the text:
		Data logging is used to collect:
		from the left margin.
3h	6	Replace the word **logger** with the words **data logger** wherever they occur
3i		(twice in all).
4h	7	In the footer enter:

your name u1pa1

an automatic date

an automatic filename.

4i	8	Check your text for accuracy.
3g	9	a) Using the software facilities, carry out a word count in the file.
		b) Enter the number of words on your printout at least two lines below the bulleted list. You may use any alignment for this.
3d	10	Save the file keeping the filename **loggers**.
3d	11	Print one copy of the file **loggers**.
3j	12	Close all files and folders.
		Make sure you check your printouts for accuracy.
1d		You should have the following printouts:

your screen print(s)

control

1e	**loggers**

Practice assignment 2

Scenario

You are working as a reporter for a local newspaper. Your job is to prepare articles on e-commerce.

Assessment Objectives	TASK 1
1a	1 During this assessment you will need a login and/or password to gain access to data. Your tutor will tell you the password and/or login and when it will be needed.
2a	2 You need to organise your files and folders.
2b	a) Rename the folder u1pras2 to be **your name (first and last name) u1pa2**.
	b) In this folder create a new sub-folder called **articles**.
2e	3 Copy the text file provided called **research** to the folder **articles**.
2d	4 Move the text file provided called **temp** from the folder **files** into the folder **articles**.
2c	5 Delete the folder **files** and its contents.
1b	6 a) Take a screen print as evidence of the folder called **your name (first and last name) u1pa2** and the contents of this folder.
1d	b) Take a screen print of the sub-folder called **articles** and the contents of this folder.
1e	c) In the footer of the page(s) displaying the screen prints, enter **your name u1pa2** and **today's date**.
3g	d) Save the screen print(s) within your filing structure. The file(s) do not need to be displayed in the folder structure on the screen print.
	e) Print the file(s) containing the screen prints. Make sure that all the contents of the folder and sub-folder are clearly visible on the print(s).
	7 Close any open files.

Assessment Objectives	TASK 2
1b	1 Create a new word-processing document.
3a	2 Set the page orientation to **portrait**.
3b	3 Set the **top**, **left** and **right** page margins to **2.3 cm**.
4a	4 Set the font to a **Tahoma** font type.
4b	5 Set the font size to **11**.

3c	6 a)	Enter the following text in **single line spacing**.
3d	b)	Make sure that the text is **left justified**.
4h		**Cheque clearing**

When a cheque has been written and paid into the bank a process called clearing begins. This describes the steps that take place before the amount written on the cheque is transferred to the account of the person whose name is on the cheque.

The first stage of the clearing process takes place at the bank where the cheque was paid in. The amount written on each cheque is input by hand and printed at the bottom of the cheque using special magnetic ink. Every day each bank sends all the cheques that have been paid in that day to a central processing centre called a clearing house.

At the clearing house data printed on the cheques is automatically input by passing them through special magnetic ink readers. Details of all the amounts to be added to and deducted from customer accounts are then sent to each bank's computer centre. Once the banks receive this information customer accounts are updated and money is transferred. The cheque clearing process is summarised in the table below.

3g	7 a)	Check the file for any errors and carry out a spell check.
	b)	In the header, enter **your name u1pa2** and your **centre number**.
	c)	In the footer, insert an **automatic date** and an **automatic filename**.
1d	8 a)	Save the file using the filename **cheques** in the sub-folder called **articles**.
	b)	Close the file.

Assessment Objectives	**TASK 3**
	1 Open your saved file called **cheques**.
1c	2 A table needs to be inserted at the end of the document.
3d	a) Insert a paragraph break and a clear line space at the end of the final paragraph
3e	immediately after the text ending:
3f	**...the table below**.
4d	b) Create a table with 2 columns and 6 rows.
	c) Enter the data below in the table:

Day	Activity
1	Cheques paid in at bank
2	Cheques processed at clearing centres
3	Account update information sent to banks
4	Banks update accounts
5	Money available in payee accounts

d) Make sure all borders will be displayed for the table on the printout.

e) Make sure all data in the table is fully displayed.

4c	3	Format the headings **Day** and **Activity** to be bold.
3c	4	a) Centre only heading and numbers in the first column.
		b) The remaining text must be left-aligned.
1d	5	Save your file keeping the filename **cheques**.
1e	6	Print one copy of the file **cheques**.
	7	Close the file called **cheques**.

Assessment Objectives | **TASK 4**

You will need to make the amendments below in a file that has been provided for you.

1c	1	a) Open the file provided called **atms** that is in your folder called **your name (first and last name) u1pa2**.
1d		b) Save the file using the new filename **cash machines** in your folder called **articles**.
4e	2	Go to the paragraph that starts **Once a correct PIN...**

Insert the following text as a new sentence after **... the available choices.**

If cash is being withdrawn the amount must be entered and the cash point checks the current balance of the customer's account to see if they have enough money.

4g	3	Go to the paragraph that starts **Banks use mainframe ...**

Delete the text/sentence:

This is the main service used by bank customers.

4f	4	In the paragraph that starts **A debit or credit ...**

Move only the text (not the clear line space after it).

This is a security measure, which is used to prevent unauthorised access to accounts.

to follow the sentence ending ...**number, or PIN.**

3h	5	a) Apply a bullet character to the following [number] lines of text:
3i		**withdraw cash;**
		check an account balance;
4h		**order a statement or print a 'mini statement';**
		order a cheque book.

    b)   Apply **double linespacing** to the bulleted text only.

    c)   Indent the text:

        Typically, an ATM can be used to:

        from the left margin.

3g   6   Replace the words **cash point** with the word **ATM** wherever they occur (twice in all).

3d   7   In the footer enter:

    your name u1pa2

    an **automatic date**

    an **automatic filename**.

3j   8   Check your text for accuracy.

1d   9   a)   Using the software facilities, carry out a word count in the file.

1e   b)   Enter the number of words on your printout at least two lines below the bulleted list. You may use any alignment for this.

10 Save the file keeping the filename **cash machines**.

11 Print one copy of the file **cash machines**.

12 Close all files and folders.

    Make sure you check your printouts for accuracy.

    You should have the following printouts:

    your screen print(s)

    cheques

    cash machines

Practice assignment 3

Scenario

You are working as a Customer Support Officer for a company that sells computer equipment. Your job is to prepare help sheets for customers.

Assessment Objectives	TASK 1
1a	1 During this assessment you will need a login and/or password to gain access to data. Your tutor will tell you the password and/or login and when it will be needed.
2a	2 You need to organise your files and folders.
2b	a) Rename the folder u1pras3 to be **your name (first and last name) u1pa3**.
	b) In this folder create a new sub-folder called **help sheets**.
2e	3 Copy the text file provided called **control** to the folder **help sheets**.
2d	4 Move the text file provided called **temp** from the folder **files** into the folder **help sheets**.
2c	5 Delete the folder **files** and its contents.
1b	6 a) Take a screen print as evidence of the folder called **your name (first and last name) u1pa3** and the contents of this folder.
1d	b) Take a screen print of the sub-folder called **help sheets** and the contents of this folder.
1e	c) In the footer of the page(s) displaying the screen prints, enter **your name u1pa3** and **today's date**.
3g	d) Save the screen print(s) within your filing structure. The file(s) do not need to be displayed in the folder structure on the screen print.
	e) Print the file(s) containing the screen prints. Make sure that all the contents of the folder and sub-folder are clearly visible on the print(s).
	7 Close any open files.

Assessment Objectives	TASK 2
1b	1 Create a new word-processing document.
3a	2 Set the page orientation to **portrait**.
3b	3 Set the **top**, **left** and **right** page margins to **1.7 cm**.
4a	4 Set the font to an **Arial** font type.

| 4b | 5 | Set the font size to **14**. |

| 3c | 6 | a) | Enter the following text in **single linespacing**. |
| 3d | | b) | Make sure that the text is **fully justified**. |

4h

Computers

There are many different types of computer available today. These range from giant supercomputers to small hand-held electronic personal organisers and microprocessors.

Mainframe computers cost millions of pounds to buy and install. They can process massive amounts of data extremely quickly, which is stored on hundreds of disk drives. A mainframe can have hundreds of terminals and users connected to it at the same time. The most powerful mainframes are called supercomputers.

The microcomputer is the most common type of computer. Microcomputers are used in the workplace, schools and homes. Microcomputers are usually called desktop personal computers or desktop PCs. The current 'entry level' specification for a PC is shown in the table below.

7   a)   Check the file for any errors and carry out a spell check.

b)   In the header, enter **your name u1pa3** and your **centre number**.

c)   In the footer, insert an **automatic date** and an **automatic filename**.

3g   8   a)   Save the file using the filename **computers** in the sub folder called **help sheets**.

b)   Close the file

Assessment Objectives | **TASK 3**

1d   1   Open your saved file called **computers**.

2   A table needs to be inserted at the end of the document.

a)   Insert a paragraph break and a clear linespace at the end of the final paragraph immediately after the text ending:

...the table below.

b)   Create a table with 2 columns and 4 rows.

1c   c)   Enter the data below in the table:

3d

Device	Size
Processor speed (GHz)	1
Memory (GB)	2
Hard disk drive (GB)	40

3e	d)	Make sure all borders will be displayed for the table on the printout.
3f	e)	Make sure all data in the table is fully displayed.
4d	3	Format the headings **Device** and **Size** to be bold.
	4 a)	The heading and numbers in the second column must be centre aligned.
	b)	The remaining text must be left-aligned.
	5	Save your file keeping the filename **computers**.
4c	6	Print one copy of the file **computers**.
	7	Close the file called **computers**.

Assessment Objectives

TASK 4

You will need to make the amendments below in a file that has been provided for you.

3c	1 a)	Open the file provided called **storage** that is in your folder called **your name (first and last name) u1pa3**.
1d	b)	Save the file using the new filename **memory** in your folder called **help sheets**.
1e	2	Go to the paragraph that starts **The software and …**

Insert the following text as a new sentence after **… cannot be changed.**

When the computer is switched off, the contents of ROM are not lost.

1c	3	Go to the paragraph that starts **The software and …**

1d   Delete the text/sentence:

This program loads the operating system from backing storage.

4e	4	In the paragraph that starts **RAM is the …**

Move only the text (not the clear line space after it)

Once the data has been collected it can be analysed by the computer.

to follow the sentence ending …**and data temporarily**.

4g	5 a)	Apply a bullet character to the following 2 lines of text:

Programmable Read Only Memory (PROM)
Erasable Programmable Read Only Memory (EPROM)

b)   Apply double line spacing to the bulleted text only.

4f	c)	Indent the text:

Other types of memory include:

from the left margin.

3h, 3i	6	Replace the word **software** with the word **programs** wherever it occurs (3 times in all).
4h	7	In the footer enter:

       your name u1pa3

       an **automatic date**

       an **automatic filename**.

4i   8   Check your text for accuracy.

3g   9   a)   Using the software facilities, carry out a word count in the file.

          b)   Enter the number of words on your printout at least two lines below the bulleted list. You may use any alignment for this.

     10   Save the file keeping the filename **memory**.

     11   Print one copy of the file **memory**.

3d   12   Close all files and folders.

        Make sure you check your printouts for accuracy.

3j   You should have the following printouts:

1d   **your screen print(s)**

1e   **computers**

        memory

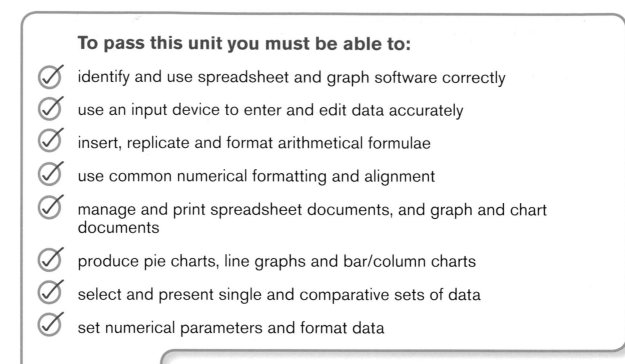

To pass this unit you must be able to:

- identify and use spreadsheet and graph software correctly
- use an input device to enter and edit data accurately
- insert, replicate and format arithmetical formulae
- use common numerical formatting and alignment
- manage and print spreadsheet documents, and graph and chart documents
- produce pie charts, line graphs and bar/column charts
- select and present single and comparative sets of data
- set numerical parameters and format data

Before you start this chapter, you or your tutor should download a zipped file called **Resources for Chapter 2** from **www.payne-gallway.co.uk/newclait/student**. It will automatically unzip. Specify that the contents are to be saved in your My Documents folder.

Spreadsheet packages

A **spreadsheet package** is a general purpose computer package that is designed to perform **calculations**. A spreadsheet is a table which is divided into **rows** and **columns**. Columns have a letter at the top and rows have a number at the side. Lines divide the rows and columns up into boxes called **cells**. A cell can contain **text**, a **number** or a **formula**. Individual **cells** are identified by their **cell reference number** which normally contains a column letter and a row number. **Microsoft® Excel® XP** (referred to as **Excel**) is a popular spreadsheet package.

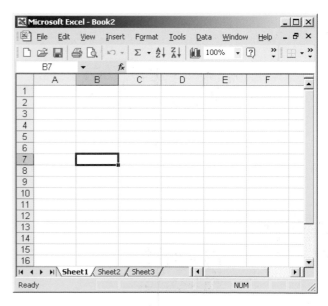

Figure 2.1

The practice tasks that follow cover all the techniques you need to learn in order to pass a New CLAiT Unit 2 **CREATING SPREADSHEETS AND GRAPHS** assignment.

Practice tasks

Task 1   Creating a new spreadsheet

This task takes you through the steps you need to follow when setting up a new spread sheet in Excel.

Starting Excel

You can load Excel in one of two ways:

- *Either* double-click the **Microsoft Excel** icon on the **Desktop** in **Windows**,

- *or* click the **Start** button at the bottom left of the screen, then click **All Programs Microsoft Excel**.

Figure 2.2

The main Excel window will be displayed – it should look like the one below with a blank **workbook** ready to start work on. In Excel, individual spreadsheets are called **worksheets**. A new workbook normally contains three blank worksheets.

Microsoft Office
Excel 2003

Excel icon

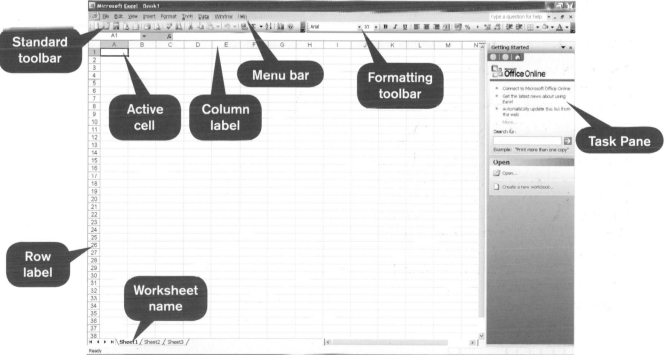

Figure 2.3

You'll find out what the different parts of the Excel window are used for as you work through the practice tasks in this chapter.

If you can't see a blank workbook:

New button

- ▶ Either click the **New** button on the **Standard** toolbar,
- ▶ or click **Create a new workbook** in the **Task Pane**.

TIP

If you want to find out what a toolbar button does just hold the mouse pointer over it for a few seconds. A **ToolTip** will appear with a brief description.

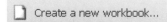
Create a new workbook...

Figure 2.4

You now have the option of either entering text into the current blank workbook or opening an existing one. During Unit 2 assignments you'll be asked to create and format new spreadsheets and draw graphs or charts using pre-prepared spreadsheets.

To get started you're going to create a new spreadsheet. The spreadsheet will provide a summary of sales information for the Area Manager of a sandwich shop company. The data you are going to enter is shown below.

April Sales Figures						
Sandwich	North Row	High Street	Kings Road	South Street	Total	Profit
BLT	457	347	218	121		
Cheese and pickle	322	234	129	109		
Chicken salad	479	219	134	242		
Egg mayonnaise	345	312	163	347		
Ham and cheese	267	208	127	262		
Ham salad	289	309	104	209		
Salmon and cucumber	379	245	182	314		
Tuna salad	226	179	141	292		

When you open a new workbook, cell **A1** is highlighted on the first worksheet called **Sheet 1** – this is the **active cell**.

Entering text in a spreadsheet

- ▶ Make sure cell **A1** is highlighted – if it isn't just click in it.
- ▶ Type the heading **April Sales Figures**. You'll notice **Column A** isn't wide enough for this heading – don't worry about this for now – we'll enter the rest of the data before looking at how to change column widths.
- ▶ Click in cell **A3**, then type in **Sandwich**.

▷ Move to cell **B3**, and type **North Row**.

▷ Work your way across **Row 3** entering the rest of the headings. When you've finished, your spreadsheet should look like the one here.

	A	B	C	D	E	F	G
1	April Sales Figures						
2							
3	Sandwich	North Row	High Stree	Kings Roa	South Stre	Total	Profit
4							
5							

Figure 2.5

Next we'll enter the data underneath the headings in each column starting with **Column A**.

▷ Click in cell **A4**, type **BLT** then press **Enter**. Excel will guess that you want to enter data down this column and will move automatically to the next cell down, **A5**.

▷ Work your way down **Column A**, entering the rest of the sandwich names. When you've finished, your spreadsheet should look like this:

	A	B	C	D	E	F	G
1	April Sales Figures						
2							
3	Sandwich	North Row	High Stree	Kings Roa	South Stre	Total	Profit
4	BLT						
5	Cheese and pickle						
6	Chicken salad						
7	Egg and cress						
8	Ham and cheese						
9	Ham salad						
10	Salmon and cucumber						
11	Tuna salad						
12							

Figure 2.6

Now we'll look at how to change the width of **Column A** so that all the text can be seen in full.

▷ Position the mouse pointer on the line between the column headers **A** and **B**. The pointer will change to a double-headed arrow.

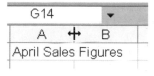

Figure 2.7

▷ Press and hold down the left mouse button.

TIP

For New CLAiT all of the data in each column must be visible. You will lose marks if the contents of any cell cannot be seen in full.

▶ Drag the mouse to the right – the column will start to widen. Let go of the mouse button when all the sandwich names can be seen in full.

	A	B
1	April Sales Figures	
2		
3	Sandwich	North Row Hig
4	BLT	
5	Cheese and pickle	
6	Chicken salad	
7	Egg mayonnaise	
8	Ham and cheese	
9	Ham salad	
10	Salmon and cucumber	
11	Tuna salad	
12		

Figure 2.8

TIP

If you see ##### displayed in a cell. This means the numerical contents of the cell cannot be displayed because it is too narrow. If this happens just make the column wider.

Next we'll use a different technique to change the width of the other columns.

▶ Position the mouse pointer on the line between the column headers B and C. The pointer will change to a double-headed arrow.

▶ Double-click the left mouse button. Column **B** will automatically widen to fit the contents.

▶ Widen columns **C**, **D** and **E** the same way. Your spreadsheet should look like the one below when you've finished.

	A	B	C	D	E	F	G
1	April Sales Figures						
2							
3	Sandwich	North Row	High Street	Kings Road	South Street	Total	Profit
4	BLT						
5	Cheese and pickle						
6	Chicken salad						
7	Egg and cress						
8	Ham and cheese						
9	Ham salad						
10	Salmon and cucumber						
11	Tuna salad						
12							

Figure 2.9

Entering numerical data in a spreadsheet

Now we need to enter the data for columns **B**, **C**, **D** and **E**.

▶ Click in cell **B4**, type **457**, then press **Enter**.

▶ Work your way down **Column B** entering the rest of the sales figures for **North Row**.

Your spreadsheet should look like the one below when you've finished.

	A	B	
1	April Sales Figures		
2			
3	Sandwich	North Row	Hig
4	BLT	457	
5	Cheese and pickle	322	
6	Chicken salad	479	
7	Egg mayonnaise	345	
8	Ham and cheese	267	
9	Ham salad	289	
10	Salmon and cucumber	379	
11	Tuna salad	226	
12			

Figure 2.10

▶ Click in cell **C4**, type **347** then press **Enter**.

▶ Work your way down **Column C** entering the rest of the sales figures for **High Street**. Your spreadsheet should look like the one below when you've finished.

	A	B	C
1	April Sales Figures		
2			
3	Sandwich	North Row	High Street
4	BLT	457	347
5	Cheese and pickle	322	234
6	Chicken salad	479	219
7	Egg mayonnaise	345	312
8	Ham and cheese	267	208
9	Ham salad	289	309
10	Salmon and cucumber	379	245
11	Tuna salad	226	179
12			

Figure 2.11

▶ Click in cell **D4**, type **218** then press **Enter**.

▶ Work your way down **Column D** entering the rest of the sales figures for Kings Road.

▶ Click in cell **E4**, type **121** then press **Enter**.

▶ Work your way down **Column E** entering the rest of the figures for **South Street**.

Saving the spreadsheet

▶ *Either* click **File** on the menu bar, then click **Save**,

▶ *or* click the **Save button** on the **Standard** toolbar. The **Save** dialogue box will appear.

Save button

The name highlighted in the **File name** box is the default filename. This is normally something like **Book1** or **Book2** and can be changed to whatever you like.

⦿ Type the name, **sandwich**, then click the **Save** button. The **Save** dialogue window will disappear, and the filename **sandwich** will displayed at the top of the screen. Your workbook will now be saved with this name whenever you click the **Save** button on the **Standard** toolbar.

>
> **TIP**
>
> Excel workbooks are automatically saved in a folder called **My Documents**. If your teacher wants you to save documents in a different place they will explain how to do this.

Finally you need to close **Excel**:

⦿ *Either* click **File** on the menu bar, then click **Exit**,

⦿ *or* click **X** in the top right-hand corner of the desktop.

Task 2   Creating formulae

During a Unit 2 assignment you'll be asked to enter simple formulae on a worksheet. **Formulae** are used on spreadsheets to perform calculations automatically using the numbers in other cells. The results of calculations are displayed in the cells where the formulae have been entered. For New CLAiT you need to be able to enter simple formulae to add, subtract, multiply or divide numbers. The mathematical symbols you'll use to do this are:

+   to **add**

-       to **subtract**

*   to **multiply**

/   to **divide**

⦿ Load **Excel**.

To work through this task you need to load the workbook called **sandwich** that you have already created and saved.

⦿ *Either* click **File** on the menu bar, then click **Open**,

⦿ *or* click the **Open** button on the **Standard** toolbar. The **Open** dialogue box will appear.

Open button

⦿ Click on **sandwich**, then click **Open**.

>
> **TIP**
>
> Ask your tutor to help you find this file if it isn't in the list on your screen.

Inserting and replicating formulae

First we need to enter a formula in cell **E4** to calculate the **Total** for **BLT** sandwiches. We'll use the **AutoSum** function to do this.

▷ Click in cell **F4**, then click the **AutoSum** button on the **Standard** toolbar. Excel will automatically outline cells **B4** to **E4** and the formula **=SUM(B4:E4)** will be displayed in cell **F4**.

AutoSum button

	A	B	C	D	E	F	G	H
1	April Sales Figures							
2								
3	Sandwich	North Row	High Street	Kings Road	South Street	Total	Profit	
4	BLT	457	347	218	121	=SUM(B4:E4)		
5	Cheese and pickle	322	234	129	109	SUM(**number1**, [number2], ...)		
6	Chicken salad	479	219	134	242			
7	Egg mayonnaise	345	312	163	347			

Figure 2.12

▷ Press **Enter**.

> **TIP**
>
> You'd get the same answer by entering the formula: **=B4+C4+D4+E4**. The **AutoSum function** just provides a quicker way to calculate totals if all the numbers are together in one row or column.

Now we need to copy or 'replicate' this formula down **Column F** so the **Total** is shown for each type of sandwich.

▷ Click back in cell **F4**. Look carefully at this cell. You'll see a small black square in the bottom right-hand corner – this is called the **fill handle**.

Figure 2.13

▷ Move the pointer over the fill handle – it will change into a thin black cross.

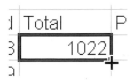

Figure 2.14

▷ Click and hold the left mouse button, then drag the mouse down the column as far as cell **F11**.

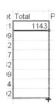

Figure 2.15

Let go of the mouse button. The formula will be replicated in cells **F5** to **F11**. Your spreadsheet should now look like the one below.

	A	B	C	D	E	F	G
1	April Sales Figures						
2							
3	Sandwich	North Row	High Street	Kings Road	South Street	Total	Profit
4	BLT	457	347	218	121	1143	
5	Cheese and pickle	322	234	129	109	794	
6	Chicken salad	479	219	134	242	1074	
7	Egg mayonnaise	345	312	163	347	1167	
8	Ham and cheese	267	208	127	262	864	
9	Ham salad	289	309	104	209	911	
10	Salmon and cucumber	379	245	182	314	1120	
11	Tuna salad	226	179	141	292	838	
12							

Figure 2.16

Auto Fill
Options button

The **Auto Fill Options** button might appear after you've used the fill handle – you don't need to use this – just ignore it.

> **TIP**
>
> If you make a mistake when you're using the **Fill** handle just click the **Undo** button on the **Standard toolbar** and try again.
>
>
>
> Undo button

Inserting a new column or row, and adding data

Next we are going to add some data to the spreadsheet about the Cost Prices of the sandwiches. We need this data to calculate the **Profit** for each sandwich. The data will be entered in a new column between **Column F (Total)** and **Column G (Profit)**.

Right-click the header for **Column G**, then click **Insert** on the shortcut menu,

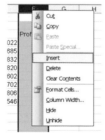

...a new column will appear.

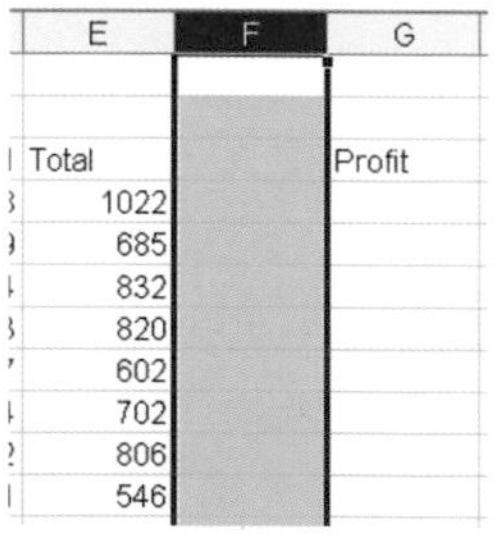

Figure 2.17

Click in **Cell G3**, type **Cost Price** then press **Enter**.

Enter the data shown below in the **Cost Price** column:

> **TIP**
>
> You could be asked to insert a new row rather than a new column. The technique is almost the same – just right-click the row label just under where you want the new row to be inserted, and then click **Insert** on the shortcut menu.

Sandwich	Cost Price
BLT	1.95
Cheese and pickle	2.1
Chicken salad	2.2
Egg mayonnaise	1.75
Ham and cheese	1.8
Ham salad	2.2
Salmon and cucumber	1.8
Tuna salad	1.75

Now we can enter a formula in cell **H4** to calculate the **Profit** for BLT by multiplying the **Total** in cell **F4** by the **Cost Price** in cell **G4**, and then multiply this figure by **0.6**.

> **TIP**
>
> The last part of the **Profit** formula ***0.6** adds a profit of 60%. Unit 2 assignments may ask you to add an extra part like this to a formula rather than just using something like a straightforward multiplication of two or more cells.

- Click in cell **H4** and type = .
- Click in cell **F4** and type *.
- Click in cell **G4** and type *0.6 .
- The formula in cell **H4** should now look like this: **=F4*G4*0.6**. If it doesn't, press the **Backspace** key to delete it then repeat the steps above.
- Press **Enter**, then use the **fill handle** to copy the formula into cells **H5 to H11.** Your spreadsheet should look like the one below.

	A	B	C	D	E	F	G	H
1	April Sales Figures							
2								
3	Sandwich	North Row	High Street	Kings Road	South Street	Total	Cost Price	Profit
4	BLT	457	347	218	121	1143	1.95	1337.31
5	Cheese and pickle	322	234	129	109	794	2.1	1000.44
6	Chicken salad	479	219	134	242	1074	2.2	1417.68
7	Egg mayonnaise	345	312	163	347	1167	1.75	1225.35
8	Ham and cheese	267	208	127	262	864	1.8	933.12
9	Ham salad	289	309	104	209	911	2.2	1202.52
10	Salmon and cucumber	379	245	182	314	1120	1.8	1209.6
11	Tuna salad	226	179	141	292	838	1.75	879.9
12								

Figure 2.18

Entering information into a header or footer

Now we'll add some information to the header section of the workbook and save it.

- Click **View** on the menu bar, and then click **Header and Footer**. The **Page Setup** dialogue box will be displayed with the **Header/Footer** tab selected.
- Click the **Custom Header** button. The **Header** dialogue box will be displayed.

⊙ Click in the **Left section** and type your name.

⊙ Click in the **Center section** and type your centre number.

Insert Date button

⊙ Click in the **Right section** and click the **Insert Date** button. Your **Header** dialogue box should now look something like the one here.

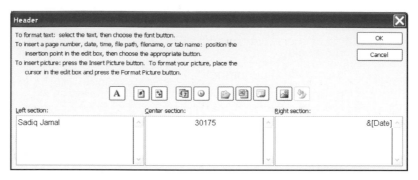

To format text: select the text, then choose the font button.
To insert a page number, date, time, file path, filename, or tab name: position the insertion point in the edit box, then choose the appropriate button.
To insert picture: press the Insert Picture button. To format your picture, place the cursor in the edit box and press the Format Picture button.

Left section:	Center section:	Right section:
Sadiq Jamal	30175	&[Date]

Figure 2.19

⊙ Click **OK** to return to the **Page Setup** dialogue box, then **OK** again to exit.

Save button

⊙ Click the **Save** button on the **Standard** toolbar to save the workbook, keeping the same name **sandwich**.

TIP

If you want to insert information into a Footer, in the second step above, click the **Custom Footer** button in the **Header dialogue** box, then follow the same procedure.

Printing a spreadsheet showing data as a table – without gridlines

To print the spreadsheet on one page in **landscape orientation**:

⊙ Click **File** on the menu bar, and then click **Page Setup**. The **Page Setup** dialogue box will appear.

⊙ Click the **Page** tab if it isn't already selected.

⊙ In the **Orientation** section click the radio button next to **Landscape**.

⊙ In the **Scaling** section click the radio button for **Fit to:** and leave the other options as **1 page wide by 1 page tall**.

⊙ Click **Print Preview**. The spreadsheet will be displayed exactly as it will be printed – it should look like the example below.

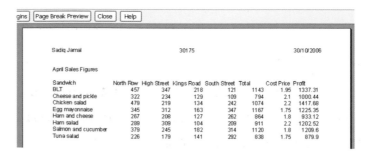

Figure 2.20

Click the **Print** button at the top of the screen. The **Print** dialogue box will appear.

 TIP

You might also need to choose a printer at this stage – if you do, your tutor will tell you what to do.

 Click **OK** to print the table, then close **Excel**.

TIP

You'll be asked to produce two types of printout during a spreadsheet assignment. The first and most straightforward of these is a printout showing the 'figures'. This is the default style for Excel printouts, and prints just the text and numbers on a worksheet. The second is a printout showing the 'formulae' – we'll cover this later. Always check printouts carefully to make sure all the information on the screen is shown clearly on them. You'll lose marks if information is missing from a printout.

Task 3 Formatting numbers and text

During a Unit 2 assignment you'll be asked to format numbers and text on a worksheet. The formatting options available on the Formatting toolbar are shown below.

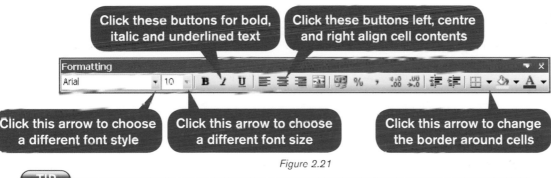

Figure 2.21

TIP

More formatting options are available by clicking **Format** on the menu bar and then **Cells**. You can try some of these out but they won't be needed during a New CLAiT assignment.

 Load **Excel**, then open your copy of the workbook called **sandwich**.

Formatting text

We'll start by centre aligning the heading **Sandwich** in **Cell A3** and making the text bold.

 Click in **Cell A3**, then click the **Centre** button on the Formatting toolbar.

 Click the **Bold** button on the Formatting toolbar.

Bold button

Centre button

Next we'll right align the headings for columns **B, C, D, E, F** and make the text italic.

⊚ Click in cell **B3**, hold the left mouse button, then drag the mouse to the right, as far as cell **F3**.

⊚ Let go of the mouse button – the cells we want to format are now highlighted.

> **TIP**
>
> If you don't highlight the correct group of cells just click back where you started and try again. Cells can also be highlighted by clicking where you want to start, holding the **SHIFT** key down and using the arrow keys.

Right Align
button

⊚ First click the **right align** button, then the **italic** button on the formatting toolbar, and apply these formats to your spreadsheet:

Italic button

⊚ Centre the column label **April Sales Figures** in **Cell A1** and make the text bold, increasing the column width if necessary.

⊚ Centre the column label **Profit** in **Cell H3** and make the text bold and italic.

⊚ Make all the sandwich names in **Cells A4** to **A11** italic. When you've finished your spreadsheet should look like the one below.

	A	B	C	D	E	F	G	H
1	**April Sales Figures**							
2								
3	**Sandwich**	*North Row*	*High Street*	*Kings Road*	*South Street*	*Total*	Cost Price	**Profit**
4	*BLT*	457	347	218	121	1143	1.95	1337.31
5	*Cheese and pickle*	322	234	129	109	794	2.1	1000.44
6	*Chicken salad*	479	219	134	242	1074	2.2	1417.68
7	*Egg mayonnaise*	345	312	163	347	1167	1.75	1225.35
8	*Ham and cheese*	267	208	127	262	864	1.8	933.12
9	*Ham salad*	289	309	104	209	911	2.2	1202.52
10	*Salmon and cucumber*	379	245	182	314	1120	1.8	1209.6
11	*Tuna salad*	226	179	141	292	838	1.75	879.9

Figure 2.22

> **TIP**
>
> Excel applies standard or 'default' alignment options when you first enter data in cells. When text is entered in a cell it is automatically left aligned. Similarly when numbers are entered in cells they are automatically right aligned. If you're asked to left align text or right align numbers in an assignment you won't need to do anything.

Formatting numbers

Next we need to format the numbers on the spreadsheet. The number formats you'll need to use during a spreadsheet assignment are **decimal**, **integer** and **currency**.

We'll start by formatting the cost prices of the sandwiches in **Column G** so they're displayed with a **currency symbol** and **2 decimal places**.

▶ Highlight cells **G4** to **G11**.

F	G	H
Total	Cost Price	**Profit**
1143	1.95	1337.31
794	2.1	1000.44
1074	2.2	1417.68
1167	1.75	1225.35
864	1.8	933.12
911	2.2	1202.52
1120	1.8	1209.6
838	1.75	879.9

Figure 2.23

▶ Click **Format**, then **Cells** on the menu bar. The **Format Cells** dialogue box will be displayed.

▶ Click the **Number** tab if it isn't already selected, then click **Currency** in the **Category** list.

▶ The value in the box next to **Decimal places** will already be set to **2**, and the **Symbol** box should contain a **£** sign (click the down arrow on the right of the box and choose **£** from the list if any other symbol is displayed).

▶ Click **OK**.

Next we'll format the Profits in **Column H** so they're displayed with a **currency symbol** and **no decimal places** (integer format).

▶ Highlight cells **H4** to **H11**.

▶ Click **Format**, then **Cells**.

▶ Click **Currency** in the **Category** list on the **Number** tab.

▶ Change the value in the **Decimal places** box to **0** by clicking the small down arrow twice, then click **OK**.

Now we'll format all the other numbers on the spreadsheet to be displayed with no **decimal places** (integer format).

▶ Highlight cells **B4** to **F11**.

▶ Click **Format**, then **Cells**.

▶ Click **Number** in the **Category** list on the **Number** tab, change the number of **Decimal places** to **0**, then click **OK**.

You won't see any obvious change in the appearance of the numbers this time. Check this formatting by clicking in any cell in **column B**, **C**, **D**, **E** or **F** and entering a number containing a decimal place. The digits after the decimal point should disappear when you press **Enter**. The value you entered will be rounded up or down to the nearest whole number. Click the **Undo** button on the **Standard** toolbar once you've tried this.

Undo button

Your spreadsheet should look like the one below.

	A	B	C	D	E	F	G	H
1	**April Sales Figures**							
2								
3	**Sandwich**	*North Row*	*High Street*	*Kings Road*	*South Street*	*Total*	Cost Price	**Profit**
4	*BLT*	457	347	218	121	1143	£1.95	£1,337
5	*Cheese and pickle*	322	234	129	109	794	£2.10	£1,000
6	*Chicken salad*	479	219	134	242	1074	£2.20	£1,418
7	*Egg mayonnaise*	345	312	163	347	1167	£1.75	£1,225
8	*Ham and cheese*	267	208	127	262	864	£1.80	£933
9	*Ham salad*	289	309	104	209	911	£2.20	£1,203
10	*Salmon and cucumber*	379	245	182	314	1120	£1.80	£1,210
11	*Tuna salad*	226	179	141	292	838	£1.75	£880
12								

Figure 2.24

TIP

If your spreadsheet doesn't look like the one above check to make sure that all the columns are wide enough to display the text labels in full.

The last formatting this spreadsheet needs is a border around all the column labels from **Sandwich** to *Profit*.

▶ Highlight cells **A3** to **H3**.

	A	B	C	D	E	F	G	H
1	**April Sales Figures**							
2								
3	**Sandwich**	*North Row*	*High Street*	*Kings Road*	*South Street*	*Total*	Cost Price	**Profit**
4	*BLT*	457	347	218	121	1143	£1.95	£1,337

Figure 2.25

Outside Border button

▶ Click the down arrow next to the **Borders** button on the formatting toolbar, then click the **Outside Borders** button in the list of border options.

Figure 2.26

▶ Click away from the highlighted cells on any blank part of the spreadsheet. The column labels on your spreadsheet should now look like those shown below.

	A	B	C	D	E	F	G	H
2								
3	**Sandwich**	*North Row*	*High Street*	*Kings Road*	*South Street*	*Total*	Cost Price	**Profit**

Figure 2.27

Finally we'll save this spreadsheet with a different name.

⊙ Click **File** on the menu bar, and then click **Save As**.

⊙ Type the new name **sanbox**, click the **Save** button, then close **Excel**.

Task 4   Editing a spreadsheet

During a Unit 2 assignment you'll be asked to edit a spreadsheet by inserting and deleting rows or columns, making changes to the values in some cells and adding new formulae. We'll start by deleting a row.

⊙ Load **Excel**, then open your copy of the workbook called **sanbox**.

Deleting a row

Cheese and pickle sandwiches are being withdrawn from sale because of complaints from customers. This means that **Row 5** must be deleted.

⊙ Right-click the label **Cheese and pickle** for **Row 5** (the row will be highlighted), then click **Delete** on the shortcut menu. The row and all its contents will disappear.

	A	B	C	D	E	F	G	H
1	April Sales Figures							
2								
3	Sandwich	North Row	High Street	Kings Road	South Street	Total	Cost Price	Profit
4	BLT	467	247	218	121	1143	£1.95	£1,337
5	Cheese and pickle	322	234	129	109	794	£2.10	£1,000
6	Cut	479	219	134	242	1074	£2.20	£1,418
7	Copy	345	312	163	347	1167	£1.75	£1,225
8	Paste	267	208	127	262	864	£1.80	£933
9	Paste Special...	289	309	104	209	911	£2.20	£1,203
1	Insert	379	245	182	314	1120	£1.80	£1,210
1	Delete	226	179	141	292	838	£1.75	£880
1	Clear Contents							
1	Format Cells...							
1	Row Height...							
1	Hide							
1	Unhide							

Figure 2.28

Deleting a column

A different Area Manager is now responsible for the shop at South Street. This means that your manager does not need figures for this shop and **Column E** must be deleted.

⊙ Right-click the header for **Column E** to highlight the column, then click **Delete** on the shortcut menu as illustrated below. The column and all its contents will disappear.

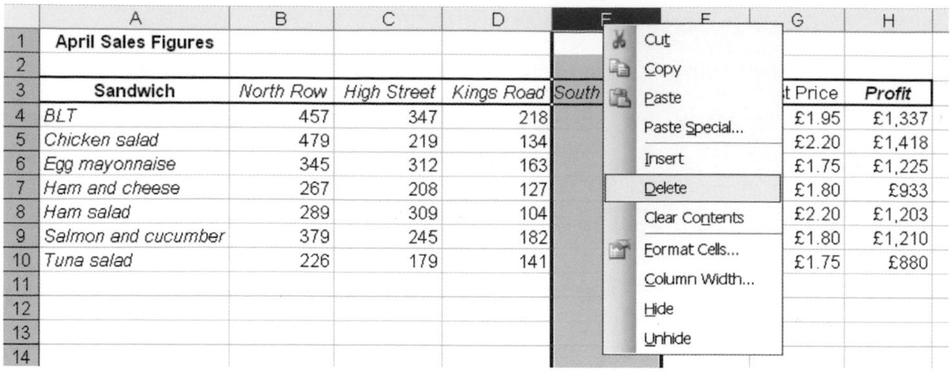

Figure 2.29

Now we need to save this version of the spreadsheet with a different name.

▶ Click **File** on the menu bar, then click **Save As**.

▶ Type the new name, **sandfinal**, and click on **Save**.

Amending text and numerical data

Egg mayonnaise sandwiches are being replaced by **Egg and cress**. We need to change this text label.

▶ Double-click in **Cell A6**, then press the **Backspace** key until the text **mayonnaise** is completely deleted.

▶ Type **and cress**, then press **Enter**.

The sales figures for **Ham salad** sandwiches at North Row are wrong. The correct amount is **398**. You need to change this amount.

▶ Click in **Cell B8**, type **398** then press **Enter**.

The **Cost Price** for **Salmon and cucumber** sandwiches during April was actually **£1.95**. You need to change this price.

▶ Click in **Cell F9**, type **1.95** (you don't need to include a £ sign here), then press **Enter**.

When you've made all these changes your spreadsheet should look like the one below.

	A	B	C	D	E	F	G
1	**April Sales Figures**						
2							
3	**Sandwich**	*North Row*	*High Street*	*Kings Road*	*Total*	Cost Price	*Profit*
4	*BLT*	457	347	218	1022	£1.95	£1,196
5	*Chicken salad*	479	219	134	832	£2.20	£1,098
6	*Egg mayonnaise*	345	312	163	820	£1.75	£861
7	*Ham and cheese*	267	208	127	602	£1.80	£650
8	*Ham salad*	398	309	104	811	£2.20	£1,071
9	*Salmon and cucumber*	379	245	182	806	£1.95	£943
10	*Tuna salad*	226	179	141	546	£1.75	£573
11							

Figure 2.30

Adding a new formula

Next you need to add a new formula in **Cell G11** to calculate the **Total Profit** by adding up all the totals. First we need to enter a new text label:

▶ Click once in **Cell F11**, type the label **Total Profit**, then press **Enter**.

Now we'll use the **AutoSum** feature to enter the formula.

▶ Click in cell **G11**.

▶ Click the **AutoSum** button on the **Standard** toolbar. Cells **G4** to **G10** will be outlined and the formula **=SUM(G4:G10)** will appear in **Cell G11**.

AutoSum button

	F	G	H	I
	Cost Price	*Profit*		
2	£1.95	£1,196		
2	£2.20	£1,098		
0	£1.75	£861		
2	£1.80	£650		
1	£2.20	£1,071		
3	£1.95	£943		
6	£1.75	£573		
	Total Profit	=SUM(G4:G10)		
		SUM(**number1**, [number2], ...)		

Figure 2.31

▶ Press **Enter**.

▶ Format the text in **Cell F11** as bold and increase the width of the column so that it still fits. Your spreadsheet should now look like the one below.

	A	B	C	D	E	F	G
1	**April Sales Figures**						
2							
3	**Sandwich**	*North Row*	*High Street*	*Kings Road*	*Total*	Cost Price	**Profit**
4	*BLT*	457	347	218	1022	£1.95	£1,196
5	*Chicken salad*	479	219	134	832	£2.20	£1,098
6	*Egg mayonnaise*	345	312	163	820	£1.75	£861
7	*Ham and cheese*	267	208	127	602	£1.80	£650
8	*Ham salad*	398	309	104	811	£2.20	£1,071
9	*Salmon and cucumber*	379	245	182	806	£1.95	£943
10	*Tuna salad*	226	179	141	546	£1.75	£573
11						**Total Profit**	£6,392

Figure 2.32

▶ Save the workbook keeping the same name **sandfinal**, by clicking the **Save** button on the **Standard** toolbar.

Save button

Press F9 if you are asked to make sure formulae are recalculated after changes have been made to a workbook.

Printing a spreadsheet showing data as a table – with gridlines

Now we'll print a copy of the spreadsheet in **landscape orientation** with the **gridlines** displayed.

- ▶ Click **File** on the menu bar, and then click **Page Setup**. The **Page Setup** dialogue box will appear.

- ▶ Click the **Page** tab if it isn't already selected.

- ▶ In the **Orientation** section click the radio button next to **Landscape**.

- ▶ In the **Scaling** section click the radio button for **Fit to:** and leave the other option as **1 page wide by 1 page tall**.

- ▶ Click the **Sheet** tab and in the **Print** section click the check box next to **Gridlines**.

- ▶ Click the **Print Preview** button The spreadsheet will be displayed exactly as it will be printed – it should look like the example below.

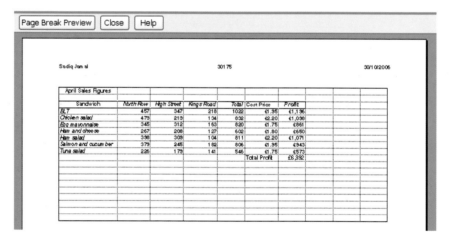

Figure 2.33

Print Preview
print button

Click the **Print** button at the top of the screen. The **Print** dialogue box will appear.

- ▶ Click **OK** to print the spreadsheet.

Printing a spreadsheet showing gridlines, headings and formulae

Next we'll print another copy of the spreadsheet in **landscape orientation** with the **gridlines**, **row and column headings** and **formulae** displayed. This printout will be used when your work is marked to check you've entered all the required formulae correctly.

- ▶ Click **Tools** on the menu bar and then **Options**. The **Options** dialogue box will appear.

- ▶ Click the **View** tab if it isn't already selected, and in the **Window options** section click the check box next to **Formulas**.

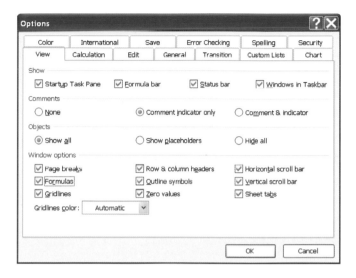

Figure 2.34

▶ Click **OK**. All the formulae will be displayed on the worksheet – the column widths will adjust automatically so the formulae can be seen in full.

▶ Click **File**, on the menu bar then **Page Setup**, and select the **Sheet** tab.

▶ In the **Print** section click the check box next to **Row and column headings** (the check box next to **Gridlines** should still be selected; if it isn't, click this as well).

▶ Click **Print Preview**. The spreadsheet will be displayed exactly as it will be printed, and should look like the example below.

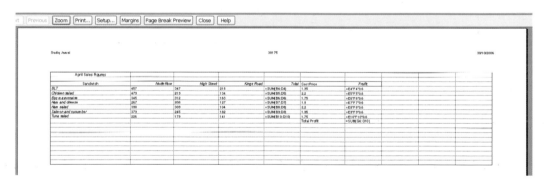

Figure 2.35

Finally we need to save this version of the spreadsheet with a different name.

▶ Click **File** on the menu bar, select **Save As**, then type the new name, **sandform**.

▶ Click the **Save** button then close **Excel**.

Task 5   Graphs and charts

During a Unit 2 assignment you'll be asked to use the data in a pre-prepared spreadsheet to create a line graph, pie chart or bar chart.

To draw graphs in **Excel**, a special tool called the **Chart Wizard** is provided.

 Load **Excel**.

> **TIP**
>
> This task describes the steps you need to work through to create each of the graphs. During a Unit 2 assignment you'll normally only be asked to create just one of these graphs.

Now you need to load a pre-prepared workbook called **salesfigs**. Your tutor will tell you where to find this workbook. In the example below it is inside a folder called **Resources**.

To load this workbook:

 Either click **File** on the menu bar, and then click **Open**,

 Open button

 or click the **Open button** on the **Standard** toolbar. The **Open** dialogue box will appear.

 Click on the file called **salesfigs**, and then click **Open**. The workbook will be opened – it should look exactly like the one below.

	A	B	C	D	E	F	G
1	Half Yearly Sales						
2							
3	Shop	Jan	Feb	Mar	Apr	May	Jun
4	North Row	1349	1438	1739	1993	2386	2321
5	High Street	1161	1241	1476	1672	1841	1992
6	Kings Road	1089	1121	1346	1519	1694	1832
7							

Figure 2.36

Creating a line graph

The first type of graph we're going to draw is a **comparative line graph**. This will display the half-yearly sales figures for North Row and High Street as two separate lines on a graph.

To draw this graph we need to highlight the column headings for the months and the sales data for each shop displayed underneath.

 Click in cell **A3**.

 Hold down the left mouse button and drag diagonally through to cell **G5** to select the data to be used for the graph.

	A	B	C	D	E	F	G
1	Half Yearly Sales						
2							
3	Shop	Jan	Feb	Mar	Apr	May	Jun
4	North Row	1349	1438	1739	1993	2386	2321
5	High Street	1161	1241	1476	1672	1841	1992
6	Kings Road	1089	1121	1346	1519	1694	1832

Figure 2.37

⊳ Let go of the mouse button.

⊳ Click the **Chart Wizard** button on the **Standard** toolbar. The Chart Wizard dialogue box will be displayed.

⊳ Click **Line** in the **Chart type** list.

⊳ Leave the fourth **Chart sub-type** selected.

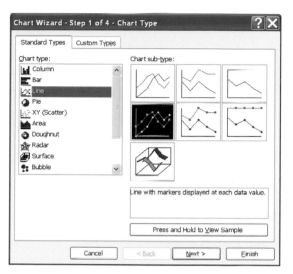

Chart Wizard button

Figure 2.38

⊳ Click **Next**. You'll be moved on to Step 2 of the Chart Wizard. A preview of the graph will be displayed – a legend has been added automatically to identify which line corresponds to which shop. You don't need to do anything else here at this stage.

⊳ Click **Next**. You'll be moved on to Step 3 of the Chart Wizard where you need to enter a title for the graph and labels for the axes.

⊳ Click in the **Chart title** box and type **Half Year Sales**.

⊳ Click in the **Category (X) axis** box and type **Month**.

⊳ Click in the **Value (Y) axis** box and type **Total Sales**.

⊳ Click **Next**. You'll be moved on to the final step 4 of the Chart Wizard process.

⊳ Click **As new sheet** to display the finished graph on a sheet of its own.

⊳ Click **Finish**. The line graph will appear in a new **Chart Sheet** – it should look like the one below.

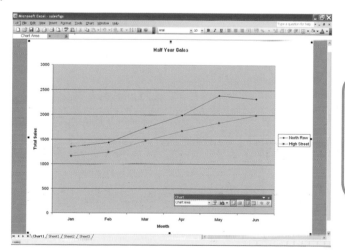

TIP

The **Chart toolbar** might appear automatically with the graph – you won't need this – just click **X** in the corner of the toolbar to close it.

Figure 2.39

There are quite large gaps on this graph, above and below the lines showing the sales figures for each shop. This can be improved by reducing the range of numbers the Y-axis is set to display.

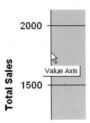

Figure 2.40

▶ Position the mouse pointer on the left of the Y-axis between any of the value labels.

▶ Double-click the left mouse button. The **Format Axis** dialogue box will be displayed.

▶ Select the **Scale** tab, click in the **Minimum** box and change the value to **1000**, and then the **Maximum** box value to **2500**.

▶ Click **OK**. Your graph should now show the new scale with 2400 near the top and both plot lines nearer to the X-axis.

TIP

If you are asked to change the scale on the X-axis of a graph the technique is exactly the same. Simply position the pointer just under the X-axis between any of the value labels. Double-click the left mouse button, and then use the **Format Axis** dialogue window to enter the values you want.

Showing labels and emphasising data points

Next we're going to make the data points on each line stand out more by increasing their size. We'll also display the actual sales figure for each point next to it as well.

▶ Position the pointer on one of the data points along the line for **North Row**.

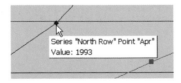

Figure 2.41

▶ Double-click the left mouse button. The **Format Data Series** dialogue box will be displayed.

TIP

Double-clicking on a data point to show the **Format Data Series** dialogue box can be quite difficult. If you have problems with this, click once anywhere on the line, and then click **Format, Selected Data Series** on the menu bar.

▶ The **Patterns** tab should be selected – if it isn't click on it.

▶ In the Marker section, click the small up arrow next to **Size** and change the value displayed to **10 pts**.

▶ Click the **Data Labels** tab, click the check box next to **Value** in the **Label Contains** section, then click **OK**. The data points on the **North Row** line will now be much larger and the actual sales figure for each point will be displayed next to it.

▶ Repeat this process for the **High Street** line. When you've finished, your graph should look like the one below.

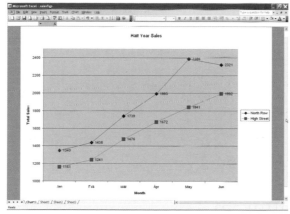

Figure 2.42

Amending the page header and printing the graph

▶ Click **View** on the menu bar, then click **Header and Footer**. The **Page Setup** dialogue box will be displayed with the **Header/Footer** tab selected.

▶ Click the **Custom Header** button. The **Header** dialogue box will be displayed.

▶ Click in the **Left section** and type your name.

▶ Click in the **Center section** and type your centre number.

▶ Click in the **Right section**, then click the **Insert Date** button. The finished header should look similar to the one in Figure 2.18. Click **OK**.

Insert Date button

▶ Click the **Page** tab in the **Page Setup** dialogue box, and make sure **Landscape** is selected in the **Orientation** section.

▶ Click the **Print** button. The **Print** dialogue box will be displayed.

▶ Check the correct printer is selected – ask your tutor if you're not sure about this – then click **OK**.

Save this spreadsheet with a different name:

▶ Click **File** on the menu bar, and then click **Save As**.

▶ Type the new name **sandgraphs**, click the **Save** button.

Creating a pie chart

The next type of graph we're going to draw is a **pie chart**, which will display the January sales figures for all three shops as different sized slices of a pie.

▶ Click on the **Sheet1** tab at the bottom of the screen.

▶ Highlight cells **A4** to **B6**, then click the **Chart Wizard** button.

▶ Click **Pie** in the **Chart type** list.

▶ Leave the first **Chart sub-type** selected

▶ Move to **Step 3** of the Chart Wizard by clicking the **Next** button twice, and click the **Titles** tab if it isn't already selected.

▶ Click in the **Chart title** box and type **January Sales**

Replacing a legend with labels

Next we're going to remove the legend from the chart – you might be asked to do this during an assignment. We'll replace the legend with labels on the pie chart showing the shop names and the percentage of total sales represented by each segment.

▶ In **Step 3** of the Chart Wizard, click the **Legend** tab and uncheck the **Show Legend** box.

▶ Click the **Data Labels** tab, and tick the **Category name** and **Percentage** boxes in the **Label Contains** list, then click **Next**.

▶ Click **As new sheet** to place the pie chart in a separate chart sheet.

▶ Click **Finish**. The pie chart will appear in a new **Chart Sheet** – it should look like the one below.

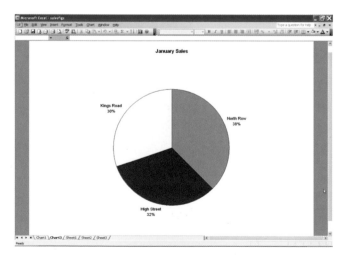

Figure 2.43

Changing the segment colours

Now we'll look at how to change the colour of individual segments in the pie chart – you might need to do this if the colours that Excel chooses don't stand out clearly from each other.

▶ Click once anywhere on the pie chart.

▶ Hold down the **Shift** key and click once on the **North Row** segment. This segment of the pie chart will be selected.

▶ Double-click anywhere on the selected **North Row** segment. The **Format Data Series** dialogue window will appear.

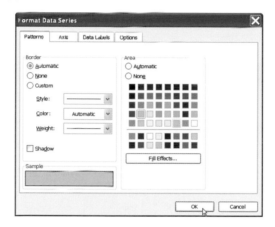

Figure 2.44

▶ Click on a colour in the area section that stands out from the other colours on the pie chart, then click **OK**. The pie chart will be displayed with the **North Row** segment re-coloured.

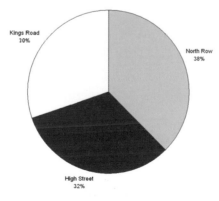

Figure 2.45

If you have time try changing the colours of the other segments on the pie chart.

▶ Print a copy of your pie chart.

Creating a bar/column chart

The last type of graph we're going to draw is a **column chart**, which will display the monthly sales figures for the North Row shop from January to June as a series of columns.

▶ Click on the **Sheet1** tab at the bottom of the screen.

▶ Highlight cells **A3** to **G4**, click the **Chart Wizard** button, then click **Column** in the **Chart type** list.

▶ Leave the first **Chart sub-type** selected, then move to **Step 3** of the Chart Wizard by clicking the **Next** button twice.

▶ Click the **Titles** tab if it isn't already selected, then click in the **Chart title** box and type **January Sales – North Row**

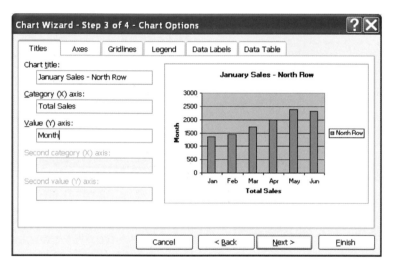

Figure 2.46

The legend on this chart doesn't provide any useful information about the data – so we can remove it:

▶ Click the **Legend** tab and uncheck the **Show Legend** box, then click **Next**.

▶ Click **As new sheet** to place the chart in a separate chart sheet, then click **Finish**. The column chart will appear in a new **Chart Sheet** – it should look like the one below.

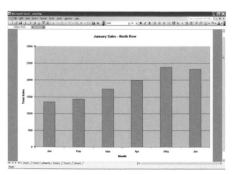

Figure 2.47

Changing column colours and adding labels

To change the colour of the columns on the chart and add labels to show the actual sales amount represented by each one:

▶ Double-click any column. The **Format Data Series** dialogue window will appear.

▶ Click the **Patterns** tab if it isn't already selected, and click on a different colour in the area section that stands out from the background on the column chart.

▶ Click the **Data labels** tab, then tick the **Value** box in the **Label Contains** list.

▶ Click **OK**. The chart will be displayed with the columns re-coloured and labelled with the sales figures.

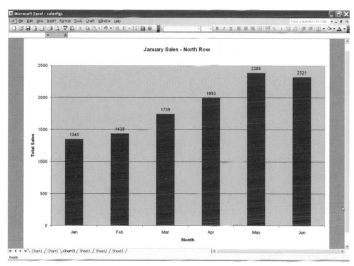

Figure 2.48

▶ **Print** a copy of your column chart, **Save** the spreadsheet keeping the filename **sandgraphs**, then **Close** Excel.

That's the end of the practice tasks. Now try the full New CLAiT assignments that follow.

Practice assignment 1

Scenario

You are working as a Financial Officer for a company that operates a number of theme parks around the country. Your job is to prepare reports on the performance of the parks for senior managers. You have been asked to report on the number of adults visiting each park and the income these visits generate.

Assessment Objectives	TASK 1	
5b	1 a)	Create a new spreadsheet.
	b)	Set the page orientation to **landscape**.
1a	2	Enter the following data, leaving the Total Visitors and Income columns blank as shown.

Theme Park Visits							
Park	April	May	June	July	August	Total Visitors	
African Adventure	13957	10543	14387	9663	8827		
Walley Word	8586	11084	12551	10988	13767		
Space Camp Europe	10284	5352	10841	5468	7251		
Partington Safari Park	5335	9955	10462	5856	6817		
Flixton Castle	7888	5042	8437	8065	5924		
West Word	9397	11064	8628	12044	8823		

5c	3	In the header enter:
		your name
		your centre number
		an **automatic date**.
5a	4	Save the spreadsheet using the filename **parks**.

Your Manager wants you to make some calculations.

2a	5 a)	In the Total Visitors column, use the Autosum function to calculate the Total for the African Adventure data from April to August.
2b	b)	Replicate this formula to show the **Total Visitors** for all the other theme parks.

| 1a | 6 | a) | Insert a new column with the label **Ticket Price** between Total Visitors and Income. |
| 1b | | b) | Enter data into the **Ticket Price** column as follows: |

Park	Ticket Price
African Adventure	13.75
Walley Word	19.2
Space Camp Europe	16.5
Partington Safari Park	11.99
Flixton Castle	8.5
West World	11.5

Your manager has asked you to calculate the income figures.

2a	7	a)	Insert a formula to calculate the Income for the African Adventure data by multiplying the Total Visitors by the Ticket Price.
2b		b)	Replicate this formula to show the **Income** for all the other theme parks.
5a	8		Save the spreadsheet keeping the filename parks.
5d	9	a)	Make sure all the data is displayed in full.
		b)	Print one copy of the spreadsheet **on one page** in **landscape** orientation, showing the figures, not the formulae.

| **Assessment Objectives** | **TASK 2** |

Your Manager has asked you to make some changes to the spreadsheet file called **parks**.

1c	1	**Partington Safari Park** has been sold to another company.
		a) Delete this row.
		b) Make sure blank cells do not remain.
4a	2	Apply the following alignments:
		a) Centre the column label **Park**.
		b) **All** other text in the first column should be displayed as left-aligned.
		c) Display all numeric data as right-aligned.
4b	3	Format the numbers as follows:
		a) Display the figures in the **Ticket Price** column with a **currency symbol** and to **2** decimal places.
		b) Display the figures in the **Income** column with a **currency symbol** and in **integer** format (zero decimal places).
		c) Display the figures in the other columns in **integer** format (zero decimal places).

| 4c | 4 | Add a single outside border around all the column labels starting with Park and ending with **Income**. |
| 5a | 5 | Save the spreadsheet with the new filename **performance**. |

Assessment Objectives	**TASK 3**	
1d 2c	1	Make the following changes to the spreadsheet file called **performance**.
		a) The **African Adventure** park has been renamed **Safari World**.
		b) The **June** figure for visitors to **Flixton Castle** must be changed to **9178**.
		c) The **Ticket Price** for **Walley World** must be changed to **21.80** (the currency symbol must remain displayed).
		d) Make sure that the **Income** figures have been updated as a result of these changes.
1a 2a 4b 5a 5b 5d	2	a) In the **Ticket Price** column, in the row below **West World**, enter the label **Total Income**.
		b) Format the **Total Income** label as bold.
		c) In the **Total Income** row, at the bottom of the **Ticket Price** column, use the **Autosum** function to calculate the total of the Income column.
		d) Make sure the **Total Income** figure is displayed with a **currency symbol** and in **integer** format (zero decimal places).
		e) Save the spreadsheet keeping the filename **performance**.
		f) Make sure **gridlines** will be displayed on the printout.
		g) Print one copy of the spreadsheet on one page in landscape orientation showing the **figures**, not the formulae.
5a 5b 5e	3	a) Display the formulae. Make sure the formulae are displayed in full.
		b) Make sure the page orientation is **landscape** and the spreadsheet fits on one page.
		c) Make sure that **gridlines** and **row and column headings** (1, 2, 3 and A, B, C...) will be displayed when printed.
		d) Save the spreadsheet formulae using the filename **performs**.
		e) Print the entire spreadsheet on **one page** in **landscape** orientation showing the **formulae**.
		f) Make sure all formulae are displayed in full and are readable on your printout.
		g) Close the file **performs**.
5a	4	Close all open files.

Assessment Objectives	TASK 4
	Your Manager has asked you to produce a graph to show the number of adult visitors to Safari World over the last two years.
	1 Using suitable software for creating graphs, open the datafile **visitscomp** which contains data on the number of adults that visited **Safari World** between **April** and **August** in **2004** and **2005**.
3a 3b	2 a) Create a comparative line graph showing the number of adults that visited **SafariWorld** between **April** and **August** in **2004** and **2005**.
4d	b) Display the months along the X-axis.
4e	c) Give the graph the heading **Safari World (adult visitors 2004 and 2005)**.
4f	d) Give the X-axis the title **Month**.
4g	e) Give the Y-axis the title **Number of adult visitors**.
4h	f) Use a legend to identify each line. Make sure that the lines and/or data points are distinctive and can be clearly identified when printed.
	g) Display the values (numbers) for each data point on both lines.
	h) Make sure that the chart is created on a full page on a sheet that is separate from the source data.
	i) Set the Y-axis range from **8000** to **15000**.

5c	3 In the header enter:
	      your name
	      your **centre number**
	      an **automatic date**.

5a	4 Save the file using the filename **visitsgraph**.
5f	5 Print one copy of the line graph.
5a	6 Close the file and exit the software.
	7 Make sure you check your printouts for accuracy.

	You should have four printouts in the following order:
	      parks
	      performance
	      performs
	      visitsgraph

Practice assignment 2

Scenario

You are working as an Administration Officer for a company that sells computer equipment. Part of your job is to process mileage claims for sales representatives.

Assessment Objectives	TASK 1
5b	1 a) Create a new spreadsheet. b) Set the page orientation to **landscape**.
1a	2 Enter the following data, leaving the **Total** and **Amount** columns blank as shown.

Mileage Claims							
Employee	Week 21	Week 22	Week 23	Week 24	Week 25	Total	Amount
Ashman, Janis	284.6	159.8	238.5	171.1	220.2		
Brice, Dean	196.8	298.2	138.8	102.4	198.3		
Cornes, Ruth	175.9	123.2	300.7	173.6	106.4		
Johnson, Scott	130.1	161.2	242.2	189.7	298.4		
Kahn, Tariq	286.2	174.1	151.1	107.7	133.5		
Singh, James	159.4	173.3	284.1	156.8	172.9		
Smith, Tracey	219.6	112.4	184.1	264.9	118.1		

5c	3 In the header enter: **your name** **your centre number** an **automatic date**.
5a	4 Save the spreadsheet using the filename **mileage**
	Your Manager wants you to make some calculations.
2a	5 a) In the **Total** column use the Autosum function to calculate the **Total** for the **Ashman, Janis** data (Week 21 to Week 25 inclusive).
2b	b) Replicate this formula to show the **Total** for all the other sales representatives.
1a	6 a) Insert a new column with the label **Rate** between **Total** and **Amount**.

1b

b) Enter data into the **Rate** column as follows:

Employee	Rate
Ashman, Janis	**0.39**
Brice, Dean	**0.4**
Cornes, Ruth	**0.39**
Johnson, Scott	**0.39**
Kahn, Tariq	**0.32**
Singh, James	**0.34**
Smith, Tracey	**0.3**

Your Manager has asked you to calculate the **Amount** figures.

2a

7 a) Insert a formula to calculate the **Amount** for the **Ashman, Janis** data by multiplying the **Total** by the **Rate**.

2b

b) Replicate this formula to show the **Amount** for all the other sales representatives.

5a

8 Save the spreadsheet keeping the filename **mileage**.

5d

9 a) Make sure all the data is displayed in full.

b) Print one copy of the spreadsheet **on one page** in **landscape** orientation, showing the figures, not the formulae.

Assessment Objectives

TASK 2

Your Manager has asked you to make some changes to the spreadsheet file called **mileage**.

1c

1 The figures for **Week 21** have already been included on another spreadsheet.

a) Delete this column.

b) Make sure blank cells do not remain.

4a

2 Apply the following alignments:

a) Centre the column labels **Employee** and **Rate** and format the text as bold.

b) **All** other text should be displayed as left-aligned.

c) Display all numeric data in the **Rate** column as centre-aligned.

d) Display **all** other numeric data as right-aligned.

4b

3 Format the numbers as follows:

a) Display the figures in the **Rate** column to **2** decimal places.

b) Display the figures in the **Amount** column with a **currency symbol** and to **2** decimal places.

c) Display the figures in the other columns in **integer** format (zero decimal places).

4c	4 Add a single outside border around all the column labels starting with **Employee** and ending with **Amount**.
5a	5 Save the spreadsheet with the new filename **payments**.

Assessment Objectives	**TASK 3**
1d 2c	1 Make the following changes to the spreadsheet file called **payments**.
	a) Employee **Cornes**, **Ruth** has changed her name to **Hammond**, **Ruth**.
	b) The **Week 23** mileage figure for **Brice**, **Dean** must be changed to **193**.
	c) The **Rate** for **Kahn**, **Tariq** must be changed to **0.42**.
	d) Make sure that the **Amount** figures have been updated as a result of these changes.
1a 2a	2 a) In the **Rate** column, in the row below **Smith**, **Tracey**, enter the label **Payment Total**.
4b	b) Right align the row label **Payment Total** and format the text as bold.
5a 5b	c) In the **Payment Total** row, at the bottom of the **Rate** column, use the Autosum function to calculate the total of the **Total Claimed** column.
5d	d) Make sure the **Payment Total** figure is displayed with a with a **currency symbol** and to **2** decimal places.
	e) Save the spreadsheet keeping the filename **payments**.
	f) Make sure **gridlines** will be displayed on the printout.
	g) Print **one copy** of the spreadsheet **on one page** in **landscape** orientation showing the **figures**, not the formulae.
5a 5b	3 a) Display the formulae. Make sure the formulae are displayed in full.
	b) Make sure the page orientation is **landscape** and the spreadsheet fits on one page.
5e	c) Make sure that **gridlines** and **row and column headings** (1, 2, 3 and A, B, C...) will be displayed when printed.
	d) Save the spreadsheet formulae using the filename **payform**.
	e) Print the entire spreadsheet on **one page** in **landscape** orientation showing the **formulae**.
	f) Make sure all formulae are displayed in full and are readable on your printout.
	g) Close the file **payform**.
5a	4 Close all open files.

Assessment Objectives	TASK 4

Your Manager has asked you to produce a graph to show the mileage claimed by **Asman, Janis** from **January** to **June**.

1   Using suitable software for creating graphs, open the datafile **mileagesum** which contains data on mileage claimed by the sales representatives from January to June.

3a
3b

2   a)   Create a column (bar) chart showing the mileage claimed by **Ashman, Janis** from **January** to **June**.

4d

    b)   Display the months along the X-axis.

4e

    c)   Give the graph the heading **Mileage for Ashman, Janis**.

4f

    d)   Give the X-axis the title **Month**

4g

    e)   Give the Y-axis the title **Miles**

4h

    f)   Do not include a legend.

    g)   Make sure that the chart is created on a full page on a sheet that is separate from the source data.

    h)   Set the Y-axis range from **0** to **600**.

5c

3   In the header enter:

      your name

      your **centre number**

      an **automatic date**.

5a

4   Save the file using the filename **mileagechart**.

5f

5   Print one copy of the column chart.

5a

6   Close the file and exit the software.

7   Make sure you check your printouts for accuracy.

You should have four printouts in the following order:

      mileage

      payments

      payform

      mileagechart

Practice assignment 3

Scenario

You are working for a national chain of newsagents. Your manager has asked you to prepare a spreadsheet for one of the shops showing their newspaper sales last week.

Assessment Objectives

TASK 1

5b

1 a)   Create a new spreadsheet.

   b)   Set the page orientation to **landscape**.

1a

2   Enter the following data, leaving the **Total Sales** and **Profit** columns blank as shown.

Weekly Sales								
Newspaper	Mon	Tue	Wed	Thu	Fri	Sat	Total Sales	Profit
Herald	145	101	107	72	83	93		
Messenger	60	38	35	56	47	51		
Record	64	85	133	138	93	113		
Reporter	72	96	86	110	140	77		
Sentinel	50	49	31	69	44	74		
Standard	90	92	117	98	94	103		

5c

3   In the header enter:

   your name

   your centre number

   an **automatic date**.

5a

4   Save the spreadsheet using the filename **newspapers**.

Your manager wants you to make some calculations.

2a

5 a)   In the **Total Sales** column, use the SUM function to calculate the **Total Sales** for the **Herald** data from Mon to Sat.

2b

   b)   Replicate this formula to show the **Total Sales** for all the other newspapers.

1a

6 a)   Insert a new column with the label **Cost Price** between Total Sales and Profit.

1b

   b)   Enter data into the **Cost Price** column as follows:

Newspaper	Cost Price
Herald	**0.3**
Messenger	**0.36**
Record	**0.34**
Reporter	**0.42**
Sentinel	**0.4**
Standard	**0.37**

2a	7	a)	Insert a formula to calculate the **Profit** for the **Herald** by multiplying the **Total Sales** by the **Cost Price** then multiplying this figure by **1.15**.
		b)	Replicate this formula to show the **Profit** for all other newspapers.
5a	8		Save the spreadsheet keeping the filename **newspapers**.
5d	9	a)	Make sure all the data is displayed in full.
		b)	Print one copy of the spreadsheet **on one page** in **landscape** orientation, showing the figures, not the formulae.

Assessment Objectives | **TASK 2**

Your Manager has asked you to make some changes to the spreadsheet file called **newspapers**.

1c	1		The figures for the **Sentinel** are not required.
		a)	Delete this row.
		b)	Make sure blank cells do not remain.
4a	2		Apply the following alignments:
		a)	Centre the column label **Newspaper** and format the text as bold.
		b)	**All** other text in the first column should be displayed as left-aligned.
		c)	Centre **all** the column labels from **Mon** to **Sat**.
		d)	Display all numeric data as right-aligned.
4b	3		Format the numbers as follows:
		a)	Display the figures in the **Cost Price** column to **2** decimal places.
		b)	Display the figures in the **Gross Profit** column with a **currency symbol** and to **2** decimal places.
		c)	Display the figures in the other columns in **integer** format (zero decimal places).
4c	4		Add a single outside border around all the column labels starting with **newspaper** and ending with **profit**.
5a	5		Save the spreadsheet with the new filename **weeksales**.

Assessment Objectives	TASK 3

1d
2c
	1. Make the following changes to the spreadsheet file called **weeksales**.
	
	   a) The newspaper **Reporter** must be renamed **Evening Tribune**.
	
	   b) The **Tue** figure for **Messenger** must be changed to **56**.
	
	   c) The **Cost Price** of **Herald** must be changed to 0.28.
	
	   d) Make sure that the **Gross Profit** figures have been updated as a result of these changes.

1a
2a
 	
4b
 	
5a
 	
5b
 	
5d
	2 a) In the **Cost Price** column, in the row below the **Standard**, enter the label **Total Profit**.
	
	   b) Right align the column label **Total Profit** and format the text as bold.
	
	   c) In the **Total Profit** row, at the bottom of the **Gross Profit** column, use the Autosum function to calculate the total of the **Gross Profit**.
	
	   d) Make sure the **Total Profit** figure is displayed with a **currency** symbol and **2 decimal places**.
	
	   e) Save the spreadsheet keeping the filename **weeksales**.
	
	   f) Make sure **gridlines** will be displayed on the printout.
	
	   g) Print **one copy** of the spreadsheet **on one page** in landscape orientation showing the **figures**, not the formulae.

5a
 	
5b
 	
5e
	3 a) Display the **formulae**. Make sure the formulae are displayed in full.
	
	   b) Make sure the page orientation is **landscape** and the spreadsheet fits on one page.
	
	   c) Make sure that **gridlines** and **row and column headings** (1, 2, 3 and A, B, C…) will be displayed when printed.
	
	   d) Save the spreadsheet formulae using the filename **weeksform**.
	
	   e) Print the entire spreadsheet on **one page** in **landscape** orientation showing the **formulae**.
	
	   f) Make sure all formulae are displayed in full and are readable on your printout.
	
	   g) Close the file **weeksform**.

5a	4 Close all open files.

Assessment Objectives	TASK 4

Your manager has asked you to produce a graph showing last year's newspapers sales figures for the North West region.

1   Using suitable software for creating graphs, open the datafile **salescomp** which contains data on last year's newspaper sales in the North West and North East regions.

3a 3b	2 a)	Create a pie chart showing last year's newspapers sales figures for the **North West** region.
4d	b)	Give the chart the heading **North West Sales**.
4e 4f	c)	Make sure that each sector of the chart is distinctive and can be clearly identified when printed.
4g	d)	Label each sector of the chart with the name of the newspaper and the percentage of sales represented.
4h	e)	Make sure that the chart is created on a full page on a sheet that is separate from the source data.

5c   3   In the header enter:

your name

your **centre number**

an **automatic date**.

5a   4   Save the file using the filename **nwpie**.

5f   5   Print one copy of the pie chart.

5a   6   Close the file and exit the software.

7   Make sure you check your printouts for accuracy.

You should have four printouts in the following order:

newspapers

weeksales

weeksform

nwpie

To pass this unit you must be able to:

☑ identify and use database software correctly

☑ enter data in an existing database and present and print database files

☑ create simple queries/searches on one or two criteria and sort data

☑ produce appropriate pre-defined reports from databases using shortcuts

☑ present data in full

Before you start this chapter, you or your tutor should download a zipped file called **Resources for Chapter 3** from **www.payne-gallway.co.uk/newclait/student**. It will automatically unzip. Specify that the contents are to be saved in your My Documents folder.

Computer databases

Computer **databases** have been used to store information since the middle of the last century. A **database** is a collection of **related records**. The term *related records* means that each record in a **database** contains the same sort of information as all the other records. Every record must have at least one **field**. A **field** contains one individual item of data. In order to identify individual records one field is normally defined as the **key field**. The **key field** in each record of a data file must be unique and cannot be duplicated in any other record.

In the example below a school is storing information about its pupils in a **database**. Each pupil has their own row; this is their **record**. On a pupil's record certain things about them are recorded like name and date of birth; these individual pieces of information are called **fields**. The **key field** in each record is the pupil number – this is different for each pupil.

UPN	Forename	Surname	Date of Birth	Teacher	Record
217364	James	Singh	12-11-1991	Mr Hillman	
400832	Harry	Portman	21-09-1991	Ms Berrisford	
545977	Lucy	Saunders	17-10-1991	Mr Sumal	

Field

Figure 3.1

The practice tasks that follow cover all the techniques you need to learn in order to pass a New CLAiT Unit 3 assignment.

Practice tasks

Task 1   Loading Microsoft Access 2003

The first part of an assessment task for this unit requires that you use a **login** – also called a **user name** – and/or **password** to gain access to data. Your tutor will give you this information and explain what to do.

During this task you'll need to take screen prints to provide evidence of what you've done. We are going to use Word to display and print out these screen prints.

Computer databases

You can load Access in one of two ways:

Microsoft Office
Access 2003

(►) *Either* double-click the **Microsoft Access 2003** (referred to as **Access**) icon on the Desktop in Windows,

Microsoft Office
Access 2003

(►) *or* click the **Start** button at the bottom left of the screen, then click **All programs**, then click

Figure 3.2

The main **Database** window will be displayed – it should look like the one below.

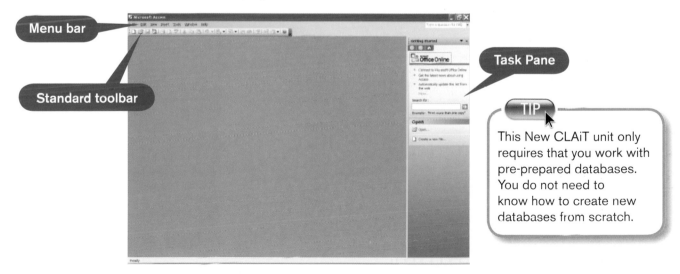

Figure 3.3

You now have the option of either opening an existing **database** or creating a new one. To get started you need to load a sample **Access database**.

Opening an existing database

Click **Open** on the **Standard** toolbar to open an existing **database**. A list of **Access** databases will be displayed.

Figure 3.4

The **database** you need to load is called **HOUSES**. Your tutor will tell you where to find this file if you can't see it in the list on your screen.

Click on **HOUSES** and **Open**. The database window will appear.

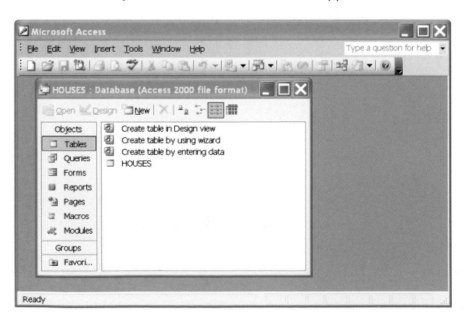

Figure 3.5

▶ **Tables** should already be selected; if it isn't just click once on it.

▶ Open the database table **HOUSES** by double-clicking it. A database table containing twelve records will appear as shown below.

	Property number	Type	Street	Town	Postcode	Beds	Baths	Price
▶	1200	Terraced	21 Lowther Street	Canford	CN21 9XJ	2	1	£119,995
	1201	Semi-detached	74 Grange Road	Canford	CN17 2BF	3	1	£144,995
	1202	Semi-detached	33 Haywood Street	Canford	CN20 8HQ	4	2	£160,000
	1203	Bungalow	14 Taybor Avenue	Gorton	GR11 3JB	4	2	£175,495
	1204	Detached	181 High Lane	Canford	CN17 8JU	5	2	£209,995
	1205	Terraced	42 Cornwallis Street	Canford	CN27 1BQ	2	1	£132,495
	1206	Detached	28 Horton Drive	Gorton	GR15 9FX	4	2	£200,000
	1207	Semi-detached	78 Grange Road	Canford	CN17 2BF	3	1	£143,495
	1208	Flat	1219 Cresta Court	Gorton	GR9 11PK	2	1	£109,495
	1209	Bungalow	27 Braymar Avenue	Canford	CN22 6CT	3	1	£154,995
	1210	Detached	45 Sherwood Road	Canford	CN26 9TY	4	2	£175,995
	1211	Terraced	17 Skaymar Court	Gorton	GR12 6GP	3	1	£125,000
*						0	0	£0

Figure 3.6

Changing page orientation

The first thing you'll be asked to do during a Unit 3 assignment is change the page orientation to landscape and print the records in table format. The steps below describe how to do this.

▶ Click **File** on the menu bar, and then click **Page Setup**.

The **Page Setup** dialogue box will appear.

▶ Click the **Page** tab.

Figure 3.7

▶ In the **Orientation** section click the radio button on the right for **Landscape**.

▶ Click **OK**.

▶ Click the **Print** button on the **Standard** toolbar.

▶ Close the database table by clicking **X** in the top right corner of the **Table** window.

Print button

Copying a database table

After printing the database table you'll be asked to make a copy of it and add your name to the table name. You must use this copy of the database table for the rest of the assignment. If you make any mistakes during the assignment you can always use the original copy of the database table to work out where you went wrong and make corrections.

To make a copy of the database table:

- **Tables** should already be selected in the window – if it isn't just click once on it.
- Click once on the database table **HOUSES**.
- Click **Copy**, then **Paste** on the **Standard** toolbar. You will see this message:

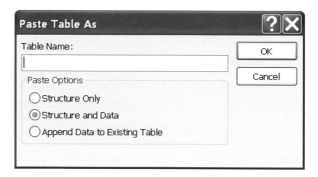

Figure 3.8

- Enter **HOUSES** followed by **(YOUR NAME)** in **the Table Name** box. For example: **HOUSES CHESTER WHEAT.**
- Click **OK**. The copy of the database table will appear in the **Database** window.

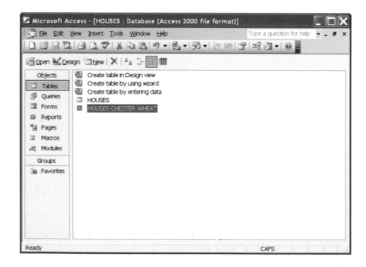

Figure 3.9

Task 2   Adding and deleting records

During a Unit 3 assignment you'll be required to make changes to an existing database by adding new records, deleting existing records and editing data inside individual fields. This task takes you through the first two of these techniques.

Design View and Datasheet View

There are two **view modes** to choose from when changes need to be made to an Access database. **Design View** is used to change the database **structure**. This might, for example, involve deleting or adding fields.

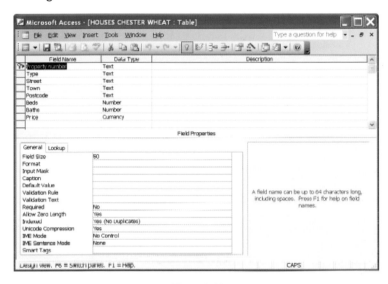

Figure 3.10

Datasheet View is used for editing existing data or adding new data to a database – this is the only view mode you will need to use for Unit 3 assignments.

 Open **your copy** of the **HOUSES** table.

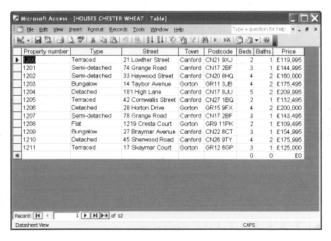

Figure 3.11

Deleting records

We'll try deleting some records first. Suppose we needed to delete the record for **42 Cornwallis Street** because it had been sold.

▶ Click anywhere in this record.

Delete Record
Icon

▶ Click the **Delete Record** icon on the **Table Datasheet** toolbar. You will see this message:

Figure 3.12

▶ Click **Yes** to delete the record.

▶ Now use the same technique to delete the records for these properties:

33 Haywood Street

74 Grange Road

When you've finished, your database table should look exactly like the one below.

	Property number	Type	Street	Town	Postcode	Beds	Baths	Price
▶	1200	Terraced	21 Lowther Street	Canford	CN21 9XJ	2	1	£119,995
	1203	Bungalow	14 Taybor Avenue	Gorton	GR11 3JB	4	2	£175,495
	1204	Detached	181 High Lane	Canford	CN17 8JU	5	2	£209,995
	1206	Detached	28 Horton Drive	Gorton	GR15 9FX	4	2	£200,000
	1207	Semi-detached	78 Grange Road	Canford	CN17 2BF	3	1	£143,495
	1208	Flat	1219 Cresta Court	Gorton	GR9 11PK	2	1	£109,495
	1209	Bungalow	27 Braymar Avenue	Canford	CN22 6CT	3	1	£154,995
	1210	Detached	45 Sherwood Road	Canford	CN26 9TY	4	2	£175,995
	1211	Terraced	17 Skaymar Court	Gorton	GR12 6GP	3	1	£125,000
*						0	0	£0

Figure 3.13

Adding records to a table

Next we'll add some new records to the **HOUSES** (your name) database. There are two ways to add a new record:

▶ *Either* click in the blank line at the bottom of the table,

	1211	Terraced	17 Skaymar Court	Gorton	GR12 6GP	3	1	£125,000
*						0	0	£0

Figure 3.14

or click the **New Record** icon on the toolbar at the top of the screen.

Try using both of these techniques to add the new records shown in the table below.

New Record
Icon

Property number	Type	Street	Town	Postcode	Beds	Baths	Price
1212	Detached	36 Horton Drive	Gorton	GR15 9FX	4	2	£181,995
1213	Semi-detached	19 Norton Ave	Canford	CN16 2SY	3	1	£110,995
1214	Detached	12 Castle Row	Canford	CN11 1LJ	4	2	£220,450

Figure 3.15

Your database table should now look exactly like the one below.

Property number	Type	Street	Town	Postcode	Beds	Baths	Price
1200	Terraced	21 Lowther Street	Canford	CN21 9XJ	2	1	£119,995
1203	Bungalow	14 Taybor Avenue	Gorton	GR11 3JB	4	2	£175,495
1204	Detached	181 High Lane	Canford	CN17 8JU	5	2	£209,995
1206	Detached	28 Horton Drive	Gorton	GR15 9FX	4	2	£200,000
1207	Semi-detached	78 Grange Road	Canford	CN17 2BF	3	1	£143,495
1208	Flat	1219 Cresta Court	Gorton	GR9 11PK	2	1	£109,495
1209	Bungalow	27 Braymar Avenue	Canford	CN22 6CT	3	1	£154,995
1210	Detached	45 Sherwood Road	Canford	CN26 9TY	4	2	£175,995
1211	Terraced	17 Skaymar Court	Gorton	GR12 6GP	3	1	£125,000
1212	Detached	36 Horton Drive	Gorton	GR15 9FX	4	2	£181,995
1213	Semi-detached	19 Norton Avenue	Canford	CN16 2SY	3	1	£110,995
1214	Detached	12 Castle Row	Canford	CN11 1LJ	4	2	£220,450
					0	0	£0

Figure 3.16

Always check new records carefully to make sure they match those shown in the table on your assignment. Mistakes made when creating new records are a common reason for candidates failing Unit 3 assignments.

Closing the database table and exiting Access

Now we'll save the database table and close Access before moving on to the next task.

- Close the **HOUSES (your name)** database table by clicking **X** in the top right-hand corner of the table window
- Click **Yes** to save the changes you've just made to the database table

To close **Access**:

- *Either* click **File** on the menu bar, and then click **Exit**,
- *or* click **X** in the top right-hand corner of the screen

Task 3   Editing records

As well as adding and deleting records you will also be asked during Unit 3 assignments to edit the data in some of the records. This will involve changing the values of individual fields for some records and replacing all the values in one field for every record with special codes.

First we'll change the values of individual fields in some of the records.

- ▶ Load **Access**.
- ▶ Open **your copy** of the **HOUSES** database.
- ▶ Open the **HOUSES (your name)** database table in **Datasheet View**.

Suppose we needed to make the following change to the table: The vendors of property number **1204** want a quick sale – the price of this property has been reduced to **£198,000**.

- ▶ Click in the **Price** field of property number **1204**.
- ▶ Delete the current value for **Price** using the **Backspace** key.
- ▶ Type **198000** and press **Enter** – this field is formatted to automatically display numbers with a pound sign and comma, so you can leave these out.

Now make these changes to the **HOUSES (your name)** database table:

- ▶ Change the number of bedrooms for the property at **45 Sherwood Road** to **3**.
- ▶ Change the location of property number **1203** to **Canford**.

Once you've made these changes your database table should look exactly like the one here.

Property number	Type	Street	Town	Postcode	Beds	Baths	Price
1200	Terraced	21 Lowther Street	Canford	CN21 9XJ	2	1	£119,995
1203	Bungalow	14 Taybor Avenue	Canford	GR11 3JB	4	2	£175,495
1204	Detached	181 High Lane	Canford	CN17 8JU	5	2	£198,000
1206	Detached	28 Horton Drive	Gorton	GR15 9FX	4	2	£200,000
1207	Semi-detached	78 Grange Road	Canford	CN17 2BF	3	1	£143,495
1208	Flat	1219 Cresta Court	Gorton	GR9 11PK	2	1	£109,495
1209	Bungalow	27 Braymar Avenue	Canford	CN22 6CT	3	1	£154,995
1210	Detached	45 Sherwood Road	Canford	CN26 9TY	3	2	£175,995
1211	Terraced	17 Skaymar Court	Gorton	GR12 6GP	3	1	£125,000
1212	Detached	36 Horton Drive	Gorton	GR15 9FX	4	2	£181,995
1213	Semi-detached	19 Norton Avenue	Canford	CN16 2SY	3	1	£110,995
1214	Detached	12 Castle Row	Canford	CN11 1LJ	4	2	£220,450
					0	0	£0

Figure 3.17

TIP

Check your database table carefully after editing records to make sure the changes you've made to individual fields match those described in the assignment task. Mistakes made when editing records are a common reason for candidates failing Unit 3 assignments.

Using Find and Replace

When data is input using a manual input device such as a keyboard, errors often occur owing to values being entered incorrectly. One method that can be used to cut down on errors like this is to use **coded values** for a field. During Unit 3 assignments you will be asked to replace all the entries in one field with codes, to make entering data for that field easier and less error-prone. We'll look at how to do this now using the **Find and Replace** facility in **Access**.

Suppose we wanted to replace every entry in the **Type** field with the following codes:

Detached	**DET**
Semi-detached	**SEM**
Terraced	**TER**
Flat	**FLA**
Bungalow	**BUN**

We'll start by replacing every entry for **Terraced** with the code **TER**.

▶ Double-click anywhere in the **Type** column where the value **Terraced** appears.

▶ Click **Edit**, then **Replace** on the menu bar. The **Find and Replace** dialogue box will appear.

Figure 3.18

▶ **Terraced** will be displayed in the **Find What** box – this is because we've already double-clicked in a record where the value for the **Type** field is **Terraced**.

▶ Click in the **Replace With** box and type **TER**.

▶ Click **Replace All**. You will see the following message:

Figure 3.19

⊙ Click **Yes**. The **Type** column in your database table should now look exactly like the one below.

Property number	Type	Street	Town	Postcode	Beds	Baths	Price
1200	TER	21 Lowther Street	Canford	CN21 9XJ	2	1	£119,995
1203	Bungalow	14 Taybor Avenue	Canford	GR11 3JB	4	2	£175,495
1204	Detached	181 High Lane	Canford	CN17 8JU	5	2	£198,000
1206	Detached	28 Horton Drive	Gorton	GR15 9FX	4	2	£200,000
1207	Semi-detached	78 Grange Road	Canford	CN17 2BF	3	1	£143,495
1208	Flat	1219 Cresta Court	Gorton	GR9 11PK	2	1	£109,495
1209	Bungalow	27 Braymar Avenue	Canford	CN22 6CT	3	1	£154,995
1210	Detached	45 Sherwood Road	Canford	CN26 9TY	3	2	£175,995
1211	TER	17 Skaymar Court	Gorton	GR12 6GP	3	1	£125,000
1212	Detached	36 Horton Drive	Gorton	GR15 9FX	4	2	£181,995
1213	Semi-detached	19 Norton Avenue	Canford	CN16 2SY	3	1	£110,995
1214	Detached	12 Castle Row	Canford	CN11 1LJ	4	2	£220,450
					0	0	£0

Figure 3.20

Next we need to replace every entry for **Semi-detached** with the code **SEM**. The **Find and Replace** dialogue box is still displayed so we can carry on using it.

⊙ Press the **Backspace** key to clear the value displayed in the **Find What** box.

⊙ Type **Semi-detached**.

⊙ Click in the **Replace With** box and type **SEM**.

⊙ Click **Replace All**.

⊙ Click **Yes** when the warning message appears.

⊙ Now repeat these steps and replace all the other entries in the **Type** field with the corresponding codes given earlier.

⊙ When you've finished click **X** in the top right hand-corner of the **Find and Replace** dialogue box to close it.

⊙ Check through the **Type** column in your database table to make sure it looks exactly like the one shown below.

Property number	Type	Street	Town	Postcode	Beds	Baths	Price
1200	TER	21 Lowther Street	Canford	CN21 9XJ	2	1	£119,995
1203	BUN	14 Taybor Avenue	Canford	GR11 3JB	4	2	£175,495
1204	DET	181 High Lane	Canford	CN17 8JU	5	2	£198,000
1206	DET	28 Horton Drive	Gorton	GR15 9FX	4	2	£200,000
1207	SEM	78 Grange Road	Canford	CN17 2BF	3	1	£143,495
1208	FLA	1219 Cresta Court	Gorton	GR9 11PK	2	1	£109,495
1209	BUN	27 Braymar Avenue	Canford	CN22 6CT	3	1	£154,995
1210	DET	45 Sherwood Road	Canford	CN26 9TY	3	2	£175,995
1211	TER	17 Skaymar Court	Gorton	GR12 6GP	3	1	£125,000
1212	DET	36 Horton Drive	Gorton	GR15 9FX	4	2	£181,995
1213	SEM	19 Norton Avenue	Canford	CN16 2SY	3	1	£110,995
1214	DET	12 Castle Row	Canford	CN11 1LJ	4	2	£220,450
					0	0	£0

Figure 3.21

- Print the **HOUSES (your name)** database table in table format (if you can't remember how to do this follow the steps listed at the end of Task 1).

- Close the database table.

- Close **Access**.

Task 4   Searching and sorting

Searching a database involves looking for an individual record or group of records that match certain conditions. To carry out a search the user must create a **query**.

For Unit 3 the most straightforward type of query you'll be asked to create will search a database to find all the records matching a single condition. We're going to work through the steps needed to do this by setting up a query in the **HOUSES** database that will:

- find all **HOUSES** with a selling price **greater than £175,000**

- sort the data into **ascending order of price**

- display *only* the **Type**, **Street**, **Town** and **Price** fields.

Creating a new query

- Load Access and open the **HOUSES** database.

- Click **Queries** in the Database window – you will see two options.

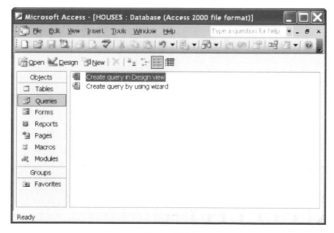

Figure 3.22

- Double-click **Create query in Design view** – this is the option you should use for all your queries. The **Show Table** window will appear.

Figure 3.23

▶ Click **HOUSES (your name)** and **Add**.

▶ Click **Close** to close the **Show Table** window – an empty query grid like the one that follows will appear.

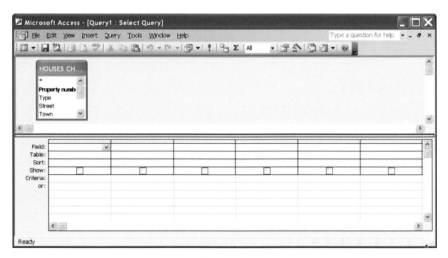

Figure 3.24

Selecting which fields to display

For this query we only need to search the **Price** field and display the **Type**, **Street**, **Town** and **Price** fields in the list of matching records.

Double-click the fields **Type, Street, Town** and **Price** to put them on the query grid.

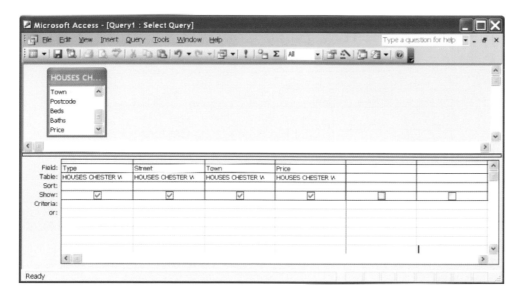

Figure 3.25

Sorting on a particular field

Click in the **Sort** row under the **Price** column.

Click the small down-arrow, and then **Ascending**.

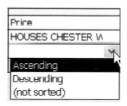

Figure 3.26

Entering search criteria

Click in the **Criteria** row under the **Price** column and type **>175000**.

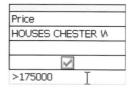

Figure 3.27

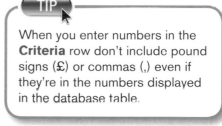

TIP

When you enter numbers in the **Criteria** row don't include pound signs (£) or commas (,) even if they're in the numbers displayed in the database table.

Running a query

That's the query ready – all we need to do now is run it to see the results.

Run button

▶ Click the **Run** button on the **Query Design** toolbar. You should see a table of results the same as the following:

	Type	Street	Town	Price
	BUN	14 Taybor Avenue	Canford	£175,495
	DET	181 High Lane	Canford	£198,000
	DET	28 Horton Drive	Gorton	£200,000
	DET	45 Sherwood Road	Canford	£175,995
	DET	36 Horton Drive	Gorton	£181,995
	DET	12 Castle Row	Canford	£220,450
▶				£0

Figure 3.28

Saving a query

Now we need to save the query.

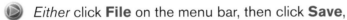

Save button

▶ *Either* click **File** on the menu bar, then click **Save**,

▶ *or* click the **Save** button on the **Standard** toolbar. The dialogue box will appear:

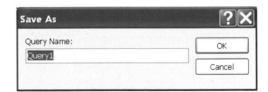

Figure 3.29

The name highlighted in the **File name** box is the default filename which is normally something like **Query**. This can be changed to whatever you like.

▶ Type the name, **PRICEGT (your name)**, for example, **PRICEGT CHESTER WHEAT**, and then click **OK**.

Now the query has been saved, it can be run any time by double-clicking its name in the **Database** window – try this if you have time.

Printing the query results

The last thing we need to do is print the query results in **Table** format.

▶ Click **File** on the menu bar and then click **Page Setup**. The **Page Setup** dialogue box will appear.

▶ Click the **Page** tab.

Figure 3.30

In the **Orientation** section click the radio button on the right for **Landscape**.

Click **OK**.

Click the **Print** button on the **Standard** toolbar

Print button

Close the query by clicking **X** in the top right corner of the **Query** window.

Now try repeating the steps described above to create a slightly different query that will:

- find all houses with a selling price **less than £125,000**.

- sort the data into **descending order of price**.

- display only the **Street**, **Town** and **Price** fields.

Save this query with the name, **PRICELT (your name).** For example: **PRICELT CHESTER WHEAT**, and then click **OK**.

> **TIP**
>
> Use the < symbol when entering the condition for a **less than** query in the **Criteria** row. To enter a less than or equal to query use the <= symbols.

Queries with multiple criteria

For Unit 3, the most complicated type of query you'll be asked to create will search a database to find all the records matching *two* conditions. We'll work through the steps needed to do this by setting up a query in the **HOUSES** database that will:

- find all **semi-detached** houses with **4 bedrooms**

- sort the data into **descending order of price**

- display only the **Street**, **Town** and **Price** fields.

- Click **Queries** in the Database window.
- Double-click **Create query in Design view**.
- Click **HOUSES (your name)** and **Add**.
- Click **Close** to close the **Show Table** window – a new empty query grid will appear.

For this query we need to search both the **Type** *and* **Beds** fields but display only the **Street**, **Town**, **Beds** and **Price** fields in the list of matching records.

- Double-click the fields **Type, Street, Town, Beds** and **Price** to put them on the query grid.
- Click in the **Sort** row under the **Price** column. Click the small down-arrow and select **Descending**.
- Click in the **Criteria** row under the **Type** column, type **SEM**.
- Click in the **Criteria** row under the **Beds** column, type **4**.

Hiding a field in the Query result table

We don't want the **Type** field to be shown in the list of matching records for this query. You'll see that there is a **Show** row above the **Criteria** row with all the boxes ticked. To do this we need to un-tick the box for this field.

- Click in the **Show** row in the **Type** column.
- Un-tick the box for this field.

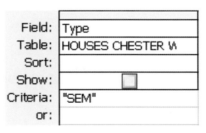

Field:	Type
Table:	HOUSES CHESTER W
Sort:	
Show:	☐
Criteria:	"SEM"
or:	

Figure 3.31

When you've finished, the query grid should look like the one here:

Field:	Type	Street	Town	Beds	Price
Table:	HOUSES CHESTER W	HOUSES CHESTER W	HOUSES CHESTER W	HOUSES CHESTER W	HOUSES CHESTER W
Sort:					Descending
Show:	☐	☑	☑	☑	☑
Criteria:	"SEM"			3	
or:					

Figure 3.32

That's the query ready – all we need to do now is run it to see the results.

Run button

○ Click the **Run** button on the **Query Design** toolbar. You should see a table of results the same as the one below.

	Street	Town	Beds	Price
	78 Grange Road	Canford	3	£143,495
	19 Norton Avenue	Canford	3	£110,995
▶			0	£0

Figure 3.33

○ Save this query with the name, **PRTYPE (your name).** For example: **PRTYPE (CHESTER WHEAT)**, and then click **OK**.

○ Print the query results table.

○ Close the query by clicking **X** in top right corner of the query window.

○ Close **Access**.

Task 5   Reports

Reports are used to summarise and print out information from a database. Reports are often used to display the information found by a query. During a Unit 3 assignment you'll be asked to create and print a report based on one of the queries you've created. We're going to work through the steps needed to do this by creating a report to display and print the information found by the query **PRTYPE** on **one page** in **landscape** orientation.

○ Load Access and open the **HOUSES** database.

Creating a report

○ Click **Reports** in the Database window - you will see two options.

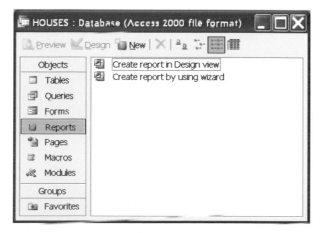

Figure 3.34

- Double-click **Create report by using wizard** – this is the option you should always use for reports. The **Report Wizard** window will appear.

- Click the small down arrow under **Tables/Queries**.

- Click **Query: PRTYPE (your name)** in the drop-down list.

- Click **>>** to include all the fields in this query in the report.

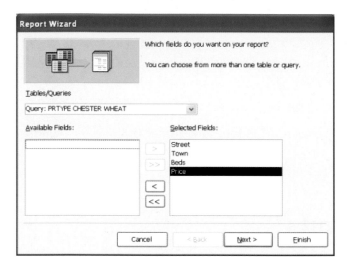

Figure 3.35

- Click **Next**.

- Click **Next** when you're asked if you want to add any grouping levels.

- Click **Next** when you're asked which sort order you want for your records.

- You'll be asked how you would like to lay out your report. In the **Orientation** section, click the radio button for **Landscape** then click **Next**.

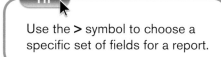

TIP

Use the **>** symbol to choose a specific set of fields for a report.

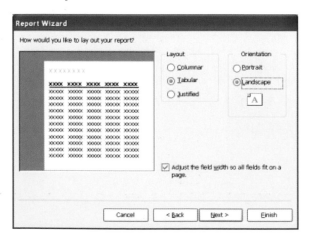

Figure 3.36

You'll be asked what style you would like for your report. Choose any style from the list, and then click **Next**.

Figure 3.37

You'll be asked what title you would like for your report. Enter the title **TYPEREPORT (your name)** – for example, **TYPEREPORT CHESTER WHEAT**, and then click **Finish**.

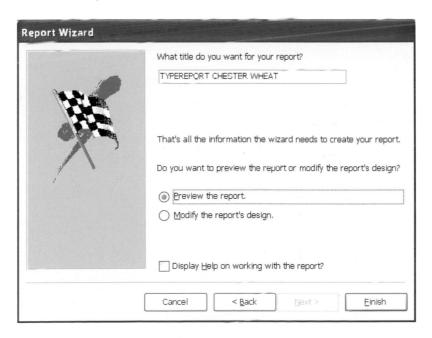

Figure 3.38

The report will appear.

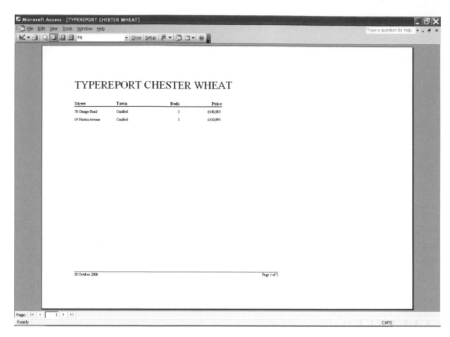

Figure 3.39

Saving the report format

Now you need to save and print the report.

⊳ Click **File** on the menu bar, and then click **Save As**.

⊳ Type the name, **TYPEREPORT (your name)** in the **Save Report** box, for example **TYPEREPORT CHESTER WHEAT**, then click **OK**.

Print button

⊳ Click the **Print** button on the **Standard** toolbar to print the report.

⊳ Close **Access**.

That's the end of the practice tasks. Now try the full New CLAiT assignments that follow.

Practice assignment 1

Scenario

You are the Data Manager of Castle Car Sales. One of your duties is maintaining a database of cars currently available for sale.

Assessment Objectives	TASK 1
1a	**1** Open the Access database called **CARS**.

The database table consists of the following fields:

FIELD HEADING	DESCRIPTION OF DATA
REGISTRATION	The car's registration number
MAKE	The name of the car's manufacturer
MODEL	The model name of the car
YEAR	The year of the car's first registration
PRICE	The selling price of the car
MILEAGE	The current mileage of the car

1g **2** Set the page orientation to **landscape**.

    a) Print all the records in **table** format, making sure all **data** and **field** headings are fully visible.

    b) Close the table.

1a
1f **3** Rename the database table **CARS** and add your name to the table name.

For example: **CARS CHESTER WHEAT**

    a) Open the database table **CARS (YOUR NAME)**.

    b) You must use this database table for all the tasks below.

1c **4** The car with registration number **FD03 MBY** has been sold. Delete this record from your database table.

1e **5** Using codes for the **MAKE** field would be more efficient. Find the existing entries and replace them with the three letter codes below:

FORD	**FOR**
PEUGEOT	**PEU**
VOLKSWAGEN	**VOK**
VOLVO	**VOL**

6   Four records have been omitted from the database.

Create records for the following four cars:

REGISTRATION	MAKE	MODEL	YEAR	PRICE	MILEAGE
HB03 LEP	VOL	V40	2003	£7,995	36432
KL02 KSR	VOL	S60	2002	£9,370	7563
ML01 NFP	VOK	Polo	2001	£5,495	22328

Check the new records to make sure you have entered all the data accurately. Make sure all data is fully displayed.

Some changes need to be made to your database.

7   Make the following amendments:

a)   Change the car registration **FE02 JDP** to **FB02 JDR**.

b)   For the car with registration number **BD00 LMT** change the **MAKE** code to **VOK** and the **MILEAGE** to **48692**.

8   Save the database table keeping the name **CARS (YOUR NAME)**.

9   a)   Set the page orientation to **Landscape**.

b)   Print all data in table format, making sure that all data and field headings are displayed in full.

c)   Make sure fields are wide enough to display all data in full on the printout.

TASK 2

A customer has asked for a list of all cars priced at more than £9000.

1   Set up the following database query:

a)   Select all cars with **PRICE more than £9000**.

b)   Sort the data in descending order of **PRICE**.

c)   Display only the **REGISTRATION**, **MAKE**, **MODEL** and **PRICE** fields.

d)   Save the query as   **PRGT (YOUR NAME)**

For example: **PRGT CHESTER WHEAT**

e)   Print the results of the query in **table** format.

A customer wants to buy a car with a mileage of less than 8000 miles.

2   Set up the following database query:

a)   Select all cars with **MILEAGE less than 8000**.

b)   Sort the data in ascending order of **MILEAGE**.

2a	c) Display only the **REGISTRATION, MAKE, MODEL, YEAR** and **MILEAGE** fields.
2c	d) Save the query as **MLLT (YOUR NAME)**
	For example: **MLLT CHESTER WHEAT**
2d	e) Print the results of the query in **table** format.

Assessment Objectives | **TASK 3**

A customer wants to buy a Ford car for less than £8,000.

1f	1 Set up the following database query:
1g	a) Select all cars with a **PRICE less than £8,000** and a **MAKE** code of **FOR.**
2b	b) Sort the data in descending order of **PRICE**.
2c	c) Display only the **REGISTRATION, MODEL, PRICE** and **MILEAGE** fields
2d	d) Save the query as **PRMK (YOUR NAME)**
	For example: **PRMK CHESTER WHEAT**
	e) Print the results of the query in **table** format.

Assessment Objectives | **TASK 4**

	1 Using the query saved in Task 3:
1f	a) Create a tabular report in landscape orientation.
1g	b) Title the report as **PRMKREPORT (YOUR NAME)**
3a	For example: **PRMKREPORT CHESTER WHEAT**
3b	c) Save the report as **PRMKREPORT (YOUR NAME)**
3c	For example: **PRMKREPORT CHESTER WHEAT**
3d	d) Print the report on **one page** in **landscape** orientation.

2 Exit the software with all updated data saved.

Make sure you check your printouts for accuracy. You should have six printouts in the following order:

     CARS

     CARS (YOUR NAME)

     PRGT (YOUR NAME)

     MLLT (YOUR NAME)

     PRMK (YOUR NAME)

     PRMKREPORT (YOUR NAME)

Practice assignment 2

Scenario

You have just started work at a local travel agency. The manager has asked you to make some changes to the holiday offers database.

Assessment Objectives	**TASK 1**
1a	1 Open the Access database called **HOLIDAYS**.
	The database table consists of the following fields:
1g	

FIELD HEADING	DESCRIPTION OF DATA
DESTINATION	The holiday resort
AIRPORT	The departure airport
DEPARTS	The departure date
DAYS	The length of the holiday in days
PRICE	The price per person of the holiday
BOARD	The board basis of the holiday
OPERATOR	The tour operator offering the holiday

2   Set the page orientation to **landscape**.

1a   a)   Print all the records in table format, making sure all data and field headings are fully visible.

1f   b)   Close the table.

1c   3   Rename the database table **HOLIDAYS** to add your name to the table name.

For example: **HOLIDAYS CHESTER WHEAT**

a)   Open the database table **HOLIDAYS (YOUR NAME)**.

b)   You must use this database table for all the tasks below.

4   The holiday to **Sharm-El-Sheik** offered by the tour operator **Worldbreaks** has been withdrawn. Delete this record from your database table.

1e   5   Using codes for the **BOARD** field would be more efficient. Find the existing entries and replace them with the three-letter codes below:

ALL INCLUSIVE	**ALL**
HALF BOARD	**HBD**
FULL BOARD	**FBD**
SELF CATERING	**SCA**

6 Four records have been omitted from the database.

1b Create records for the following four holidays:

RESORT	AIRPORT	DEPARTS	DAYS	PRICE	BOARD	OPERATOR
Ibiza	Birmingham	16/08/2006	7	£659	HBD	Sun Tours
Majorca	Manchester	11/07/2006	14	£749	HBD	Global
Majorca	Gatwick	24/08/2006	7	£499	SCA	Sun Tours
Dubai	Manchester	28/06/2006	7	£989	FBD	Global

Check the new records to make sure you have entered all the data accurately.
Make sure all data is fully displayed.

1d Some changes need to be made to your database.

7 Make the following amendments:

a) Change the **AIRPORT** for the Sun Tours holiday to Majorca on 01/07/2006 to **Manchester**.

b) For the Global holiday to Egypt on 17/06/2006 change the **BOARD** code to **ALL** and the **COST** to **£1,299**

1f 8 Save the database table keeping the name **HOLIDAYS (YOUR NAME)**.

9 Set the page orientation to **Landscape**.

a) Print all data in table format, making sure that all data and field headings are displayed in full.

b) Make sure fields are wide enough to display all data in full on the printout.

Assessment Objectives | **TASK 2**

Your manager has asked you for a list of holidays available after 01/08/2006.

1f 1 Set up the following database query:

1g a) Select all holidays with **DEPARTS** dates **greater than 01/08/2006**.

2a b) Sort the data in ascending order of **DEPARTS** dates.

2c c) Display only the **RESORT**, **DEPARTS**, **DAYS** and **PRICE** fields.

2d d) Save the query as   **DEGT (YOUR NAME)**

For example: **DEGT CHESTER WHEAT**

e) Print the results of the query in table format.

2 A customer has asked if there are any holidays available for less than £600.

Set up the following database query:

1f a) Select all holidays with **PRICE less than £600**.

1g	b)	Sort the data in descending order of **PRICE**.
2a	c)	Display only the **RESORT**, **AIRPORT**, **DAYS**, **PRICE** and **BOARD** fields.
2c	d)	Save the query as **PRLT (YOUR NAME)**
		For example: **PRLT CHESTER WHEAT**
2d	e)	Print the results of the query in table format.

Assessment Objectives **TASK 3**

A customer wants to book a half board holiday costing less than £700.

1   Set up the following database query:

1f	a)	Select all holidays with **PRICE less than £700** and a **BOARD** code of **HBD**.
1g	b)	Sort the data in ascending order of **PRICE**.
2b	c)	Display only the **RESORT**, **AIRPORT**, **DEPARTS**, **DAYS** and **PRICE** fields.
2c	d)	Save the query as **PRBD (YOUR NAME)**
		For example: **PRBD CHESTER WHEAT**
2d	e)	Print the results of the query in table format.

Assessment Objectives **TASK 4**

1	1	Using the query saved in Task 3:
3a	a)	Create a tabular report in landscape orientation.
3b	b)	Title the report as **PRBDREPORT (YOUR NAME)**
		For example: **PRBDREPORT CHESTER WHEAT**
3c	c)	Save the report as **PRBDREPORT (YOUR NAME)**
		For example: **PRBDREPORT CHESTER WHEAT**
3d	d)	Print the report on **one page** in **Landscape** orientation.

2   Exit the software with all updated data saved.

Make sure you check your printouts for accuracy. You should have six printouts in the following order:

HOLIDAYS

HOLIDAYS (YOUR NAME)

DEGT (YOUR NAME)

PRLT (YOUR NAME)

PRBD (YOUR NAME)

PRBDREPORT (YOUR NAME)

Practice assignment 3

Scenario

You are working as an administrative assistant for a large college that runs evening courses for adults on three different sites.

Assessment Objectives		
	TASK 1	
1a	1	Open the Access database called **COURSES**.

The database table consists of the following fields:

FIELD HEADING	DESCRIPTION OF DATA
CODE	The identifying code for a course
TITLE	The name of the course
TUTOR	The name of the course tutor
SITE	The college site where the course is held
DURATION	The length of the course in weeks
COST	The total cost of the course

1g appears beside the fields table.

2 a) Set the page orientation to **Landscape**.

   b) Print all the records in **table** format, making sure all **data** and **field** headings are fully visible.

   c) Close the table.

1a

3 a) Rename the database table **COURSES** to add your name to the table name.
       For example: **COURSES CHESTER WHEAT**

1f

   b) Open the database table **COURSES (YOUR NAME)**.

1c

   You must use this database table for all the tasks below.

4 Course **108** has been cancelled because of low student numbers.
   Delete this record from your database table.

1e

5 Using codes for the **SITE** field would be more efficient.

   Find the existing entries and replace them with the three letter codes below:

CRANBURY	**CRN**
HEBDEN	**HEB**
LANGLEY	**LNG**

6 Four records have been omitted from the database.

Create records for the following four courses:

CODE	TITLE	TUTOR	SITE	DURATION	COST
104	Latin dance	Miss Martin	CRN	12	£90
106	Basic Spanish	Mrs O'Sullivan	HEB	30	£145
110	Bricklaying	Mr. Jackson	HEB	24	£170
122	Hobby craft	Mr. Dean	LNG	12	£75

Check the new records to make sure you have entered all the data accurately. Make sure all data is fully displayed.

Some changes need to be made to your database.

7 Make the following amendments:

a) Change the **TUTOR** for course **121** to **Miss Bertrand**.

b) For course **119** change the **SITE** code to **HEB** and the **DURATION** to **24**.

8 Save the database table keeping the name **COURSES (YOUR NAME)**.

9 Set the page orientation to **Landscape**.

a) Print all data in table format, making sure that all data and field headings are displayed in full.

b) Make sure fields are wide enough to display all data in full on the printout.

Assessment Objectives

TASK 2

Your manager has asked for a list of all the courses that run for 12 weeks or less.

1 Set up the following database query:

a) Select all courses with **DURATION less than or equal to 12**.

b) Sort the data in descending order of **DURATION**.

c) Display only the **TITLE**, **TUTOR** and **COST** fields.

Save the query as   **DURA (YOUR NAME)**

For example: **DURA CHESTER WHEAT**

d) Print the results of the query in table format.

The charges for courses costing less than £50 are being reviewed. A list of these courses is needed by the college Bursar.

2 Set up the following database query:

a) Select all courses with **COST less than £50**.

b) Sort the data in ascending order of **COST**.

Margin labels: 1b, 1d, 1f, 1g, 1f, 1g, 2a, 2c, 2d, 1f, 1g

2a	c)	Display only the **CODE**, **TUTOR**, **SITE** and **COST** fields.
2c	d)	Save the query as **COLT (YOUR NAME)**
		For example: **COLT CHESTER WHEAT**

Assessment Objectives | **TASK 3**

Your manager has asked for a list of all courses at the Hebden site that cost more than £200.

1   Set up the following database query:

1f	a)	Select all courses with **COST more than £200** and a **SITE** code of **HEB**.
1g	b)	Sort the data in descending order of **COST**.
2b	c)	Display only the **CODE**, **TITLE**, **TUTOR**, **DURATION** and **COST** fields.
2c	d)	Save the query as **COSI (YOUR NAME)**
		For example: **COSI CHESTER WHEAT**.
2d	e)	Print the results of the query in table format.

Assessment Objectives | **TASK 4**

1f/1g	1	Using the query saved in Task 3:
3a	a)	Create a tabular report in landscape orientation.
3b	b)	Title the report as **COSIREPORT (YOUR NAME)**
		For example: **COSIREPORT CHESTER WHEAT**
3c	c)	Save the report as **COSIREPORT (YOUR NAME)**
		For example: **COSIREPORT CHESTER WHEAT**
3d	d)	Print the report on **one page** in **Landscape** orientation.

2   Exit the software with all updated data saved.

Make sure you check your printouts for accuracy. You should have six printouts in the following order:

     COURSES

     COURSES (YOUR NAME)

     DURA (YOUR NAME)

     COLT (YOUR NAME)

     COSI (YOUR NAME)

     COSIREPORT (YOUR NAME)

To pass this unit you must be able to:

- ⊘ identify and use publication software correctly
- ⊘ set up a standard page layout and text properties
- ⊘ use basic tools and techniques appropriately
- ⊘ import and place text and image files
- ⊘ manipulate text and images to balance a page

Before you start this chapter, you or your tutor should download a zipped file called **Resources for Chapter 4** from **www.payne-gallway.co.uk/newclait/student**. It will automatically unzip. Specify that the contents are to be saved in your My Documents folder.

Desk top publishing

Desk top publishing, or **DTP** for short, is the use of a desk top publishing package on a computer to produce publications such as newsletters, magazines, leaflets, posters, and books.

The **DTP** process is mainly concerned organising the layout and appearance of text and graphics in a publication. The contents of the publication should already have been prepared, using a word processing package for text and graphics packages for pictures, diagrams and illustrations.

Many word processing packages like **Word** can be used for simple **Desk Top Publishing** tasks but the tools they offer for positioning text and images to achieve a particular page layout are quite limited and difficult to use. **DTP** packages don't have these limitations because they are **frame-based**. This means that text and graphics are placed inside special rectangular boxes called **frames** which can be easily arranged in layers on top of each other. Another key difference between Word Processing and **DTP** packages is in the printing facilities they offer. A professional **DTP** package will include a large variety of specialised printing options that commercial printing companies need.

Figure 4.1

In this chapter you will learn how to use **Microsoft Publisher XP** (referred to as **Publisher**) which is a common **DTP** package found in schools and colleges. **Publisher** offers many of the typical features that you would expect to find in a commercial **DTP** package.

The practice tasks that follow cover all the techniques you need to learn in order to pass a New CLAiT Unit 4 E-PUBLICATION CREATION assignment.

Practice tasks

Task 1   Creating a master page

The first thing you'll be asked to do during a Unit 4 assignment is set up a master page or template to a specified layout. This task takes you through the steps you'll need to follow to do this.

Starting Publisher

To get started we need to load **Publisher** – this can be done by:

Microsoft Office
Publisher 2003

- *Either* double-clicking the **Publisher** icon on the main screen in Windows,
- *or* clicking the **Start** button at the bottom left of the screen, then clicking **Programs**, and

Figure 4.2

The main **Publisher** window will be displayed – it should look like the one below with a blank publication ready to start work on.

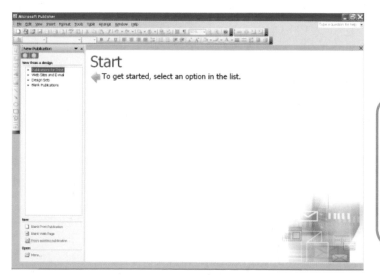

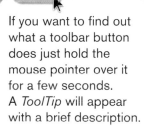

TIP

If you want to find out what a toolbar button does just hold the mouse pointer over it for a few seconds. A *ToolTip* will appear with a brief description.

Figure 4.3

We'll explore what the different parts of the **Publisher** window are used for as you work through these practice tasks.

Creating a new publication

You now have the options of creating a new publication or opening and working on an existing publication. We'll start by creating a new publication and creating a standard layout on the **master page**.

 Click **Blank print publication** in the **Task Pane**. The **Publication Designs** pane will appear – you don't need to use this so click **X** in the top right hand corner of the pane to close it.

> **TIP**
>
> Publisher has a wide range of different publication templates and layouts to choose from. These can save time when setting up a publication but make a lot of decisions about layout and style for you. Unit 4 assignments will ask you to create your own publication templates from scratch to match specified layouts.

 Click **View** on the menu bar, and then click **Master Page**. The **master page** will look like the one shown below with the **Edit Master Pages** toolbar displayed.

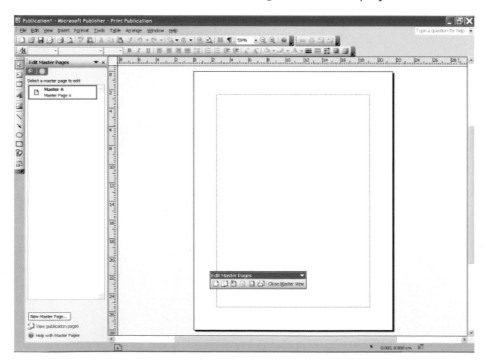

Figure 4.4

The first thing we're going to do is set the page orientation for the publication.

- Click **File** on the menu bar, then click **Page Setup**. The **Page Setup** dialogue box will appear.

- Click the **Layout** tab if it isn't already selected. The **Publication type** should already be set as **Full page** – if it isn't scroll though the list and click on this option.

- Click the radio button next to **Portrait** in the Orientation section if it isn't already selected. Then click **OK**.

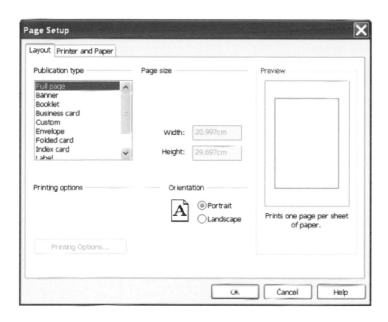

Figure 4.5

Next we'll set the page margins for the publication.

- Click the **Layout Guides** button on the **Edit Master Pages** toolbar. The Layout Guides dialogue box will appear.

- Click the **Margin Guides** tab if it isn't already selected.

Layout Guides button

The first thing you'll be asked to do during a New CLAiT e-Publication assignment is create a new publication and set the margins and page orientation.

Setting margins

We're going to set the left and right margins for this publication to **3 cm**.

▶ Click inside the boxes for the **left** and **right** margins. Replace each value with **3 cm**.

We're going to set the top and bottom margins for this publication to **2 cm**.

▶ Click inside the boxes for the **top** and **bottom** margins. Replace each value with **2 cm**.

Setting the page format

Next we're going to set up a newsletter format for the page layout by creating areas for two equally-spaced columns of text.

▶ Click the **Grid Guides** tab.

▶ Change the value next to **Columns** to **2** by clicking the small up arrow once, and the value next to **Spacing** to **1 cm** by clicking the small up arrow twice. This will leave 1 cm of empty space between the columns.

▶ Click **OK**. Your master page should look like the one below.

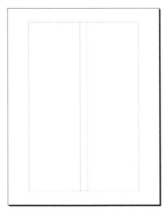

Figure 4.6

Adding a text box

Next we're going to add a text box at the top of the page and enter a heading.

Text Box button

▶ Click the **Text Box** button in the **Objects** toolbar. The mouse pointer will change to a thin cross shape.

Mouse pointer

▶ Position the pointer on the top left corner of the first column.

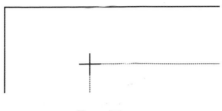

Figure 4.7

 Click and hold the left mouse button.

 Drag down and across to the right side of the right column. As you drag, an outline will show what size the text box will be when you let go of the mouse button. When the text box is roughly the same size as the one shown below, let go of the mouse button.

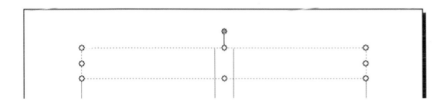

Figure 4.8

TIP

The text box for the page heading must extend across both columns. You can adjust the **width of the text box** using the handles on either side. The height of the text box is also important – if it is too tall the heading will end up taking over the whole page – a value of up to 2 cm is normally fine for this. You can adjust the **height of the text box** using the handles at the top and bottom; the exact height of the text box will be displayed in the bottom right corner of the Publisher window as you do this.

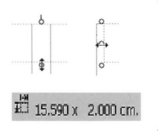

Next we need to enter a page heading in the text box and format the text to fill the box.

 Click in the text box and type **ELECTRONIC COMMUNICATION**.

 Highlight the text by clicking the mouse button three times – you can click and drag if you prefer.

Choosing a font and aligning the text

Once the text is highlighted you need to choose a font type and size for the page heading. There are two basic types of font, called **Serif** and **Sans Serif**. Serif fonts have little tails – called serifs – at the top and bottom of each letter. This sentence is written in a Serif font called Times New Roman. Serif fonts are used for large amounts of text that will be read quickly, such as in newspapers or books. The serifs 'lead your eye' from one word to the next. Sans Serif fonts don't have any tails on the letters and are used in places where text needs to be clear and easy to read, such as road signs and text books. This book has been written in a Sans Serif font. We're going to use a Sans Serif font for the page heading.

Figure 4.9

▶ Click the down-arrow in the **Font name** box at the top of the screen.

▶ Scroll through the list of fonts and click on the font called **Arial**.

▶ Click the small arrow on the right of the **Font Size** box at the top of the screen.

▶ Scroll through the list of sizes and click on **26.**

> **TIP**
>
> The page heading must fill the text box so that it extends across the columns underneath. You will need to try out different font sizes to get this exactly right during an assignment. A font size in the range 24 to 28 points is typical for a page heading. If you need a size that's not shown in the drop down list, click in the font size box, type the required number and press **Enter**.

Centre button

B

Bold button

Now we'll centre align the text and format it as bold.

▶ Click the **Centre** button on the **Formatting** toolbar.

▶ Click the **Bold** button on the **Formatting** toolbar. Your page heading should now look like the one below.

ELECTRONIC COMMUNICATION

Figure 4.10

Now you need to add your name to the footer section in the margin area at the bottom of the page.

▶ Click **View** on the menu bar, then click **Header and Footer**. The **Header and Footer** toolbar will appear. The cursor will be flashing in the header section.

Figure 4.11

▶ Click the **Show Header/Footer** button on the **Header and Footer** toolbar. The cursor will start flashing in the footer section.

Show Header/
Footer button

▶ Type **your name**. Your page footer should now look something like the one below.

Figure 4.12

▶ Click the **Close** button on the **Header and Footer** toolbar.

Close button

Finally we need to save the new page template and close **Publisher**.

▶ Click the **Close Master View** button on the **Edit Master Pages** toolbar, then,

Close Master
View button

▶ *either* click **File** on the menu bar, and then click **Save**,

▶ or click the **Save** button on the **Standard** toolbar. The **Save As** dialogue box will appear. The name highlighted in the **File name** box is the default filename which is normally something like **Publication1**. This can be changed to whatever you like.

Save button

▶ Type the name **ecom1** and click the **Save** button, then

▶ *either* click **File** on the menu bar, and then click **Exit**,

▶ or click **X** in the top right-hand corner of the screen to close **Publisher**.

Task 2 Importing text and images

This task takes you through the steps needed to create a new publication based on the **master page** layout that you have just set up. You are going to create text frames to hold the main body text for the page, import this text from a pre-prepared file and insert an image on the page.

▷ Load **Publisher**.

To work through this task you need to load the template publication called **ecom1** that you have already created and saved.

Open button

▷ *Either* click **File** on the menu bar, and then click **Open**,

▷ *or* click the **Open button** on the Standard toolbar. The **Open dialogue** box will appear.

▷ Click on **ecom1** and **Open**. Your publication should look like the one below.

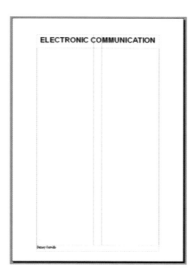

Figure 4.13

Adding text boxes

To get started we need to add some text boxes in the spaces marked out by the blue column guides.

Text Box button

▷ Click the **Text Box** button in the **Objects** toolbar on the left of the screen, and position the cross-shaped pointer on the top left corner of the first column underneath the heading text box.

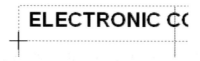

Figure 4.14

▶ Click and hold the left mouse button.

▶ Drag down and across towards the bottom right corner of this column. Let go of the mouse button when the text box is covering the blue column guides, as in the diagram on the right.

ELECTRONIC COM

Figure 4.15

Now we need to repeat this process for the second column.

▶ Click the **Text Box** button again.

Text Box button

▶ Position the cross-shaped pointer on the top left corner of the second column underneath the heading text box.

OMMUNICATION

Figure 4.16

▶ Click and hold the left mouse button, then drag down and across to the bottom right corner of the column. Let go of the mouse button when the text box is covering the blue column guides. Around both columns of your publication there should now be blue guides, overlapped by the dashed outlines of the text boxes.

Importing text

Now the text boxes have been added we can import the main **body text** for the page. The body text is in a pre-prepared text file called **communication**. Your tutor will tell you where to find this file. In the following example it is inside a folder called **Resources**.

Click in the first-column text box.

Click **Insert** on the menu bar, and then click **Text File**. The **Insert Text** dialogue box will appear.

Click on the file called **communication** and then click **OK**. You might see the following message:

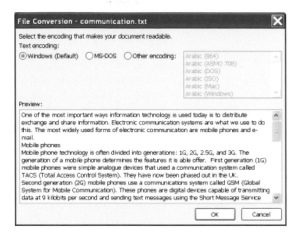

Figure 4.17

Click the radio button next to **Windows (Default)** if it isn't already selected, then click **OK**. The text file will be imported, completely filling the first column. The warning message shown here will appear.

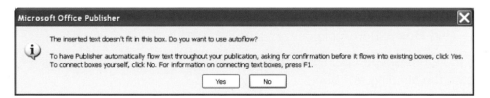

Figure 4.18

Click **Yes** to use autoflow. Publisher will automatically select the second column text box as the next closest text box with empty space available for the overflowed text. The following message will appear:

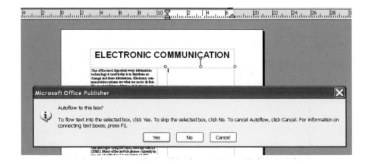

Figure 4.19

Click **Yes** again. The remaining text will appear in the second column. Your publication should now look like this:

Figure 4.20

TIP

Text sometimes fits into one column when it is first imported and overflows once it has been formatted. When this happens the **Text overflow symbol** will appear at the bottom of the first text box. To make overflowed text reappear click the **Create Text Box Link** button at the top of the screen. The pointer will change into an overflowing cup symbol, hold it over the next free text box and click the mouse button.

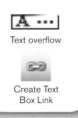

Text overflow

Create Text Box Link

Using spellcheck

Next we need to spellcheck the text and correct any errors.

 Click the **Spelling** button. The **Check Spelling** dialogue box will appear.

Spelling button

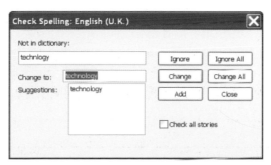

Figure 4.21

The suggested correction for the first error is correct.

▶ Click the **Change** button to accept and make the correction. The next suggested correction, **Mobley**, is not correct – the word we need is slightly further down the list of suggestions.

▶ Click the word **Mobile** in the list of suggestions, then click **Change**.

▶ Carry on working through the spellcheck – there are three more errors in total that need to be corrected.

> **TIP**
>
> An e-Publication assignment will state exactly how many errors should be found and corrected. Make sure that you have only corrected the given number of errors. Remember that spell checkers are not foolproof and often highlight 'errors' that should be ignored.

Inserting an image

Now that the text has been checked for errors and corrected, we can move on and look at how to insert an image. We are going to insert an image in the second column, underneath the text.

▶ Click in the second column just underneath the text.

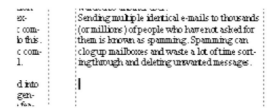

Figure 4.22

▶ Click **Insert** on the menu bar and then click **Picture, From File....** The Insert Picture dialogue box will appear. The image file you need is called **mobphone**. Your tutor will tell you where to find this file. In the following example the image file is in a folder called **Resources**.

▶ Click on the file called **mobphone**, and then click **Insert**. The image will be inserted in the publication. It will be selected with the sizing handles and the **Picture** toolbar visible.

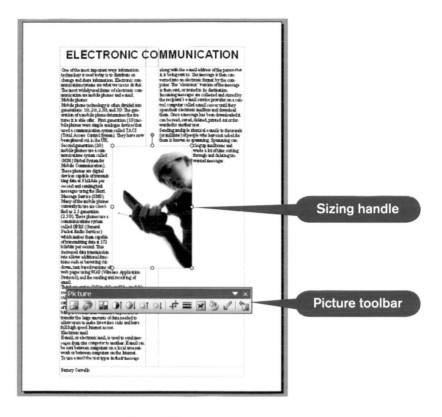

Figure 4.23

There are some parts of this image we don't need. The important part of the image is the mobile phone but there's too much of the user's right arm in the bottom of the picture. We can remove unwanted parts of an image by **cropping** it. We'll look at how to do this now.

▶ Click the **Crop** button on the **Picture** toolbar. The circular sizing handles around the image will be replaced by cropping handles.

Crop button

▶ Position the mouse pointer over the bottom centre cropping handle.

Figure 4.24

▶ Click and hold the left mouse button.

▶ Drag up towards the middle of the image. As you drag, a dashed outline will show what will be left of the image after **cropping.** When the outlined area looks like the one here, let go of the mouse button.

▶ Leave the image selected with the sizing handles visible.

The cropped parts of an image can be restored either by dragging in the opposite direction if you go too far when cropping, or clicking the **Reset Picture** button after cropping.

Reset Picture

Figure 4.25

The cropped image is still too large for the publication and needs resizing before it can be put in the correct position on the page.

▶ Move the mouse pointer over the bottom right sizing handle until it changes shape into a diagonal two-headed arrow.

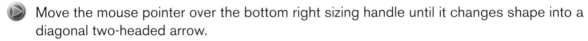

Figure 4.26

▶ Click and hold the left mouse button.

▶ Drag up and across towards the top left corner of the image. As you drag, a dotted line will show you how big the image will be when you let go of the mouse button. When the outlined area is roughly the same size as the one shown here, let go of the mouse button.

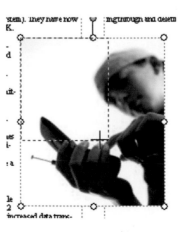

Never use the side sizing handles to resize an image – this will distort it. For e-publication assignments you should resize the images so that they stay in proportion. This means always using the corner sizing handles to resize images.

Figure 4.27

Moving the image

Next we need to move the image into the second column underneath the text. Images are moved by clicking and dragging.

▶ Click once on the image to make sure it is selected and the handles are visible.

▶ Move the mouse pointer over the image until it changes shape into a cross with four arrow heads.

Figure 4.28

▶ Click and hold the left mouse button, then drag it across to the right into the second column. As you drag, a dotted line will show you where the image will be when you let go of the mouse button.

TIP

If you don't get the image in the right position first time just try moving it again. Images should not overlap margins, columns or be placed over text unless you are specifically told to do this.

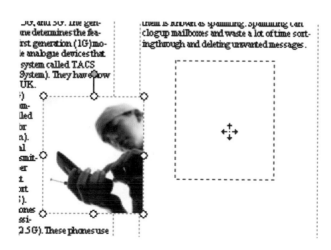

Figure 4.29

Formatting the text

Now we'll return to the body text and format it to be displayed in a **Serif** font with **left alignment**.

 Click anywhere in the first column, hold down the **Ctrl** key and press the **A** key, to select all the body text.

 Click the down arrow in the **Font name** box at the top of the screen, scroll through the list of available fonts and click on the font called **Century Schoolbook**.

> **TIP**
>
> You might have noticed that a **Serif** font – Times New Roman – was already selected for the body text. We could have left this as it was but choosing another Serif font is a good way to make sure we've definitely got *all* the body text displayed correctly. You could also be asked to choose a **Sans Serif** font for the body text – the technique is exactly the same.

Left Align button

 Leave the body text selected, then click the **left align** button on the **Formatting** toolbar.

> **TIP**
>
> If the **left align** button is **already selected** when all the body text is highlighted you won't need to do this if left alignment is specified in a task.

You'll notice that the text in the second column has expanded slightly and is now wrapping around the image.

Figure 4.30

We need to re-position the image so that it is still underneath the text.

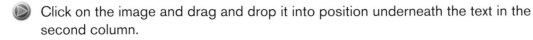 Click on the image and drag and drop it into position underneath the text in the second column.

Figure 4.31

Printing the publication

Now all we need to do is print a copy of the publication and save it.

 Click **File** on the menu bar, and then click **Print Preview**. A preview of the printout will be displayed. The publication should be shown on a single page like the one above.

 TIP

The instructions in a Unit 4 assignment may ask you to print a **composite copy** of a publication. This just means print a normal black and white copy of the page with all the text and images visible. If you were printing in colour it is possible to produce separate prints that show just the objects on a page that are a certain colour. This is a facility used by commercial printing companies but you don't need to use it for New CLAiT.

Click the **Print** button at the top of the screen to print the publication.

Print button

Finally we'll save the publication keeping the name **ecom1**.

Click the **Save** button on the **Standard** toolbar.

Close **Publisher**.

Save button

 TIP

You might need to choose a printer at this stage – if you do your tutor will tell you what to do.

Task 3 Images, borders and lines

Once you've created the first version of an e-publication you'll be asked to improve its appearance by changing and repositioning images, and to add borders and lines to separate out the different sections of the page. This task takes you through these techniques.

▶ Load **Publisher**.

▶ Open your copy of the publication called **ecom1**.

The first thing we need to do is make some more changes to the position and appearance of the image. We are going to flip the image horizontally, put a border around it, and reposition it underneath the first paragraph.

Changing the image orientation

We'll start by flipping the image horizontally.

▶ Click on the image to select it.

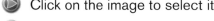
Free Rotate button

▶ Click the small down arrow next to the **Free Rotate** button on the **Standard** toolbar. A list of rotate and flip options will appear.

Figure 4.32

▶ Click **Flip Horizontal** in the list – the image will be flipped horizontally.

> TIP
>
> If you choose the wrong flip or rotate option just click the undo button on the Standard toolbar and try again. During an e-publication assignment you could be asked to use any of the rotate or flip options.

Adding a border

Next we'll add a border around the image.

Line/Border Style button

▶ Click the **Line/Border Style** button on the **Formatting** toolbar – a list of line styles will appear – and click **3pt** in the list. The image should look like the one opposite.

Figure 4.33

Next we'll reposition the image.

 Drag the image into the first column and drop it underneath the first paragraph ending **... and e-mail**, and position the image in the centre of the column, as in the example on the below.

Figure 4.34

 TIP

You may need to 'fine tune' the position of the image by dragging and dropping it up and down or from left to right. Use the arrow keys on the keyboard to do this if you're not confident controlling the mouse.

You'll notice that the text after the first paragraph has flowed around the image on both sides. We'll need to change this so that the text is placed above and below the image.

 Click the **Text Wrapping** button on the **Picture** toolbar. A list of text wrapping options will appear.

Text Wrapping button

Figure 4.35

Click **Top and Bottom** in the list. The text will be moved above and below the image. This section of your publication should now look like the one shown here. Reposition the image if your publication doesn't look like this.

Figure 4.36

TIP

You'll normally need to use either **square** text-wrapping to flow text around an image or **top and bottom** text-wrapping to place text above and below an image.

Amending text

Now we need to make a change to one of the paragraph subheadings.

 Click at the end of the paragraph subheading **Electronic mail**.

 Use the **Backspace** key to delete the text.

 Type in the new heading **E-mail**. This section of your publication should now look like the one below.

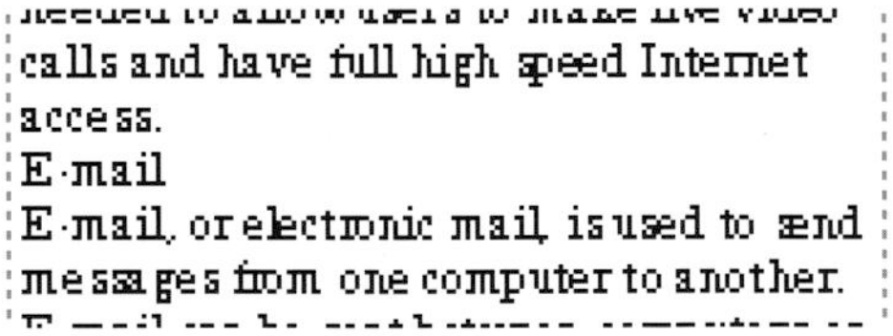

Figure 4.37

Adding borders/lines

Next we're going to draw some lines to improve the appearance of the publication. We'll start by adding lines above and below the heading to separate it more clearly from the rest of the page.

Line button

 Click the **Line** button in the **Objects** toolbar on the left of the screen.

 Position the cross-shaped pointer on the top left corner of the heading text box.

Cross-shaped pointer

 Click and hold the left mouse button.

 Press and hold down the **Shift** key – this will keep the line straight.

- Drag across towards to the top right corner of the heading text box. Let go of the **Shift** key and mouse button when the line looks like the one shown below.

Figure 4.38

- Click the **Line/Border Style** button on the **Formatting** toolbar.

- Click **1½ pt** in the list of line styles.

Line/Border
Style button

Now we need to repeat this process to draw a line underneath the heading text.

- Click the **Line** button.

- Position the pointer on the left edge of the heading text box just underneath the text.

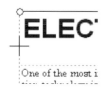

Figure 4.39

- Click and hold the left mouse button and press the **Shift** key.

- Drag across to the right edge of the heading text box. Let go of the **Shift** key and mouse button when the line looks like the one shown below.

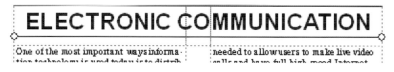

Figure 4.40

- Change the style of this line to **1½ pt**.

Now we'll draw a vertical line between the columns.

- Click the **Line** button, and position the pointer on the bottom edge of the heading text box, halfway between the guide lines separating the columns.

Figure 4.41

⊚ Click and hold the left mouse button and press the **Shift** key.

⊚ Drag down to the bottom margin guideline and let go of the mouse button and **Shift** key, then change the style of this line to **1½ pt**. Your publication should now look like the one below.

Figure 4.42

Finally we need to save the publication with a new filename and close **Publisher**.

⊚ Click **File** on the menu bar and then click **Save As**.

⊚ Type the new name, **ecom2**, click the **Save** button, then close **Publisher**.

Task 4   Reformatting text

Part of a Unit 4 assignment will ask you to make some further changes to a publication by re-formatting the subheadings and body text. This task takes you through the steps you'll need to work through.

Changing text alignment

We'll start by changing the alignment of the body text to be **fully justified**.

⊚ Click anywhere in the first column, then hold down the **Ctrl** and **A** keys to select all the body text.

Justify button

⊚ Click the **Justify** button on the **Formatting** toolbar.

Emphasising text – subheadings

Next we'll make the subheadings stand out more in the body text by changing the font to a different **serif** type, and increasing the font size.

 Click anywhere in the subheading **Mobile phones**

 Click the mouse button three times to highlight the subheading.

> **TIP**
>
> You could also highlight the subheading by clicking at the end of the line, holding the mouse button and dragging to the left. Take care to highlight just the subheading. If any other part of the body text is highlighted click away from it and try again.

 Click the down-arrow in the **Font name** box on the formatting toolbar, scroll through the list of fonts and click on the font called *Comic Sans MS*.

 Click the small arrow on the right of the **Font Size** box, and click on size **16**. This section of your publication should now look like the following example:

Figure 4.43

 Re-format the second subheading **E-mail** in exactly the same way.

> **TIP**
>
> You should format fonts consistently throughout a publication so that all the body text and subheadings appear in the same font type and size. You must use different font sizes for the main heading, subheadings and body text in a publication. Generally you should use 16 to 18 points for subheadings, and 10 to 14 points for body text. If a specific size is given for any part of the text you must use it.

Emphasising text – paragraphs

Next we'll make the paragraphs stand out more in the body text by indenting the first line of each one.

▷ Click anywhere in the first paragraph, then click the mouse button three times to highlight the whole paragraph.

TIP

You could also highlight the paragraph by clicking at the end of the last line, holding the mouse button and dragging back and up to the start of the first line. Take care to highlight *just* the paragraph. If any other part of the body text is highlighted click away from it and try again.

▷ Click **Format** on the menu bar and then click **Paragraph**. The Paragraph dialogue box will appear.

▷ The **Indents and Spacing** tab should already be selected – if it isn't, click on it.

▷ In the **Indentation** section click once on the small up arrow next to **First line**. The value in the box will change to **0.25 cm**. Click OK to continue

▷ Work through the body text, indenting the other paragraphs in exactly the same way. When you've finished, your publication should look like the example below.

Figure 4.44

Resizing text and images

Next we need to increase the size of the body text and resize the image so as to balance the length of the columns and reduce the large amount of 'white space' at the bottom of the second column.

We'll start by increasing the font size of the body text. This must be done *paragraph by paragraph* this time, to avoid reformatting the subheadings.

- Highlight the first paragraph.

- Click the small arrow on the right of the **Font Size** box, scroll through the list of available sizes and click on **11**.

- Format all the other paragraphs in exactly the same way. When you've finished, your publication should look like the example here.

Figure 4.45

Next we'll increase the size of the image slightly to take up more space on the page. This will cause more text to 'flow' into the second column getting rid of the remaining 'white space' at the bottom.

- Click on the image to select it – the sizing handles and **Picture** toolbar will appear.

- Resize and reposition the image so that it looks like the one here.

Figure 4.46

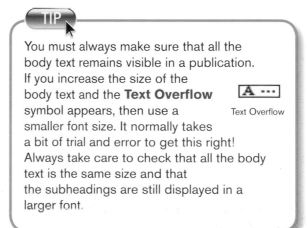

TIP

You must always make sure that all the body text remains visible in a publication. If you increase the size of the body text and the **Text Overflow** symbol appears, then use a smaller font size. It normally takes a bit of trial and error to get this right! Always take care to check that all the body text is the same size and that the subheadings are still displayed in a larger font.

Text Overflow

When you've finished, your final publication should look like the example below. Try resizing and repositioning the image again if your publication doesn't look like it.

Figure 4.47

That's the publication finished. All we need to do now print is to print a copy and save it.

Click **File** on the menu bar and then click **Print Preview**. A preview of the printout will be displayed – the publication should still be shown on one page.

Click the **Print** button on the Standard toolbar, then click **OK** to print the publication.

Print button

Save the publication, keeping the name **ecom2**, by clicking the **Save** button on the **Standard** toolbar, then close **Publisher**.

Save button

That's the end of the practice tasks. Now try the full New CLAiT assignments that follow.

Practice assignment 1

Scenario

You are working as a Help Desk assistant for a company that sells computer equipment. Part of your job is to prepare information sheets for customers.

Assessment Objectives	TASK 1
	Before you begin this task make sure that you have the text file **crime** and the image **hack**.
	1 Create a new single-page publication.
1a 1b 1c	2 a) Set up the master page or template for the page as follows:

page size	**A4**
page orientation	**portrait/tall**
left margin	**3cm**
right margin	**3cm**
top margin	**4cm**
bottom margin	**2cm**

b) In the bottom margin area key in **your name**.

Assessment Objectives	
1c 1d	3 Set up the page layout in a newsletter format to include a page-wide heading above two columns of text.

column widths	**equal**
space between columns	**1.25 cm**

Assessment Objectives	
1e 2d 3c	4 a) Enter the heading **COMPUTER CRIME** at the top of the page. b) Format the heading in a **serif** font (e.g. Times New Roman) c) Make sure the heading text extends across both columns and fills the space across the top of the page. You may increase the character spacing (kerning) and/or font size to achieve this. d) Make sure there is no more than 1 cm of white space to the left or right between the heading and the margins.
4a	5 Save the publication with the filename **dangers1**.

Assessment Objectives	TASK 2
	Continue working on the publication **dangers1**.
2a 2d	1 a) Import the text file **crime** b) The text should begin at the top of the left-hand column below the heading. It should fill the first column then flow under the heading into the second column.

		c)	Make sure all the text has been imported and is visible on the page.
3d	2	a)	Spell check the text and correct the **four** spelling errors.
		b)	Do not make any other amendments to the text file.
2b	3	a)	Import the image **hack**
2c		b)	Place it below the text in the second column.
		c)	Make sure the image does not overlap any text or extend into the margin or column space.
		d)	Make sure the image is in proportion.
1e	4	a)	Format all the imported body text to be **left-aligned.**
3a		b)	Format all the imported body text in a **sans serif** font (e.g. Tahoma).
1c	5	a)	Make sure your publication fits on one page.
		b)	Check your publication to make sure you have carried out all instructions correctly.
4a	6		Save your publication keeping the filename **dangers1**.
4b	7		Print a composite copy of the publication on one page.
	8		Check your printout for accuracy and write the filename **dangers1** on the printout.

Assessment Objectives

TASK 3

You have been asked to make some changes to your publication called **dangers1**.

3e	1	a)	Flip the **hack** image **horizontally**.
		b)	Make sure you keep the original proportions of the image.
		c)	Move the image to the top of the first column under the first paragraph.
		d)	Make sure that the image does not overlap any text or extend into the margin or column space.
3b	2		Change the subheading **The Computer Misuse Act** to be **Hackers**
2e	3	a)	Draw a **line** above the heading to separate the margin area from the text. The line must extend from the left margin to the right margin.
		b)	Draw a second **line** below the body text to separate the margin area from the text. The line must extend from the left margin to the right margin.
		c)	Draw a third **line** below the heading to separate the columns. The line must extend from the top of the body text to the bottom margin.
		d)	Make sure the lines do not touch or overlap any text.
		e)	The lines must not extend into any of the margin areas.
4a	4		Save your publication using the new filename **dangers2**.

Assessment Objectives	TASK 4

Continue working on the publication **dangers2**.

3a 1 Change the body text to be **fully justified**.

1e 2 a) Increase the size of the subheadings **Hackers** and **Viruses** so that both subheadings are the same size and are larger than the body text, but smaller than the heading.

b) Format the subheadings in a **serif** style that is different to the heading (e.g. Book Antiqua).

c) Format the subheadings to be **centre aligned**.

3a 3 a) Format the body text so that each paragraph has a **first line indent**.

b) Make sure that you do **not** insert a clear linespace between paragraphs.

c) Make sure that the subheadings are **not** indented.

3c 4 a) Change the size of the body text so that both columns are balanced at the bottom of the page.

b) Make sure that the heading, subheadings and body text are still different sizes.

c) Make sure all the original text is still displayed on the page.

d) Make sure your publication fits onto one page.

5 Check your publication to make sure you have carried out all the instructions correctly.

4a 6 Save your publication keeping the filename **dangers2**.

4b 7 Print a composite copy of the publication on one page.

4b 8 Close the publication and exit the software.

9 Check your printout for accuracy and write the filename **dangers2** on the printout.

You should have two printouts: **dangers1** and **dangers2**

Practice assignment 2

Scenario

You are working as an Education Officer for the police. Part of your job is to prepare education resources for use in schools.

Assessment Objectives		
	TASK 1	

Before you begin this task make sure that you have the text file **police** and the image **pcar**.

1   Create a new single-page publication.

1a	2 a)	Set up the master page or template for the page as follows:
1b		page size **A4**
1c		page orientation **portrait/tall**
		left margin **3 cm**
		right margin **3 cm**
		top margin **3 cm**
		bottom margin **3 cm**
	b)	In the bottom margin area key in **your name**.
1c	3	Set up the page layout in a newsletter format to include a page wide
1d		heading above two columns of text.
		column widths **equal**
		space between columns **0.5 cm**
1e	4 a)	Enter the heading **COMPUTERS AND THE POLICE** at the top of the page.
2d	b)	Format the heading in a **sans serif** font (e.g. Tahoma)
3c	c)	Make sure the heading text extends across both columns and fills the space across the top of the page. You may increase the character spacing (kerning) and/or font size to achieve this.
	d)	Make sure there is no more than 1 cm of white space to the left or right between the heading and the margins.
4a	5	Save the publication with the filename **crime1**.

Assessment Objectives		
	TASK 2	

Continue working on the publication **crime1**.

2a	1 a)	Import the text file **police**.
2d	b)	The text should begin at the top of the left-hand column below the heading. It should fill the first column then flow under the heading into the second column.

		c)	Make sure all the text has been imported and is visible on the page.
3d	2	a)	Spell check the text and correct the **three** spelling errors.
		b)	Do not make any other amendments to the text file.
2b	3	a)	Import the image **pcar.**
2c		b)	Place it below the text in the second column.
		c)	Make sure the image does not overlap any text or extend into the margin or column space.
		d)	Make sure the image is in proportion.
1e	4	a)	Format all the imported body text to be **left-aligned**.
3a		b)	Format all the imported body text in a **serif** font (e.g. Georgia).
1c	5	a)	Make sure your publication fits on one page.
		b)	Check your publication to make sure you have carried out all instructions correctly.
4a	6		Save your publication keeping the filename **crime1**.
4b	7		Print a composite copy of the publication on one page.
	8		Check your printout for accuracy and write the filename **crime1** on the printout.

Assessment Objectives

TASK 3

You have been asked to make some changes to your publication called **crime1**.

3e	1	a)	Flip the **pcar** image **horizontally**.
		b)	Make sure you keep the original proportions of the image.
		c)	Move the image to the top of the first column above the heading **Automatic Number Plate Recognition**.
		d)	Make sure that the image does not overlap any text or extend into the margin or column space.
3b	2		Change the subheading **Traffic Police** to be **Drivers**
2e	3	a)	Draw a **line** below the heading to separate the heading area from the body text. The line must extend from the left margin to the right margin.
		b)	Draw a second **line** below the heading to separate the columns. The line must extend from the top of the body text to the bottom margin.
		c)	Make sure the lines do not touch or overlap any text.
		d)	The lines must not extend into any of the margin areas.
4a	4		Save your publication using the new filename **crime2**.

Assessment Objectives	TASK 4
	Continue working on the publication **crime2**.
3a	1 Change the body text to be **fully justified**.
1e 1f 3a	2 a) Increase the size of the subheadings: **Drivers**, **Automatic Number Plate Recognition** and **Fingerprint Identification** so that all subheadings are the same size and are larger than the body text, but smaller than the heading.
	b) Format the subheadings in a **sans serif** style that is different to the heading (e.g. Verdana).
	c) Format the subheadings to be **left-aligned**.
3a	3 a) Format the body text so that each paragraph has a **first line indent**.
	b) Make sure that you do **not** insert a clear linespace between paragraphs.
	c) Make sure that the subheadings are not indented.
3c	4 a) Change the size of the body text so that both columns are balanced at the bottom of the page.
	b) Make sure that the heading, subheadings and body text are still different sizes.
	c) Make sure all the original text is still displayed on the page.
	d) Make sure your publication fits onto one page.
	5 Check your publication to make sure you have carried out all the instructions correctly.
4a	6 Save your publication keeping the filename **crime2**.
4b	7 Print a composite copy of the publication on one page.
4b	8 Close the publication and exit the software.
	9 Check your printout for accuracy and write the filename **crime2** on the printout. You should have two printouts: **crime1** and **crime2**.

Practice assignment 3

Scenario

You are working as a Teaching Assistant in a school. Part of your job is to prepare classroom resources for pupils and teachers.

Assessment Objectives	TASK 1
	Before you begin this task make sure that you have the text file **computers** and the image **pda**.
	1 Create a new single-page publication.
1a	2 a) Set up the master page or template for the page as follows:

        page size   **A4**
        page orientation   **landscape/wide**
        left margin   **3 cm**
        right margin   **3 cm**
        top margin   **2 cm**
        bottom margin   **2 cm**

      b)   In the bottom margin area key in **your name**.

1c 1d	3 Set up the page layout in a newsletter format to include a page wide heading above three columns of text.

        column widths   **equal**
        space between columns **1 cm**

1e 2d 3c	4 a) Enter the heading **TYPES OF COMPUTER** at the top of the page. b) Format the heading in a **serif** font (e.g. Batang) c) Make sure the heading text extends across all three columns and fills the space across the top of the page. You may increase the character spacing (kerning) and/or font size to achieve this. d) Make sure there is no more than 1 cm of white space to the left or right between the heading and the margins.
4a	5 Save the publication with the filename **comps1**.

Assessment Objectives	TASK 2
	Continue working on the publication **comps1**.
2a	1 a) Import the text file **computers**.
2d	b) The text should begin at the top of the left-hand column below the heading. It should fill the first column then flow under the heading into the second column.
	c) Make sure all the text has been imported and is visible on the page.
3d	2 a) Spell check the text and correct the **four** spelling errors.
	b) Do not make any other amendments to the text file.
2b	3 a) Import the image **pda**.
2c	b) Place it at the top of the third column.
	c) Make sure the image does not overlap any text or extend into the margin or column space.
	d) Make sure the image is in proportion.
1e	4 a) Format all the imported body text to be **left-aligned**.
3a	b) Format all the imported body text in a **sans serif** font (e.g. Comic Sans MS).
1c	5 a) Make sure your publication fits on one page.
	b) Check your publication to make sure you have carried out all instructions correctly.
4a	6 Save your publication keeping the filename **comps1**.
4b	7 Print a composite copy of the publication on one page.
	8 Check your printout for accuracy and write the filename **comps1** on the printout.

Assessment Objectives	TASK 3
	You have been asked to make some changes to your publication called **comps1**.
3e	1 a) Flip the **pda** image **horizontally**.
	b) Make sure you keep the original proportions of the image.
	c) Move the image to the second column above the heading **Portable computers**.
	d) Make sure that the image does not overlap any text or extend into the margin or column space.
3b	2 Change the subheading **Desktop PC** to be **Microcomputers**.
2e	3 a) Draw a **line** above the heading to separate the margin area from the text. The **line** must extend from the left margin to the right margin.

b) Draw a second **line** below the body text to separate the margin area from the text. The line must extend from the left margin to the right margin.

c) Make sure the lines do not touch or overlap any text.

d) The lines must not extend into any of the margin areas.

4a	4 Save your publication using the new filename **comps2**.

Assessment Objectives	**TASK 4**
	Continue working on the publication **comps2**.
3a	1 Change the body text to be **fully justified**.
1e	2 a) Increase the size of the subheadings: **Mainframe computers, Microcomputers, Portable computers**, and **Minicomputers** so that both subheadings are the same size and are larger than the body text, but smaller than the heading.
	b) Format the subheadings in a **sans serif** style that is different to the heading (e.g. *Comic Sans MS*).
	c) Format the subheadings to be **left-aligned**.
3a	3 a) Format the body text so that each paragraph has a **first line indent**.
	b) Make sure that you do **not** insert a clear linespace between paragraphs.
	c) Make sure that the subheadings are not indented.
3c	4 a) Change the size of the body text so that all the columns are balanced at the bottom of the page.
	b) Make sure that the heading, subheadings and body text are still different sizes.
	c) Make sure all the original text is still displayed on the page.
	d) Make sure your publication fits onto one page.
	5 Check your publication to make sure you have carried out all the instructions correctly.
4a	6 Save your publication keeping the filename **comps2**.
4b	7 Print a composite copy of the publication on one page.
4b	8 Close the publication and exit the software.
	9 Check your printout for accuracy and write the filename **comps2** on the printout.
	You should have two printouts: **comps1** and **comps2**.

To pass this unit you must be able to:

- ☑ identify and use presentation software correctly
- ☑ set up a slide layout
- ☑ select fonts and enter text
- ☑ import and insert images correctly
- ☑ use the drawing tools
- ☑ format slides and presentation
- ☑ re-order slides and produce printed handouts
- ☑ manage and print presentation files

Before you start this chapter, you or your tutor should download a zipped file called **Resources for Chapter 5** from **www.payne-gallway.co.uk/newclait/student**. It will automatically unzip. Specify that the contents are to be saved in your My Documents folder.

Presentation graphics software is used to create slide shows which can be viewed on-screen or with a data projector connected to the computer. **Microsoft PowerPoint** (referred to as **PowerPoint**) is the most commonly used presentation package. Slides in a presentation can have any combination of text images or video. Some slides in a **PowerPoint** presentation are shown below.

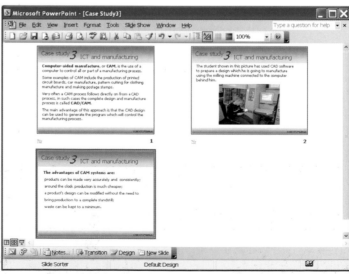

Figure 5.1

The practice tasks that follow cover all the techniques you need to learn in order to pass a **New CLAiT Unit 5** assignment.

Practice tasks

Task 1 Setting up a new presentation

You can load **PowerPoint** in one of two ways:

▶ *Either* double-click the **PowerPoint** icon on the **Desktop** in Windows,

▶ *or* click the **Start** button at the bottom left of the screen, then click **All Programs**, then click

Microsoft Office
PowerPoint
2003

PowerPoint icon

Microsoft Office PowerPoint 2003

Figure 5.2

The main **PowerPoint** window will be displayed – it should look like the one below.

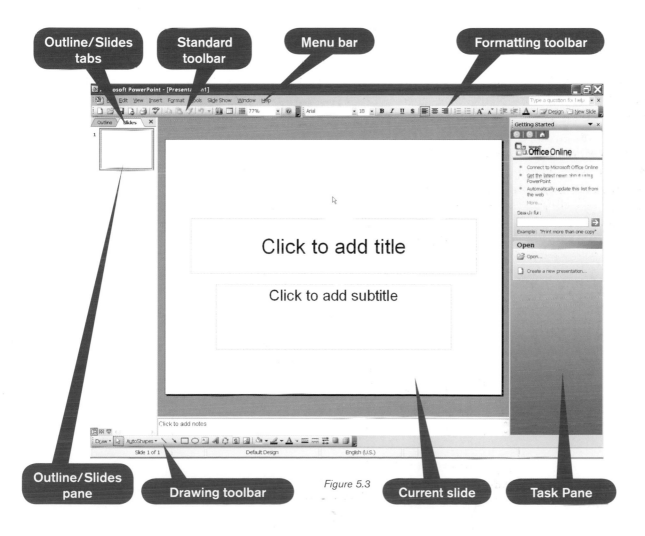

Outline/Slides tabs

Standard toolbar

Menu bar

Formatting toolbar

Outline/Slides pane

Drawing toolbar

Current slide

Task Pane

Figure 5.3

We'll explore what the different parts of the **PowerPoint** window are used for as you work through these practice tasks.

Creating a presentation

You now have the options of creating a new presentation or opening and working on an existing presentation. We'll start by creating a new presentation and specifying exactly how the slides should look.

▶ Click **Create a new presentation** in the **Task Pane**. The **New Presentation** pane will appear.

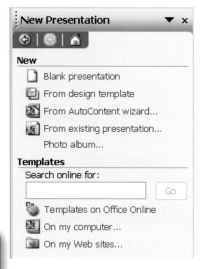

Figure 5.4

TIP

If you can't see the Task Pane click **View**, **Task Pane** on the menu bar.

▶ Click **Blank presentation**. The display will change to show the available **Slide Layout** options.

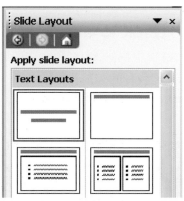

Figure 5.5

PowerPoint has automatically selected the **Title Slide** layout which is not the one we want. For Unit 5 assignments the most useful layout is **Title and Text**. This layout has a page-wide **title frame** at the top of the page with a page-wide **main frame** below it.

Click the **Title and Text** icon in the **Text Layouts** pane.

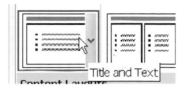

Figure 5.6

Next we need to make sure the **Master Slide** is set up correctly. The **Master slide** specifies how every slide in a presentation will look. For example, if you choose a particular background colour and font style for the master slide, this background colour and font style will be the same on every slide.

 Click **View**, **Master**, **Slide Master** on the menu bar. The **Master slide** will look like the one shown below.

Figure 5.7

The **Master slide** is used to specify how text in the title and main frames should be formatted. We're going to set up the text frame styles for this presentation as follows:

style	emphasis	size	feature	alignment
title	bold only	large	dark border	centre
1st level bullet	none	medium	any bullet character	left
2nd level bullet	italic only	small	any bullet character	left and indented from 1st level bullet

First we'll set the properties specified in the table for the text in the title frame.

▶ Click on the text **Click to edit Master title style** in the title frame.

Figure 5.8

The quickest way to alter text format is by using the buttons on the formatting toolbar at the top of the screen.

Figure 5.9

▶ Click the **Bold** button.

▶ Click the **Center** button if it isn't already selected (it is in the screenshot above).

A large size text is needed for the title frame. The preset text size of **44** shown in the **font size** box is large enough so we'll leave this as it is.

Figure 5.10

> **TIP**
>
> If the preset font size for the title isn't at least **44** click the small arrow on the right of the **Font size** box, scroll-down the list of available sizes and click on **44** with the left mouse button.

To set a **dark border** style for this frame we need to increase the thickness of the line around the frame.

Line Style
button

▶ Click the **Line Style** button on the **Drawing toolbar** at the bottom of the screen. Click **4½ pt** from the list of available line styles. The border around the title frame will now be much thicker.

Figure 5.11

> **TIP**
>
> If you can't see the **Line Style** button at the bottom of the screen click **View**, **Toolbars**, and then **Drawing** on the menu bar.

Next we'll set the properties specified in the table for the 1ˢᵗ level bullet.

▷ Click on the text **Click to edit Master text styles** in the main frame.

- **Click to edit Master text styles**
  - Second level

Figure 5.12

The only style we need to set for this bullet is a medium sized text. The preset text size of **32** shown in the **Font size** box is OK when compared with the size of the title text so we'll leave this as it is.

Arial ▾ 32 ▾

Figure 5.13

Now we'll set the properties specified in the table for the 2ⁿᵈ level bullet.

▷ Click on the text **Second level** in the main frame.

A small sized italic text is specified for this bullet. The preset text size of **28** shown in the **font size** box is slightly large compared with the size of the 1ˢᵗ level bullet text so we'll reduce this slightly.

Arial ▾ 28 ▾

Figure 5.14

▷ Click the small arrow on the right of the **font size** box. Scroll-down the list of available sizes and click on **20** with the left mouse button.

▷ Click the **Italic button** on the **Formatting** toolbar at the top of the screen.

Italic button

That's the text formatting done. Now we'll set a background colour for all the slides. The default background colour is set to white – we'll change this to a different colour.

▷ Click **Format** on the menu bar and then click **Background**. The Background dialogue box will appear.

Figure 5.15

▷ Click the small arrow underneath **Background fill**. A choice of fill options will appear.

▶ Click **More Colors...,** click any light colour on the palette, then click **OK**.

▶ In the Background dialogue box, click the **Apply to All** button. The new background colour will be shown on the master slide. The examples that follow in this chapter will have a white background – this is just to make them easy to read – you can choose any colour you like.

> **TIP**
>
> Always make sure you set the background colour specified in an assignment – if this is white you don't need to do anything.

Inserting Footer information

Next we need to put some information in the footer at the bottom of the master slide.

▶ Click the text **<date/time>** in the **Data Area** at the bottom of the screen.

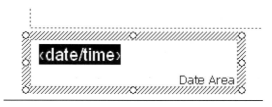

Figure 5.16

▶ Click **Insert** on the menu bar, and then click **Date and Time**. The Date and Time dialogue box will appear.

▶ Click the option in the list of available formats that shows just a date followed by the time with no seconds displayed.

Figure 5.17

▶ Click **OK**. The current date and time will be displayed in the Date Area.

▶ Click the text **<footer>** in the **Footer Area** at the bottom of the screen.

▶ Type your name followed by a few spaces and your centre number.

Figure 5.18

The last thing we need to do is add the current slide number on the bottom right corner of each slide. A space is already set up for this in the **Number Area**. We need to close the master slide before activating the numbering.

▶ Click the **Close Master View** button on the **Slide Master View** Toolbar.

<u>C</u>lose Master View

Figure 5.19

▶ Click **Insert** on the menu bar and then click **Slide Number**. The Header and Footer dialogue box will appear.

▶ Tick the **Slide number** check box, then click the **Apply to All** button. The slide number will appear in the bottom right corner of the slide. The footer area of your first slide should now look like the one below.

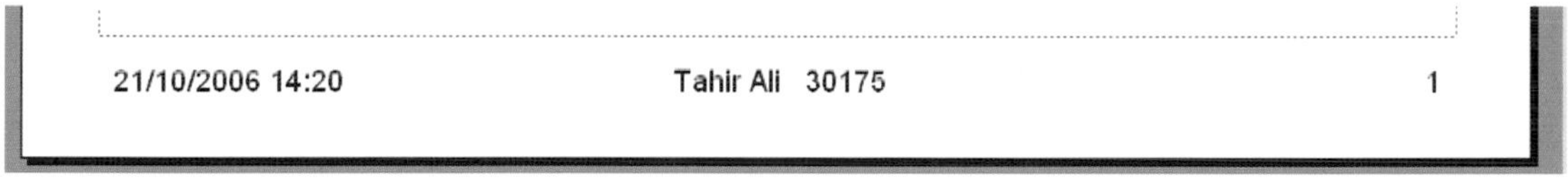

| 21/10/2006 14:20 | Tahir Ali 30175 | 1 |

Figure 5.20

Now we're ready to save the presentation:

▶ *Either* click **File** on the menu bar, then click **Save**,

▶ or click the **Save button** on the **Standard** toolbar. The **Save** dialogue box will appear.

The name highlighted in the **File name** box is the default filename which is normally something like **Presentation1** or **Presentation2**. This can be changed to whatever you like.

▶ Type the name **paradise**, then click the **Save** button. The **Save As** dialogue window will disappear and the filename **paradise** will be displayed at the top of the screen. The presentation will now be saved with this name whenever the save button on the Standard toolbar is clicked.

Save button

Finally you need to close **PowerPoint**.

▶ *Either* click **File** on the menu bar, and then click **Exit**,

▶ or click **X** in the top right-hand corner of the screen.

TIP

PowerPoint presentations are automatically saved in the **My Documents** folder. If your tutor wants you to save work in a different place, they'll explain how to do this.

Task 2   Creating and formatting slides

⊳ Load **PowerPoint**.

To work through this task we need to load the presentation called **paradise**.

Open button

⊳ *Either* click **File** on the menu bar, and then click **Open**,

⊳ *or* click the **Open button** on the **Standard** toolbar. The **Open** dialogue box will appear.

⊳ Click on **paradise** and then click **Open**.

> **TIP**
>
> Ask your tutor to help you find this file if it isn't in the list on your screen.

The presentation will open with a blank first slide like the one shown below.

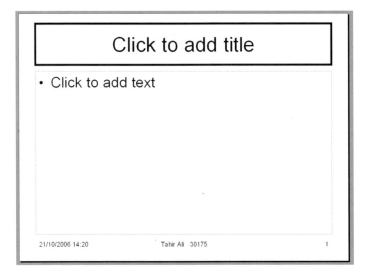

Figure 5.21

Adding a title

We'll start by adding a title to this slide.

⊳ Click on the text **Click to add title** in the title frame.

⊳ Type **PARADISE BEACH HOTEL**

Figure 5.22

Adding and formatting an image

Next we'll insert, resize and position an image underneath the title.

⊳ Click **Insert** on the menu bar, and then click **Picture, From File**. The **Insert Picture** dialogue box will appear.

The image file you need is called **beach.gif**. Your tutor will tell you where to find this file if it is not in your **My Documents** folder.

⊳ Click on the file called **beach** and then click **Insert**. The image will be inserted on the slide – it should look exactly like the one below.

Figure 5.23

Now we need to increase the size of this image and position it in the centre of the main frame. You can make an image bigger or smaller by dragging any of the corner handles.

⊳ Click once on the image to make sure it is selected and the handles are visible.

⊳ Move the mouse pointer over the top right handle until it changes shape into a diagonal two-headed arrow.

⊳ Click and hold the left mouse button.

Figure 5.24

⊳ Drag up towards the top right corner of the slide. As you drag, a dotted line will show you how big the image will be when you let go of the mouse button. When the picture is roughly the same size as the one shown below, let go of the mouse button.

 TIP

Never use the side handles to resize an image – this will distort it. For e-presentation assignments you should resize the images so that they stay in proportion. This means always use the corner handles for resizing.

Figure 5.25

Images can be moved by simply clicking and dragging. We need to move this image to the centre of the main frame.

▶ Click once on the image to make sure it is selected and the handles are visible.

▶ Move the mouse pointer over the image until it changes shape into a cross with four arrow heads.

Figure 5.26

▶ Click and hold the left mouse button, then drag down and across to the bottom left corner of the slide. As you drag a dotted line will show you where the image will be when you let go of the mouse button. When the picture is in roughly the same position as the one shown below, let go of the mouse button. You will also need to delete the text and bullet point from beneath the picture.

Figure 5.27

TIP

If you don't get the image in the right position just try moving it again. Don't worry about getting the image exactly in the middle of the main frame. Just make sure it doesn't overlap the title or any of the information in the footer at the bottom of the slide.

That's the first slide finished. Now we're ready to start work on the second one.

To create another new slide:

▶ *Either* click the **New Slide** button on the **Formatting** toolbar,

▶ *or* click **Insert** and then **New Slide** on the menu bar. A new blank slide like the one shown below will appear.

New Slide
button

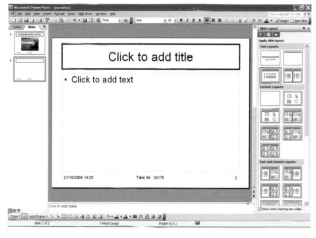

Figure 5.28

First we'll start by adding a title to this slide.

▶ Click on the text **Click to add title** in the title frame.

▶ Type **FIVE STAR HOTEL FACILITIES**

FIVE STAR HOTEL FACILITIES

• Click to add text

Figure 5.29

Next we'll add some bulleted text in the main frame.

▶ Click on the text **Click to add text** in the main frame.

▶ Type **Two outdoor swimming pools** and press **Enter**. The cursor will move down onto the next line and create another bullet.

FIVE STAR HOTEL FACILITIES

• Two outdoor swimming pools

Figure 5.30

 Enter the text shown below. Press **Enter** at the end of each line.

One for adults only with a poolside bar

Health and fitness centre

Fully equipped gym, sauna and Jacuzzi

Beauty parlour

Wide variety of popular treatments available

Now we'll demote the second line on this slide to become a 2nd level bullet.

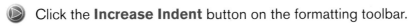 Click anywhere in the text **One for adults only with a poolside bar**.

Click the **Increase Indent** button on the formatting toolbar.

Increase
button

When you've finished your second slide should look exactly like the one shown below. Check your work and correct any mistakes before carrying on.

Figure 5.31

That's the second slide finished. Now we're ready to start work on the third and final slide.

Create another new blank slide.

Enter the title **HOTEL LOCATION**

Enter the text shown below as individual bulleted lines in the main frame.

Exclusive beachfront situation

Private beach area for hotel guests

Short drive from many popular attractions

Shops, restaurants and bars nearby

Now we'll demote some of the information on this slide to become 2nd level bullets.

- Click anywhere in the text **Private beach area for hotel guests**, then click the **Increase Indent** button.

- Repeat this step for the text **Shops, restaurants and bars nearby**.

When you've finished, your third slide should look exactly like the one shown below. Check your work and correct any mistakes before carrying on.

Figure 5.32

- Now click the **Spelling and Grammar** button on the menu bar.

- Work through the spell check, making sure that you correct any mistakes before carrying on.

Spelling and Grammar button

Printing the slides

Next we're going to print all three slides in **landscape** orientation.

- Click **File** on the menu bar and then click **Page Setup**. The **Page Setup** dialogue box will appear.

- In the **Notes, handouts & outline** section click the radio button for **Landscape**, then click **OK**.

- Click **File** on the menu bar, then click **Print**. The **Print** dialogue box will appear.

- Check **Slides** is selected underneath **Print what** adjacent to the **Handouts** section at the bottom of the screen, then click **OK**.

You might also need to choose a printer at this stage – if you do, your tutor will tell you what to do.

Finally we'll save the file keeping the same name **paradise**.

- Click the **Save** button on the **Standard** toolbar, then close the presentation and shut down **PowerPoint**.

Save button

Outlining toolbar

Task 3   Editing slides

This task describes how to edit bullets, search and replace text and add standard shapes to slides.

▶ Load **PowerPoint**.

▶ Open your saved presentation called **paradise**.

The first thing we're going to do is **promote** and **demote** some text. We'll use a slightly different technique to the one described in the last task.

▶ Click **View, Toolbars** and then **Outlining** on the menu bar. The Outlining toolbar will appear on the left of the screen.

▶ Click the **Outline** tab in the **Outline pane**.

Figure 5.33

First we'll promote some of the information on **Slide 3** to become a 1ˢᵗ level bullet.

▶ Click anywhere in the text **Shops, restaurants and bars nearby** in the **outline pane**.

Promote button

▶ Click the **Promote** button on the outlining toolbar. Slide 3 should look now like the one shown below.

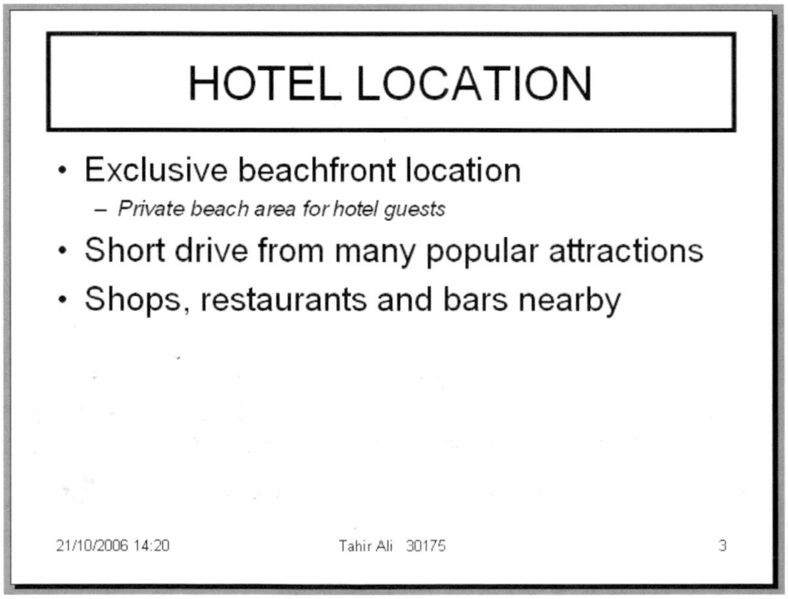

HOTEL LOCATION

- Exclusive beachfront location
  - *Private beach area for hotel guests*
- Short drive from many popular attractions
- Shops, restaurants and bars nearby

21/10/2006 14:20   Tahir Ali 30175   3

Figure 5.34

Next we'll demote some of the information on **Slide 2** to become 2nd level bullets.

▶ Click anywhere in the text **Fully equipped gym, sauna and Jacuzzi** in the Outline pane.

▶ Click the **Demote** button on the Outlining toolbar.

▶ Click anywhere in the text **Wide variety of popular treatments available** in the outline pane.

▶ Click the **Demote** button. **Slide 2** should now look like the one shown below.

Deomote button

FIVE STAR HOTEL FACILITIES

- Two outdoor swimming pools
  - *One for adults only with a poolside bar*
- Health and fitness centre
  - *Fully equipped gym, sauna and Jacuzzi*
- Beauty parlour
  - *Wide variety of popular treatments available*

21/10/2006 14:20   Tahir Ali 30175   2

Figure 5.35

▶ Click the **Slides** tab in the outline pane.

Figure 5.36

TIP

You can use whichever technique you prefer to promote and demote bulleted text. Always check your work carefully after making changes to ensure that each bullet on a slide is the level (1st or 2nd) specified in the assignment.

Replacing text

Next we'll replace some of the text in the presentation. Suppose we needed to replace the word **HOTEL** with **RESORT** throughout the presentation. The **Replace** facility offers the quickest way to do this.

▶ Click **Edit** on the menu bar and then click **Replace**. The **Replace** dialogue box will appear.

▶ Click in the **Find what** box and type **HOTEL**.

▶ Click in the **Replace with** box and type **RESORT**.

▶ Click the checkbox next to **Match case**, then click the checkbox next to **Find whole words only**. Your replace dialogue box should now look like the one below.

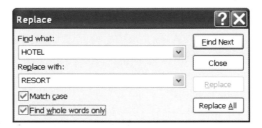

Figure 5.37

▶ Click **Replace All**. A message will appear telling you that **3** replacements have been made.

▶ Click on **OK**, then click **Close**.

Adding a slide

Now we're going to add another slide with a title and a graphic at the end of the presentation.

▶ Click on **Slide 3** in the Outline pane. We want to add the new slide after this one.

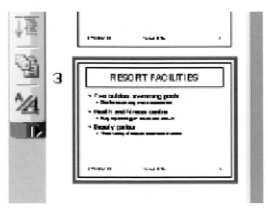

Figure 5.38

▶ Create another new blank slide and enter the title **BE TREATED LIKE A STAR**

The graphic we're going to add is a yellow star shape. Simple shapes are quite easy to add with the **AutoShapes** facility. The steps below describe how to do this.

- Click the **AutoShapes** button on the Drawing toolbar. A pop-up menu showing different options will appear.

Figure 5.39

TIP

If you can't see the Drawing toolbar click **View, Toolbars**, and then **Drawing** on the menu bar.

- Position the mouse pointer over **Stars and Banners** – another pop-up menu will appear.
- Click **5-Point Star**.

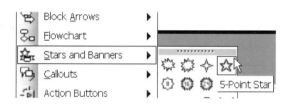

Figure 5.40

The mouse pointer will change to a thin cross shape.   +

- Click and hold the left mouse button in the main frame just underneath the text **Click to add text.**

- Drag down and across to the bottom right corner of the slide. As you drag an outline will show what size the shape will be when you let go of the mouse button. When the star is roughly the same size as the one shown below, let go of the mouse button.

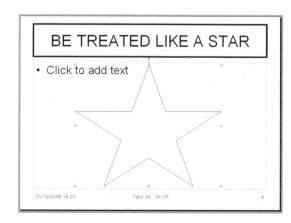

TIP

If a shape isn't the right size it can be resized using the corner handles. Make sure any shape you draw doesn't overlap the title or any of the information in the footer at the bottom of the slide. A shape in the wrong position can be moved by clicking on it, holding the left mouse button and dragging.

Figure 5.41

Now all we need to do is fill the shape with the correct colour.

Fill colour
icon

▶ Click once on the star to make sure it is still selected, then click the small down arrow next to the **Fill color** icon. A choice of fill options will appear.

▶ Click **More Fill Colors....**

▶ Click on any shade of yellow on the palette, then click **OK**. The slide should look something like the one shown below.

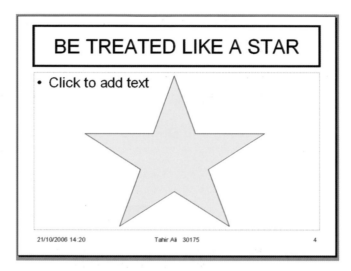

Figure 5.42

Next we'll save this edited version of the presentation with a new name.

▶ Click **File**, and then **Save As** on the menu bar. The **Save As** dialogue box will appear.

▶ Type the new name **resortinfo**, then click **Save**.

Printing as handouts

Finally we need to print just the last three slides as **handouts**.

▶ Click **File** on the menu bar, and then click **Page Setup**. The **Page Setup** dialogue box will appear.

▶ In the **Notes, handouts & outline** section click the radio button for **Portrait**, then click **OK**.

▶ Click **File** on the menu bar, and then click **Print**. The **Print** dialogue box will appear.

▶ Click the radio button next to **Slides** in the **Print range** section.

▶ Type **2,3,4** in the box next to **Slides** in the **Print range** section.

▶ Click the down arrow next to the **Print what** box adjacent to the **Handouts** section.

▶ Click **Handouts** in the drop-down list of options.

▶ Click the down arrow next to the **Slides per page** box in the **Handouts** section.

▶ Click **3** in the drop-down list of options. The options selected in your **Print** dialogue should now be the same as those shown in the example below.

▶ Click **OK**, then close the presentation and shut down **PowerPoint**.

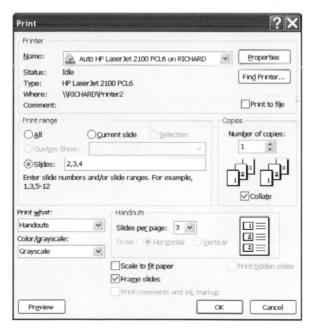

Figure 5.43

Task 4 Reordering and editing slides

During a Unit 5 assignment you'll be asked to reorder and edit slides in a presentation. This task takes you through the steps you need to follow to do this.

▶ Load **PowerPoint**.

▶ Open your saved presentation called **resortinfo**

The first thing we'll cover in this task is how to use **Slide Sorter View** to change the order of slides in a presentation. We're going to move Slide 3 so that it becomes Slide 2.

Slide Sort View button

▶ Click the **Slide Sorter View** icon on the bottom left of the screen. All the slides will be shown in number order as a series of thumbnail images.

1   2   3   4

Figure 5.44

▶ Click on **Slide 3** and hold down the left mouse button.

▶ Drag to the left so that a vertical grey line appears after **Slide 1**.

1   2

Figure 5.45

168

Let go of the mouse button – your slides should now be in the same order as those shown below.

1   2   3   4

Figure 5.46

Click the **Normal View** icon on the bottom left of the screen.

Normal View button

Editing text

Next we'll edit some of the text on one of the slides. We are going to delete the text **FIVE STAR** from the title on Slide 3.

Click on **Slide 3** in the Outline pane.

Click in the title frame after the word **STAR**.

Use the **Backspace** key to delete the text **FIVE STAR**. The slide should now look like the one below.

Figure 5.47

169

Printing as an Outline View

Now we're going to print all the slides in **Outline view** to display just the text on each slide.

▶ Click **File** on the menu bar and then click **Print**. The **Print** dialogue box will appear.

▶ Check that the radio button next to **All** in the **Print range** section is selected.

▶ Click the down arrow next to the **Print what** box adjacent to the **Handouts** section.

▶ Click **Outline View** in the drop-down list of options. The options selected in your **Print** dialogue should now be the same as those shown in the example below.

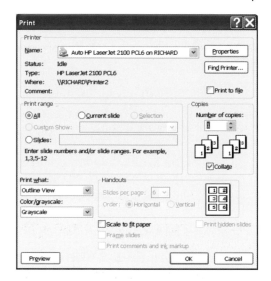

Figure 5.48

Before you print, a header or footer needs adding to the page showing your name.

▶ Click the **Preview** button in the bottom left corner of the window. A preview of the printout will be displayed.

▶ Click the **Options** button at the top of the screen, then click **Header and Footer**.

Figure 5.49

▶ Click in either the **Header** or **Footer** box and type your name, then click **Apply to All**.

▶ Click the **Print** button at the top of the screen – the **Print** dialogue window will reappear – then click **OK**.

Figure 5.50

▶ Click the **Close** button at the top of the screen to leave print preview.

Figure 5.51

Saving with a new name

Finally we'll save this edited version of the presentation with another new name.

- Click **File**, and then **Save As** on the menu bar. The **Save As** dialogue box will appear.
- In the **File name** box type the new name **resor** then click **Save**.
- Close the presentation and shut down **PowerPoint**.

That's the end of the practice tasks. Now try the full New CLAiT assignments that follow.

Practice assignment 1

Scenario

You are working as an administrative assistant for a local school. Part of your job is to prepare publicity resources about the school.

Assessment Objectives	TASK 1
	The Headteacher has asked you to create a presentation to introduce the school to prospective new parents.
1a, b, c	1 Set up a master slide as follows. This master slide layout must be used for all slides.
2e, f, g, h	a) Set the slide orientation to **landscape**.
4d, e	b) Use a placeholder (text frame) for the title towards the top of the slide.
	c) Use a placeholder (frame) for the main slide content.
	d) Set up text styles as follows:

style	emphasis	size	feature	alignment
title	bold only	large	dark border	centre
1st level bullet	bold	medium	any bullet character	left
2nd level bullet	italic	small	any bullet character	left and indented from 1st level bullet

e) Make sure there is at least one character space between the bullets and the text.

f) In the footer enter:

your **name**

your **centre number**

an **automatic date**

the **time**

	g)	Format the background to be **white**.	
	h)	Display the slide number on the bottom right of the slide.	
4a	2 a)	Save the presentation using the filename **crossways**.	
	b)	You must use the same slide layout for all the slides.	

Assessment Objectives   **TASK 2**

2a	1 a)	Create slide 1 and enter the title below. The title may be displayed on two lines.
		CROSSWAYS SCHOOL
2c	b)	Insert the image **school** below the title placeholder. You may resize this image.
3a	c)	Make sure you maintain the original proportions of the image.
	d)	Make sure the image does not touch or overlap any text.
	e)	Make sure only the image is displayed between the title and the footer.
2a	2 a)	Create slide 2 and enter the title:
		SCHOOL ICT FACILITIES
2c	b)	Enter the following text in the main placeholder (frame), with the styles shown:

300 networked computers	1st level bullet
Desktop PCs and wireless laptops	2nd level bullet
Fast internet access across the network	1st level bullet
10 Mbps broadband	2nd level bullet
Electronic whiteboards	1st level bullet
At least one in every curriculum area	2nd level bullet

2a	3 a)	Create slide 3 and enter the title:
		A TECHNOLOGY SCHOOL
2c	b)	Enter the following text in the main placeholder (frame), with the styles shown:

Specialising in four key subjects	1st level bullet
DT, ICT, Maths and Science	1st level bullet
Leading in learning through partnership	1st level bullet
Partner schools	2nd level bullet
Local businesses	2nd level bullet

2d	4	Use the spell check facility to check the accuracy of the text.
4a	5	Save the slide show keeping the filename name.
4f	6	Print out each of the 3 slides, one per page, in landscape orientation.

Assessment Objectives	TASK 3
	Your team leader has asked for a few changes to the presentation.
	1 On slide 3 titled **A TECHNOLOGY SCHOOL** demote the line **DT, ICT, Maths and Science** to become a second level bullet.
	2 a) Replace the word **SCHOOL** with the word **COLLEGE** wherever it appears in the presentation (3 times).
	b) Make sure you match the use of case.
2a 2c	3 Create slide 4 and enter the title: **CROSSWAYS**
3b	4 a) In the main placeholder, create a cross as shown below:
	b) Fill this cross with a **dark** colour.
	c) Make sure the cross does not touch or overlap any text.
	d) Make sure only the cross is displayed between the title and footer.
4b	5 Save the presentation using the new filename **newparents**.
4g	6 Print slides 2, 3 and 4 as **handouts** with 3 slides on one page.

Assessment Objectives	TASK 4
2b	1 In your presentation called **newparents** change the order of the slides so that slide 3 becomes slide 2.
2i	2 On slide 3, titled **COLLEGE ICT FACILITIES** delete the text **COLLEGE**.
4b	3 Save the amended presentation as **crossfinal**. An outline view printout will be needed.
4e	4 Enter **your name** as a header or footer for this print.
4h	5 Print the presentation in outline view to display the text on all four slides.
4c	6 Close the presentation and exit the software.
	7 Make sure you check your printouts for accuracy. You should have the following printouts: **3 individual slides** **a handout print showing slides 2, 3 and 4** **an outline view print showing slides 1, 2, 3 and 4.**

Practice assignment 2

Scenario

You are working as volunteer for a campaign group that is trying to stop the redevelopment of a local beauty spot.

Assessment Objectives		
	TASK 1	
	The campaign manager has asked you to prepare a presentation for an upcoming public meeting.	
1a, b, c 2e, f, g, h	1	Set up a master slide as follows. This master slide layout must be used for all slides.
		a) Set the slide orientation to **landscape**.
		b) Use a placeholder (text frame) for the title towards the top of the slide.
		c) Use a placeholder (frame) for the main slide content.
4d, e		d) Set up text styles as follows:

style	emphasis	size	feature	alignment
Title	bold only	large	dark border	centre
1st level bullet	bold	medium	any bullet character	left
2nd level bullet	none	small	any bullet character	left and indented from 1st level bullet

e) Make sure there is at least one character space between the bullets and the text.

f) In the footer enter:

your **name**

your **centre number**

an **automatic date**

the **time**

g) Format the background to be **light blue**.

h) Display the slide number on the bottom right of the slide.

4a   2   a) Save the presentation using the filename **carnforth**.

b) You must use the same slide layout for all the slides.

Assessment Objectives	TASK 2

2a

1 a) Create slide 1 and enter the title below. The title may be displayed on two lines.

         SAVE CARNFORTH SEAFRONT

2c

    b) Insert the image **carnforth** below the title placeholder. You may resize this image.

3a

    c) Make sure you maintain the original proportions of the image.

    d) Make sure the image does not touch or overlap any text.

    e) Make sure only the image is displayed between the title and the footer.

2a

2c

2 a) Create slide 2 and enter the title:

         SEAFRONT MARCH

    b) Enter the following text in the main placeholder (frame), with the styles shown:

March from the seafront to the town hall	1st level bullet
Meet at the Yacht Club	2nd level bullet
Tuesday 5th April	2nd level bullet
10.30 am	2nd level bullet

2a

3 a) Create slide 3 and enter the title:

         STOP THE CRAZY REDEVELOPMENT

2c

    b) Enter the following text in the main placeholder (frame), with the styles shown:

The council is planning to:	1st level bullet
Demolish the historic old Yacht Club	2nd level bullet
Drain the marshlands	2nd level bullet
Build a business park	2nd level bullet
We can't let this happen	2nd level bullet

2d

4 Use the spell check facility to check the accuracy of the text.

4a

5 Save the slide show keeping the filename **name**.

4f

6 Print out each of the 3 slides, one per page, in **landscape** orientation.

Assessment Objectives	TASK 3
	Your team leader has asked for a few changes to the presentation.
2k	1 On slide 3 titled **STOP THE CRAZY REDEVELOPMENT** promote the line **We can't let this happen** to become a first level bullet.
2j	2 a) Replace the word **SEAFRONT** with the word **BEACH** wherever it appears in the presentation (twice).
	b) Make sure you match the use of case.
2a	3 Create slide 4 and enter the title:
2c	**JOIN THE MARCH**
3b	4 a) In the main placeholder, create an arrow as shown below:
	b) Fill this arrow with a **dark** colour.
	c) Make sure the arrow does not touch or overlap any text.
	d) Make sure only the arrow is displayed between the title and footer.
4b	5 Save the presentation using the new filename **march**.
4g	6 Print slides 2 and 3 as **handouts** with both slides on one page.

Assessment Objectives	TASK 4
2b	1 In your presentation called **march** change the order of the slides so that slide 3 becomes slide 2.
2i	2 On slide 2, titled **STOP THE CRAZY REDEVELOPMENT**, delete the text **CRAZY**.
4b	3 Save the amended presentation as **campaign**.
	An outline view printout will be needed.
	4 Enter your **name** as a header or footer for this print.
	5 Print the presentation in outline view to display the text on all four slides.
	6 Close the presentation and exit the software.
	7 Make sure you check your printouts for accuracy.
	You should have the following printouts:
	3 individual slides
	a handout print showing slides 2 and 3
	an outline view print showing slides 1, 2, 3 and 4.

Practice assignment 3

Scenario

You are working as a Park Ranger for a popular country park. Part of your job is to prepare information for visitors to the park.

Assessment Objectives	TASK 1
	1 Set up a master slide as follows. This master slide layout must be used for all slides.
1a, b, c	a) Set the slide orientation to **landscape**.
2e, f, g, h	b) Use a placeholder (text frame) for the title towards the top of the slide.
	c) Use a placeholder (frame) for the main slide content
4d, e	d) Set up text styles as follows:

style	emphasis	size	feature	alignment
title	bold and italic	large	no border	centre
1st level bullet	bold	medium	any bullet character	left
2nd level bullet	italic only	small	any bullet character	left and indented from 1st level bullet

e) Make sure there is at least one character space between the bullets and the text.

f) In the footer enter:

your **name**

your **centre number**

an **automatic date**

the **time**

g) Format the background to be **light green**.

h) Display the slide number on the bottom right of the slide.

4a	**2** a) Save the presentation using the filename **ashdown**.
	b) You must use the same slide layout for all the slides.

Assessment Objectives	TASK 2

TASK 2

2a
2c

1 a) Create slide 1 and enter the title below. The title may be displayed on two lines.

ASHDOWN ESTATE

3a

b) Insert the image **horses** below the title placeholder. You may resize this image.

c) Make sure you maintain the original proportions of the image.

d) Make sure the image does not touch or overlap any text.

e) Make sure only the image is displayed between the title and the footer.

2 a) Create slide 2 and enter the title:

ESTATE ATTRACTIONS

b) Enter the following text in the main placeholder (frame), with the styles shown:

Popular park attractions include:	1st level bullet
Crazy golf course	2nd level bullet
Adventure playground	2nd level bullet
Visitor centre and lakeside restaurant	2nd level bullet
Family picnic and barbeque areas	1st level bullet

2a

3 a) Create slide 3 and enter the title:

ESTATE LOCATION DETAILS

2c

b) Enter the following text in the main placeholder (frame), with the styles shown:

Bordering beautiful Branbourne Lake	1st level bullet
Close to scenic Barton-on-Rye	1st level bullet
2 miles north of the M71, Junction 21b	2nd level bullet
3 miles south of Branbourne on the A963	2nd level bullet

2d

4 Use the spell check facility to check the accuracy of the text.

4a

5 Save the slide show keeping the filename **ashdown**.

4f

6 Print out each of the 3 slides, one per page, in **landscape** orientation.

Assessment Objectives	TASK 3
	Your team leader has asked for a few changes to the presentation.
2k	1 On slide 2 titled **ESTATE ATTRACTIONS** demote the line **Family picnic and barbeque areas** to become a second level bullet.
2j	2 a) Replace the word **ESTATE** with the word **PARK** wherever it appears in the presentation (3 times).
	b) Make sure you match the use of case.
2a	3 Create slide 4 and enter the title:
2c	**VISIT US FOR FAMILY FUN**
3b	4 a) In the main placeholder, create a smiley face as shown below:
3c	
	b) Fill the smiley face with a light colour.
	c) Make sure the smiley face does not touch or overlap any text.
	d) Make sure only the smiley face is displayed between the title and footer.
4b	5 Save the presentation using the new filename **park**.
4g	6 Print slides 2, 3 and 4 as **handouts** with 3 slides on one page.

Assessment Objectives	TASK 4
2b	1 In your presentation called **park** change the order of the slides so that slide 2 becomes slide 3.
2i	2 On slide 2, titled **ESTATE LOCATION DETAILS** delete the text **DETAILS**.
4b	3 Save the amended presentation as **visitors**.
4e	An outline view printout will be needed.
	4 Enter **your name** as a header or footer for this print.
4h	5 Print the presentation in outline view to display the text on all four slides.
4c	6 Close the presentation and exit the software.
	7 Make sure you check your printouts for accuracy. You should have the following printouts:
	3 individual slides
	a handout print showing slides 2, 3 and 4
	an outline view print showing slides 1, 2, 3 and 4.

To pass this unit you must be able to:

- ✓ identify and use image creation software correctly

- ✓ use basic file handling techniques for the software

- ✓ import, crop and resize images

- ✓ enter, amend and resize text

- ✓ manipulate and format page items

- ✓ manage and print artwork

Before you start this chapter, you or your tutor should download a zipped file called **Resources for Chapter 6** from **www.payne-gallway.co.uk/newclait/student**. It will automatically unzip. Specify that the contents are to be saved in your My Documents folder.

Image creation software is used to create and manipulate images on a computer. This type of software can be divided into two main groups – **painting packages** and **drawing packages**.

Painting packages produce images by changing the colour of small dots called **pixels** on the screen, which are then coded to create a **bitmap graphics file**. Images captured using a digital camera or by a scanner are also stored as **bitmaps**. The main advantage of using bitmap graphics is that individual pixels can be changed which makes very detailed editing possible. This is particularly useful when photographs need to be changed in some way.

The main disadvantages of using **bitmap graphics files** are:

- individual parts of an image cannot be resized – only the whole picture can be increased or decreased in size which can create empty spaces, jagged edges or produce a blurred image

- information has to be stored about every pixel in an image. This produces large files that use up a lot of space on a computer's hard disk drive.

Figure 6.1

Examples of painting packages that can produce and manipulate bitmap images include Microsoft® Paint XP, PC Paintbrush, Adobe® Photoshop®, and Corel Paint Shop Pro®. We are going to use a painting package – **Paint Shop Pro®** – to manipulate bitmap graphics in this chapter.

Drawing packages produce images made up from a combination of lines and shapes such as circles, squares and rectangles. An image produced in this way is saved as a **vector graphics file** which contains a series of instructions that describe the individual lines and shapes making up the image.

Figure 6.2

The main advantages of using **vector graphics** files are:

- they take up much less storage space than **bitmap graphics** files
- each part of an image is treated as a separate object, which means that individual parts can be easily modified
- the image can be resized without any reduction in quality.

The disadvantage of **vector graphics** is that they don't look as realistic as **bitmap graphics**, and this makes them unsuitable for storing, and for manipulating images like photographs.

Examples of drawing graphics packages include CorelDRAW®, Serif DrawPlus and Micrographx Layout sketcher. We're going to use the drawing facilities in Microsoft® **Word** to create vector graphics in this chapter because they offer all the features we need, in a program that you're already familiar with.

The practice tasks that follow cover all the techniques you need to learn in order to pass a **New CLAiT Unit 6** assignment.

Practice tasks

Task 1 Creating a new piece of artwork

This task takes you through the steps needed to create a new piece of **vector graphic** artwork in **Word**. We are going to work to the design layout sketch shown below.

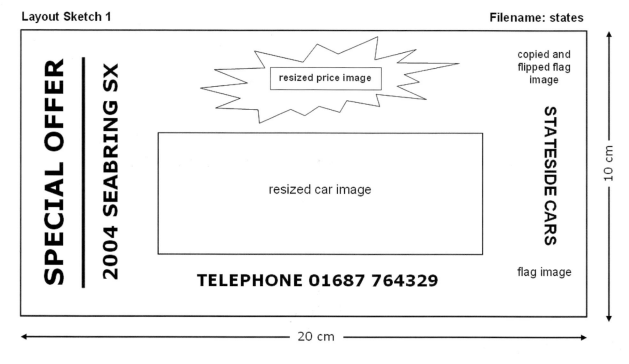

Figure 6.3

▶ Load **Word**. The main **Word** document window will be displayed with a blank document ready to start work on. If there is no blank document:

▶ *Either* click the **New** button on the **Standard** toolbar,

New button

▶ *or* click **Blank Document** in the **Task Pane**.

Page setup

The first thing we need to do is set the **page orientation** for the document to **landscape**. This will give us a better page width to create artwork on.

▶ Click **File** on the menu bar and then click **Page Setup...**

▶ The **Page Setup** dialogue box will be displayed. The **Margins** tab should already be selected – if it isn't just click on it.

▷ Click **Landscape** in the **Orientation** section. Your screen should look like the one below.

Figure 6.4

Next we need to change the page view so that the whole page is visible on the screen.

▷ Click the small down arrow next to the **Zoom** box on the **Standard** toolbar.
A list of **Zoom** options will appear.

Figure 6.5

▷ Click **Whole Page** in the list.

Creating a new drawing

▷ Click **Insert** on the menu bar and then click **Picture, New Drawing**. A blank drawing canvas will appear – this is the working area where we will create the new piece of artwork.

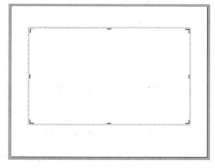

Figure 6.6

The first thing we need to do is make sure the drawing canvas is the size specified on **Layout Sketch 1.**

⊳ Click **Format** on the menu bar, then click **Drawing Canvas**. The **Format Drawing Canvas** dialogue box will appear.

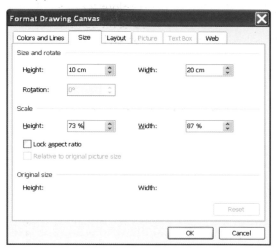

Figure 6.7

⊳ Click the **Size** tab, then In the **Scale** section click the check box next to **Lock aspect ratio** to remove the tick.

⊳ Click inside the **Height** box in the **Size and rotate** section, press the **Backspace** key to delete the current value, then type **10 cm**.

⊳ Repeat for the **Width** box and type **20 cm**.

> **TIP**
>
> Take care to make sure that the size of your drawing canvas is exactly the same size and shape as specified on the **Layout Sketch 1** design and in the instructions for any assignments.

Next we need to fill the drawing canvas with a background colour. The colour we are going to use for this artwork is yellow.

Fill colour button

⊳ On the **Drawing** toolbar, click the small down arrow next to the **Fill Color** button. A choice of fill options will appear.

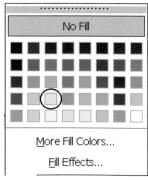

Figure 6.8

Click the yellow square on the palette.

Unit 6 assignments will specify a background colour for each piece of artwork. Always make sure you have used the colour specified. If you can't see the colour you need on the palette click **More Fill Colors**, click a colour, and then **OK**.

Your drawing canvas should look like the one below.

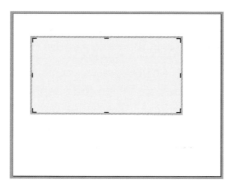

Figure 6.9

Creating basic shapes

Now we are going to add the explosion shape shown on **Layout Sketch 1**. Simple shapes like this can be added using the **AutoShapes** facility. The steps below describe how to do this.

TIP

In assignments for this unit you will be asked to create simple shapes like triangles, squares, circles and rectangles. All these shapes can be created using the **AutoShapes** facility.

 Click the **AutoShapes** button on the drawing toolbar. A pop-up menu showing different autoshapes options will appear.

Autoshapes button

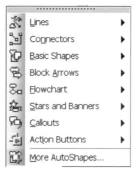

Figure 6.10

185

Position the mouse pointer over **Stars and Banners** (another pop-up menu will appear), then click **Explosion 2**.

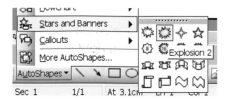

Figure 6.11

The mouse pointer will change to a thin cross shape.

 Click and hold the left mouse button in the centre of the drawing canvas.

 Drag down and across to the right. As you drag an outline will show what size the shape will be when you let go of the mouse button. When the shape is roughly the same size as the one shown in **Layout Sketch 1**, let go of the mouse button. (The image below shows the size in relation to the whole canvas.)

Figure 6.12

Positioning shapes

Now we need to move the shape into the correct position at the top of the artwork as shown on the layout sketch.

 Click once on the shape to make sure it is selected, and with the sizing handles visible, then move the mouse pointer over the shape until it changes into a cross with four arrowheads.

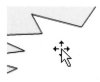

Figure 6.13

 Click and hold the left mouse button, then drag up towards the top of the drawing canvas. As you drag, a dotted line will show you where the shape will be when you let go of the mouse button. When the shape is in roughly the same position as in **Layout Sketch 1**, let go of the mouse button.

Resizing shapes

Next we need to resize the shape so that it is the same as the example in the **Layout Sketch 1** design.

 Click once on the shape to make sure it is selected and the sizing handles are visible, then move the mouse pointer over the bottom right sizing handle until it changes into a **double-headed arrow**.

Figure 6.14

 Click and hold the left mouse button, then drag up towards the top left corner of the shape. As you drag, a dotted outline will show you what size the shape will be when you let go of the mouse button.

 Use the sizing handles around the shape to resize it so that it looks like the one in **Layout Sketch 1**.

Filling shapes

Now all we need to do is fill the shape with colour. The fill colour we are going to use for this shape is red.

 Click once on the explosion shape to make sure it is still selected, then click the **Fill color** button arrow. A choice of fill options will appear.

Fill colour button

 Click the red square on the palette, then click **OK**. The shape should look like the one below.

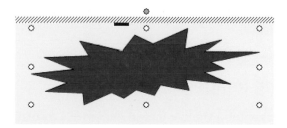

Figure 6.15

Saving a piece of artwork

Finally we need to save this new piece of artwork:

 Either click **File** on the menu bar, then click **Save**,

 or click the **Save** button on the **Standard** toolbar. The **Save** dialogue box will appear.

Save button

⊳ Type the name **states** in the **File name** box, then click the **Save** button.

The **Save** dialogue window will disappear and the filename **states** will be displayed at the top of the screen. The document will now be saved with this name whenever you click the **Save** button on the **Standard** toolbar.

Closing a piece of artwork and exiting Word

Finally you need to close this document and shut down **Word**:

⊳ *Either* click **File** on the menu bar, then click **Exit**,

⊳ *or* click the **X** in the top right-hand corner of the screen.

Task 2   Working with images

During this task we'll use the canvas that we created in Task 1, inserting images into it and resizing them, working to the **Layout Sketch 1** design. To work through this task you will need to open the saved document **states** that contains your artwork.

Opening a saved piece of artwork

⊳ Load **Word**, then

⊳ *Either* click **File** on the menu bar, and click **Open**,

Open button

⊳ *or* click the **Open** button on the **Standard** toolbar. The **Open** dialogue box will appear.

⊳ In the window, click on **states** then click **Open**.

Ask your tutor to help you find this file if it isn't in the list on your screen.

Inserting and resizing images

We will start by inserting and resizing the car image shown in **Layout Sketch 1**.

Inserting

You can insert a picture in one of two ways:

⊳ *Either* click **Insert** on the menu bar, then click **Picture, From File...**,

Insert Picture
button

⊳ *or* click the **Insert Picture** button on the **Drawing** toolbar.

The **Insert Picture** dialogue box will appear and the image file we need is called **car**. Your tutor will tell you where to find this file. In this screenshot it's in a folder called **Resources**.

Figure 6.16

Click on the file called **car**, then click **Insert**. The image will be inserted in the drawing canvas and will be selected with the sizing handles visible.

Figure 6.17

Resizing

Now we need to resize the image:

Position the mouse pointer over the bottom right sizing handle until it changes to a diagonal two-headed arrow, then click and hold the left mouse button.

Drag up and across towards the top left corner of the image. As you drag, a dotted line will show you how big the image will be when you let go of the mouse button. When the outlined area is roughly the same size as the one shown in **Layout Sketch 1** (about two thirds of its original size), let go of the mouse button.

Figure 6.18

Your drawing canvas should now look like the one below.

TIP

If you use the side sizing handles to resize an image it will become distorted. Use the **corner sizing handles** to resize an image if you want it to stay in proportion.

Figure 6.19

Moving the Image

Next we need to move the image into the position shown in **Layout Sketch 1**. Images are moved in the same way as shapes, by **clicking and dragging**.

- Click once on the image to make sure it is selected and the sizing handles are visible.

- Move the mouse pointer over the image until it changes shape into a cross with four arrowheads.

Figure 6.20

> **TIP**
>
> If you don't get the image in the right position first time just move it again. Keep trying until the image is in the position shown in the Layout Sketch 1 design.

- Click and hold the left mouse button, drag the image into the position shown in **Layout Sketch 1**, then let go of the mouse button.

Next we need to insert the price image shown in the layout sketch.

- *Either* click **Insert** on the menu bar, then click **Picture, From File…**,

- *or* click the **Insert Picture** button on the **Drawing** toolbar. The image file is called **price**. Your tutor will tell you where to find this file. In our example, the image file was in a folder called **Resources**.

- Click on the file called **price**, then click the **Insert** button. The image will be inserted in the drawing canvas.

Figure 6.21

As before, we need to move the image into the position shown in **Layout Sketch 1**.

- Click **once** on the image to make sure it is selected (with the sizing handles visible).

- Move the mouse over the image until the pointer changes to a cross, then click and hold the left mouse button, and drag the picture into the position shown below.

- When the image is correctly positioned, let go of the mouse button.

Figure 6.22

Copying and flipping images

We now need to insert the **flags** image, as in **Layout Sketch 1**.

▶ *Either* click **Insert** on the menu bar, and then click **Picture, From File...**,

▶ *or* click the **Insert Picture** button on the **Drawing** toolbar.

▶ The image file you need is called **flags**, which your tutor will tell you where to find. The file we're using here is also in the **Resources** folder.

▶ Click on the file called **flags** and then click the **Insert** button. The image will be inserted in the drawing canvas.

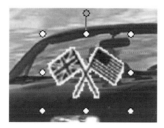

Figure 6.23

Next we need to move the flags into the position shown in the **Layout Sketch 1** design.

▶ Click once on the image to make sure it is selected with the sizing handles visible. Move the mouse over the image until the pointer changes to the cross shape, then click and hold the left mouse button.

▶ Drag the flags into the position shown below, then let go of the mouse button. This is a **drag and drop** manoeuvre.

Figure 6.24

Now we need to make a copy of the flags image, flip it horizontally and put it into the position shown on the layout sketch.

Copying

▶ Click once on the image to make sure it is selected with the sizing handles visible.

▶ On the **Standard** toolbar, first click the **Copy** button, then the **Paste** button. A copy of the flags image will appear, slightly offset from the original.

Draw button

 Click the **Draw** button on the **Drawing** toolbar. A pop-up menu showing the available drawing options will appear.

Figure 6.25

 Position the mouse pointer over **Rotate or Flip** – another pop-up menu will appear.

 Click **Flip Horizontal**. The image will be 'flipped' horizontally.

 All we need to do now is to drag and drop it to the top right-hand position, as in **Layout Sketch 1**. The full drawing canvas should now look like the one below.

Figure 6.26

Finally we'll save the artwork keeping the document name **states**.

Save button

 Click the **Save** button on the **Standard** toolbar, then close **Word**.

Task 3 Working with text

To work through this task you need to open the saved document **states**, which contains your artwork.

Opening a saved piece of artwork

Load **Word**, then,

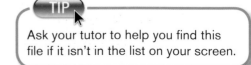
Ask your tutor to help you find this file if it isn't in the list on your screen.

 Either click **File** on the menu bar, and click **Open**,

Open button

 or click the **Open** button on the **Standard** toolbar. The **Open** dialogue box will appear.

 Click on **states** in the window, then click **Open**.

Adding and rotating text

We'll start by adding the vertically aligned text shown on the left of **Layout Sketch 1**.

- Click the **Text Box** button on the **Drawing** toolbar. The mouse pointer will change to a thin cross shape. +

- Position the pointer in the top left corner of the drawing canvas.

Text Box
button

Figure 6.27

- Click and hold the left mouse button.

- Drag down and across to the right. As you drag, an outline will show what size the text box will be when you let go of the mouse button. When the text box is roughly the same size as the one shown opposite, let go of the mouse button.

The **Text Box** toolbar will appear on the screen.

Figure 6.28

Figure 6.29

Layout Sketch 1 shows that the text in this box needs to be set vertically.

- Click the **Change Text Direction** button on the **Text Box** toolbar twice. As you click, the flashing cursor in the text box will change position. The cursor should now be at the bottom of the text box in the same position as the one shown below.

Change Text
Direction button

Figure 6.30

- Type **SPECIAL OFFER** in the textbox.

Now we'll add the second piece of vertically aligned text shown on the left of **Layout Sketch 1**.

- Click the **Text Box** button.

- Position the pointer at the top the drawing canvas on the right of the first text box.

Text Box
button

Figure 6.31

▶ Click and hold the left mouse button, drag down and across to the right, then when the text box is roughly the same size as the one shown opposite, let go of the mouse button.

Layout Sketch 1 shows that the text in this box also needs to be aligned vertically reading from bottom to top.

Change Text
Direction button

▶ Click the **Change Text Direction** button on the **Text Box** toolbar twice.

▶ Type **2004 SEABRING SX** in the text box.

Next we'll add the vertically aligned text shown on the right of **Layout Sketch 1**.

Text Box
button

▶ Click the **Text Box** button.

▶ Position the pointer on the right of the drawing canvas just under the top flags image.

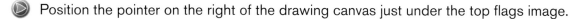

Figure 6.32

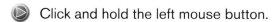

Figure 6.33

▶ Click and hold the left mouse button.

▶ Drag down and across to the right. When the text box is roughly the same size as the one shown opposite, let go of the mouse button.

Layout Sketch 1 shows that the text in this box needs to be aligned vertically reading from top to bottom.

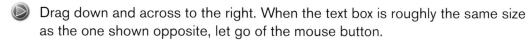

Figure 6.34

Change Text
Direction button

▶ Click the **Change Text Direction** button on the **Text Box** toolbar once. The cursor in your text box should now be in the same position as the one shown below.

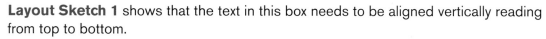

Figure 6.35

▶ Type **STATESIDE CARS**

Finally we'll add the horizontally-aligned telephone number text shown in the centre of **Layout Sketch 1**.

Text Box
button

▶ Click the **Text Box** button.

▶ Position the pointer in the bottom left of the drawing canvas underneath the car image.

Figure 6.36

▶ Click and hold the left mouse button, drag down and across to the right, and when the text box is roughly the same size as the one in **Layout Sketch 1**, let go of the mouse button.

▶ Type **TELEPHONE 01687 764329**

That's all of the text added to the artwork and aligned as specified on the layout sketch. Next we need to format the text.

Formatting text

We'll start by formatting the text on the left of the drawing canvas.

▶ Click three times inside the text box containing the text **SPECIAL OFFER** to select the text.

▶ Click the down arrow in the **Font name box** in the **Formatting** toolbar.

▶ Scroll down through the list of fonts and click on the font called **Verdana**.

▶ Click the small arrow on the right of the **Font Size** box in the **Formatting** toolbar, scroll through the list of sizes, and click on **26**.

Font size box

Figure 6.37

 TIP

Some of the text in a text box might disappear when you format it. If this happens you will need to use the sizing handles around the text box to make it bigger.
The missing text will reappear once the text box is large enough to display it in full.

▶ Click the **Bold** button on the **Formatting** toolbar (make sure the text is still selected).

B

Bold button

▶ Click the **Center** button on the **Formatting** toolbar – this will position the text centrally in the text box with an equal amount of blank space on either side.

Center button

▶ On the **Drawing** toolbar, click the **Font Color** button arrow (a choice of font colour options will appear), and click the red coloured square on the palette. This text box should now look like the one below.

Font Color button

Figure 6.38

 TIP

Once you've clicked a colour on the font colour pallette it becomes the default colour. To use the same colour again all you need to do is click the **Font Color button**. You will only need to click the small down arrow to the right of the button if a different font colour is required.

Font Color button

Now we'll format the text in the second text box on the left of the drawing canvas as in **Layout Sketch 1**.

▶ Click three times inside the text box containing the text **2004 SEABRING SX** to select the text.

▶ Use the **Font name box** to change the font type to **Verdana**.

Figure 6.39

B

Bold button

Font Colour button

▶ Use the **Font Size** box to change the font size to **20**.

▶ Click the **Bold** button to make the text bold.

▶ Click the **Center** button to position the text in the middle of the text box.

Center button

▶ Click the **Font Color** button to change the colour to red. This text box should now look like the one below.

Figure 6.40

Next we'll format the text in the text box on the right of the drawing canvas as in **Layout Sketch 1**.

▶ Click three times inside the text box containing the text **STATESIDE CARS** to select the text.

▶ Use the **Font name box** to change the font type to **Verdana**.

▶ Use the **Font Size** box to change the font size to **18**.

▶ Click the **Bold** button to make the text bold.

▶ Click the **Center** button to position the text in the middle of the text box.

▶ Click the **Font Color** button to change the colour to red. This text box should now look like the one opposite.

Figure 6.41

Finally we'll format the text at the bottom of the drawing canvas as in **Layout Sketch 1**.

▶ Click three times inside the text box containing the text **TELEPHONE 01687 764329** to select the text.

▶ Use the **Font name box** to change the font type to **Verdana**.

Figure 6.42

▶ Use the **Font Size** box to change the font size to **16**.

▶ Click the **Bold** button to make the text bold.

▶ Click the **Center** button to position the text in the middle of the text box.

▶ Click the **Font Color** button to change the colour to red. This text box should now look like the one below.

Bold button

Center button

Font Colour button

TELEPHONE 01687 764329

Figure 6.43

Adding lines

The next thing we need to do is add the vertical line between the text boxes shown on the left of **Layout Sketch 1**.

▶ Click the **Line** button in the **Drawing** toolbar.

▶ Position the cross-shaped pointer between the tops of the two text boxes on the left of the drawing canvas.

Line button

Figure 6.44

▶ Click and hold the left mouse button, press and hold the **Shift** key – this will keep the line straight – then drag down towards to the bottom of the drawing canvas. Let go of the mouse button then the **Shift** key, when the line looks like the one shown opposite.

The last thing we need to do with the line is to increase its thickness slightly.

Figure 6.45

▶ Click the **Line Style** button on the **Drawing** toolbar.

▶ Click **3 pt** in the list of line styles.

Line Style button

Formatting text boxes

To finish off this piece of artwork we need to remove the white backgrounds and black borders from all the text boxes as in **Layout Sketch 1**.

- Click inside the text box containing the text **TELEPHONE 01687 764329**, then
- Click **Format** on the menu bar, and then click **Text Box**,
- In the **Fill** section, click the down arrow next to the **Color** box and click **No Fill**.
- In the **Line** section, click the down arrow next to the **Color** box and click **No Line**.
- Click **OK**. The text box should now look like the one below.

TELEPHONE 01687 764329

Figure 6.46

- Repeat these steps to remove the white backgrounds and black borders from the remaining text boxes. When you've finished, your drawing canvas should look like the one below.

Figure 6.47

Printing artwork in colour

Finally we need to print the artwork in colour before saving it and closing **Word**.

 Click **File** on the menu bar, then click **Print**. The **Print** dialogue box will appear.

 In the **Printer** section, click the small down arrow next to **Name**. A list of available printers will appear. At this stage you need to select a suitable colour printer from the list of available printers. Your tutor will tell you which printer to choose.

 Click on the name of the printer you want to use then click **OK**.

> **TIP**
>
> When you are asked to print in colour, make sure that a suitable colour printer is available. It is not acceptable to print in black and white unless you are specifically instructed to do so.

Finally we'll save the artwork keeping the document name **states**.

Click the **Save** button on the **Standard** toolbar, then close **Word**.

Save button

Task 4   Modifying a piece of artwork

Once you've created a new piece of artwork you'll be asked to modify it to match a new design layout sketch. The new design layout we're going to use for this task is shown below.

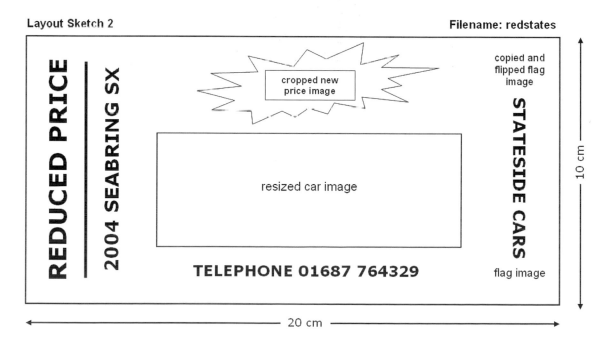

Figure 6.48

▶ Load **Word**.

▶ Open the saved document **states**, containing your artwork.

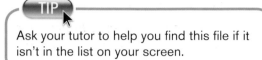

TIP

Ask your tutor to help you find this file if it isn't in the list on your screen.

Deleting images

To get started we need to delete the price image, which is going to be replaced with the price image shown on **Layout Sketch 2**.

▶ Click once on the price image to make sure it is selected with the sizing handles visible.

Figure 6.49

▶ Press the **Delete** key – the price image will disappear.

Now we can insert the new price image.

▶ *Either* click **Insert** on the menu bar, and then click **Picture, From File...**,

▶ *or* click the **Insert Picture** button on the **Drawing** toolbar. The image file you need is called **redstate**. Your tutor will tell you where to find this file. In the example here, the image file is in the **Resources** folder.

▶ Click on the file called **redstate**, and then click **Insert**. The image will be inserted in the drawing canvas.

Figure 6.50

Cropping images

The text **Price reduced to just** before the figures on the image is not needed. We must remove the unwanted parts of this image by **cropping** it. We'll look at how to do this now.

▷ Click once on the new price image to make sure it is selected, with the sizing handles visible.

▷ Click the **Crop** button on the **Picture** toolbar. The circular sizing handles around the image will be replaced by cropping handles.

Crop button

▷ Position the mouse pointer on the left edge of the image until it changes into the same shape as one of the cropping handles.

Figure 6.51

▷ Click and hold the left mouse button, then drag across towards the right of the image. As you drag, a dotted frame will show what will be left of the image after cropping. When the outlined area looks like the one below, let go of the mouse button.

Figure 6.52

▷ Click the **Crop** button again to turn cropping off. Leave the image selected with the sizing handles visible.

> **TIP**
>
> The cropped parts of an image can be restored either by dragging in the opposite direction if you go too far when cropping, or by clicking the **Reset Picture** button after cropping.
>
>
>
> Reset Picture button

Now we'll move the new price image into the position shown on **Layout Sketch 2**.

▷ Click once on the image to make sure it is selected with the sizing handles visible. Move the mouse pointer over the image until it changes to a cross shape, click and hold the left mouse button, drag the picture into the position shown on **Layout Sketch 2**, then let go of the mouse button.

Editing text

Next we need to change the text inside the first text box on the left of the screen to match **Layout Sketch 2**.

▶ Click three times inside the text box containing the text **SPECIAL OFFER** to select the text, then press the **Backspace** key to delete all of the text.

▶ Type in **REDUCED PRICE**. Your drawing canvas should now look like the one below.

Figure 6.53

Printing and saving with a new name

All we need to do now is print a copy of the modified artwork and save the file with a new name. First we'll **Save** this modified version of the artwork with a new name

▶ Click **File**, and then **Save As...** on the menu bar. The **Save As** dialogue box will appear.

▶ Type the new name **redstate** in the **File name:** box, click **Save**, then close down **Word**.

Now we'll **Print** a copy

▶ Click **File** on the menu bar, and then click **Print**. The **Print** dialogue box will appear.

▶ Choose a printer and click **OK**.

Task 5   Editing bitmap images

The last part of an **E-image creation** assignment will ask you to edit some bitmap images. The bitmap editing tools built into **Word** don't offer all the necessary functions needed to complete this task accurately. You will need to use a painting package specifically designed to edit bitmap images. We are going to use a popular painting package called **Paint Shop Pro** to complete this task.

> **TIP**
>
> Version **X** of **Paint Shop Pro** has been used for the task here. Check with your tutor if this is the version that you will be using. They will need to let you know about any differences if you are using an earlier version of this software.

You can load **Paint Shop Pro** in one of two ways:

▶ Either double-click the **Paint Shop Pro** icon on the **Desktop** in Windows,

▶ or click the **Start** button at the bottom left of the screen, then click **Programs**, **Paint Shop Pro**

The main **Paint Shop Pro** window will be displayed – it should look something like the one below.

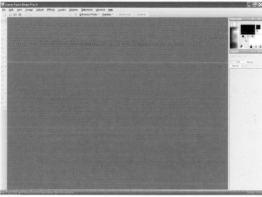

Figure 6.54

Editing a digital camera picture

To complete this part of the task we will download a picture that was taken using a digital camera. In the example below we are using a black and white picture called **fighters** that has been downloaded from a digital camera and placed in a subfolder called **Images**. Your tutor will tell you where to find this picture.

> **TIP**
>
> You don't need to take the picture or download it from a digital camera yourself to meet the requirements of this unit. It is quite acceptable to use a picture that has already been taken with a digital camera and placed on a disk or network resource drive. When you see the instruction 'download' in an assignment it simply means locate and open the image. You must not download a picture from the Internet.

▶ Either click **File** on the menu bar, then click **Open**,

▶ or click the **Open** button on the toolbar at the top of the screen. The **Open** dialogue box will appear.

▶ Click on the file called **fighters**, then click **Open**. The image will be opened – it should look exactly like the one below.

Figure 6.55

Adding text to an image

Next you need to add your name and the date anywhere on this image.

▶ Click the **Background and Fill Properties** box (circled below) on the **Materials** palette…

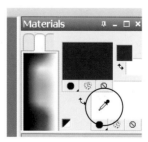

Figure 6.56

…the **Material Properties** dialogue window will appear.

TIP

If you can't see the **Materials** palette click **View**, **Palettes** and then click **Materials** on the menu bar at the top of the screen.

Position the dropper pointer over the black square at the top right-hand corner on the colour palette, then click the left mouse button.

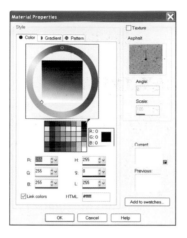

Figure 6.57

TIP

This sets the text colour to black. If you are placing text on quite a dark area of an image during an assignment, it might sometimes be better to use white text.

Click **OK**.

Click the **Text Tool** button on the **Tool Palette** on the left of the screen.

Click anywhere on the image – choose an area where text will be seen clearly. The **Text Entry** dialogue window will appear.

Type your name followed by the date in the box headed **Enter Text Here:**. The text will appear on the image as you type.

A

Text Tool
button

Figure 6.58

Click **Apply**. The text will appear on the image.

Saving and printing the modified picture

Now you need to save the modified image with a suitable filename.

⊳ On the menu bar click **File**, then **Save As...**.

⊳ Click in the **File name:** box and type the new name, **newfighters** – you can use a different name if you want to.

⊳ Click the small down arrow next to the **Save in:** box and click on your **My Documents** or network home directory folder if it is not already selected.

⊳ Click the **Save** button.

Finally you need to print the picture in black and white before closing it.

⊳ On the menu bar click **File**, then **Print**. The **Print** dialogue box will appear.

⊳ Click the **Printer** button, click on the name of a black and white printer in the list, then click **OK**. Ask your tutor for help if you're not sure which printer to choose.

⊳ Click on **OK**, then click **X** in the top right-hand corner of the image window to close the picture.

TIP

Make sure that you have printed the image using the correct type of printer – colour or black and white, depending on the instructions in the assignment.

Changing the resolution of a bitmap image

Bitmap images are made up from patterns of different coloured dots called **pixels**. You are going to change the **resolution** of a bitmap image by changing the number of **pixels per inch**.

You need to load a bitmap image called **harbour**. Your tutor will tell you where to find this image. In the example below, the image is in the **Resources** folder.

⊳ *Either* Click **File** on the menu bar, then click **Open**,

⊳ *or* click the **Open** button on the toolbar at the top of the screen. The **Open** dialogue box will appear.

⊳ Click on the file called **harbour**, then click **Open**. The image will be opened – it should look like the one below.

Figure 6.59

⊚ On the menu bar click **Image**, then **Resize**. The **Resize** dialogue box will appear.

⊚ In the **Print Size** section, click inside the **Resolution:** box, delete the current value and type in **40**, then click **OK**.

Next we'll save this changed version of the image with a new name.

⊚ On the menu bar click **File**, then **Save As...**.

⊚ Click in the **File name:** box and type the new name, **harbournew**.

⊚ Click the small down arrow next to the **Save in:** box, click on your **My Documents** or network home directory folder if it is not already selected, then click the **Save** button.

Finally you need to print this image in colour before closing it.

⊚ On the menu bar click **File**, then **Print**. The **Print** dialogue box will appear.

⊚ Click the **Printer** button, click on the name of a colour printer in the list, then click **OK**. Ask your tutor for help if you're not sure which printer to choose.

⊚ Click **OK**, then click **X** in the top right-hand corner of the **Paint Shop Pro** window to close the program.

That's the end of the practice tasks. Now try the full New CLAiT assignments that follow.

Practice assignment 1

Scenario

You are working as a Graphic Designer for a record company. You have been asked to produce a CD cover design for a popular group's new album.

Layout Sketch 1
Filename: eastcd

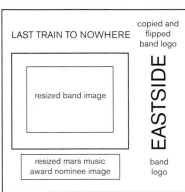

Layout Sketch 2
Filename: eastnew

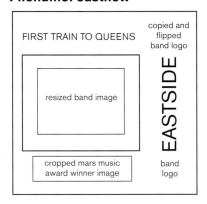

Assessment Objectives	TASK 1
	Before you begin this task make sure that you have the files **eastside.jpg** and **marsnorm.gif**.
	Refer to **Layout Sketch 1** and the Candidate Instructions for the Completion of all Tasks, when carrying out this task.
1b	1 a) Create a new piece of artwork which is **12 cm** wide by **12 cm** tall.
3a, 4a	b) Fill the background with colour.
1g	2 a) Create a **rectangle** shape in the centre left of your artwork.
3a	b) Fill this shape with **gold**.
	c) Ensure that the shape remains inside the artwork. It should fill half the height of the artwork with one quarter empty space above and below. It should fill three quarters of the width with one quarter empty space on the right.
1c	3 a) Insert the image **eastside**.
1d	b) Resize this image so that it will fit inside the rectangle.
1f	c) Position this image in centre of the rectangle shape.
4c	4 Save your artwork using the filename **eastcd**.
1c	5 a) Insert the image **marsnorm**.
1d	b) Resize this image so that it is the same width as the rectangle shape.
1f	c) Position this image below the rectangle shape.
4c	6 Save your artwork keeping the filename **eastcd**.

Assessment Objectives	**TASK 2**
	Before you begin this task make sure that you have the file **eastlogo.gif**.
	Refer to **Layout Sketch 1** and the Candidate Instructions for the Completion of all Tasks, when carrying out this task.
	Continue working on your artwork saved in called **Task 1** called **eastcd**.
1c	1 a) Insert the image **eastlogo**.
	b) Position this image in the bottom right corner of the artwork.
3d	2 a) Copy the image **eastlogo**.
3c	b) Flip the copy of the image **horizontally**.
	c) Position the copy in the top right corner of the artwork.
	d) Make sure the flipped image is the same size as the original image.
2a	3 a) Enter the following text in **white**:
3a	**LAST TRAIN TO NOWHERE**
	b) Place this text at the top of the artwork.
	c) Size this text to fit the width of the rectangle shape.
2a	4 a) Enter the following text in **yellow**:
3a	**EASTSIDE**
3b	b) Rotate this text **90° clockwise**.
	c) Place this text to **right-hand** side of the artwork.
	d) Size this text to fit the space between the **eastlogo** images.
4c	5 Save your artwork keeping the filename **eastcd**.
4d	6 Print your artwork in colour.
	7 a) On the printout, write **your name**, **your centre number** and **today's date**.
	b) Check your printout for accuracy.
	c) Make sure that you have placed all items according to **Layout Sketch 1** and that you have carried out all the instructions for the completion of the tasks.

Assessment Objectives	TASK 3
	Before you begin this task make sure that you have the file **marswin.gif**.
	Continue working on your artwork saved in **Task 2** called **eastcd**.
	Refer to **Layout Sketch 2** and the Candidate Instructions for the Completion of all Tasks, when carrying out this task.
3g	1 Delete the image **marsnorm** under the rectangle shape.
2a	2 a) Change the text **LAST TRAIN TO NOWHERE** to:
	FIRST TRAIN TO QUEENS
2b	b) Resize this text to fit the width of the rectangle shape.
1d	3 a) Insert the image **marswin**.
1e	b) Crop this image to remove the year **2006**.
	c) Position this image below the rectangle shape.
4c	4 Save your artwork using the new filename **eastnew**.
4d	5 Print your artwork in colour.
	6 a) On the printout, write **your name**, **your centre number** and **today's date**.
	b) Check your printout for accuracy.
	c) Make sure that you have placed all items according to **Layout Sketch 2** and that you have carried out all the instructions for the completion of the tasks.
4c	7 Close all open files.

Assessment Objectives	TASK 4
	Before you begin this task make sure that you have the following images:
	• **a black and white image of a city street taken using a digital camera**
	• **shore.jpg.**
	1 Open a suitable software package to enable you to download a picture taken using a digital camera.
1a	2 a) Download a suitable picture of a city street.
	b) Make sure your picture is not offensive, inappropriate or unsuitable in any way.
2a	3 a) On the image, insert **your name** and **today's date**.
	b) You may position this text anywhere on the image. Make sure this text will be clearly readable on the printout.

4c	4	Save the image using a suitable filename.
4d	5	Print the picture in black and white.
4c	6	Close the picture.
	7	Open the image **shore**.
4b	8	Change the resolution of this image to be **20 pixels/inch** or **8 pixels/cm**.
4c	9	Save the changed image using the filename **newshore**.
4d	10	Print the image **newshore**.
		On the printout, write **your name**, **your centre number** and **today's date**.
4c	11	Close the file and exit the software.
	12	Make sure you check your printouts for accuracy.

You should have the following printouts in the this order:

> **eastcd artwork**
>
> **eastnew artwork**
>
> **the digital picture of a city street**
>
> **newshore**

Make sure your name is clearly displayed on all printouts.

Practice assignment 2

Scenario

You are working as a Graphic Designer for a technology company. Your manager has asked you to produce a design for a new staff security pass.

Layout Sketch 1
Filename: Icorp

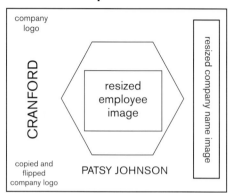

Layout Sketch 2
Filename: newcorp

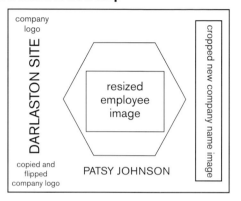

Assessment Objectives			TASK 1
			Before you begin this task make sure that you have the files **patsyj.jpg** and **corporation.gif**.
			Refer to **Layout Sketch 1** and the Candidate Instructions for the Completion of all Tasks when carrying out this task.
1b	1	a)	Create a new piece of artwork which is **8 cm** wide by **7 cm** tall.
3a, 4a		b)	Fill the background with **light blue**.
1g	2	a)	Create a **6-sided** shape (hexagon) in the centre of your artwork.
3a		b)	Fill this shape with **black**.
		c)	Make sure that this shape remains inside the artwork. It should fill three quarters of the height of the artwork with one quarter of empty space below. It should fill half the width of the artwork with one quarter of empty space on each side.
1c	3	a)	Insert the image **patsyj**.
1d		b)	Resize this image so that it will fit inside the 6-sided shape.
1f		c)	Position this image in the centre of the 6-sided shape.
4c	4		Save your artwork using the filename **Icorp**.
1c	5	a)	Insert the image **corporation**.
1d		b)	Resize this image so that it fills the height of the artwork.
1f		c)	Position this image on the **right-hand** side of the artwork.
4c	6		Save your artwork keeping the filename **Icorp**.

Assessment Objectives	TASK 2
	Before you begin this task make sure that you have the file **liqlogo.gif**.
	Refer to **Layout Sketch 1** and the Candidate Instructions for the Completion of all Tasks when carrying out this task.
	Continue working on your artwork saved in called **Task 1** called **Icorp**.
1c	**1** a) Insert the image **liqlogo**.
	b) Position this image in the top left corner of the artwork.
3d	**2** a) Copy the image **liqlogo**.
3c	b) Flip the copy of the image **horizontally**.
	c) Position the copy in the bottom left corner of the artwork.
	d) Make sure the flipped image is the same size as the original image.
2a	**3** a) Enter the following text in **gold**:
3a	**CRANFORD SITE**
3b	b) Rotate this text **90° anticlockwise**.
	c) Place this text to **left-hand** side of the artwork.
	d) Size this text to fit the space between the **liqlogo** images.
2a	**4** a) Enter the following text in **gold**:
3a	**PATSY JOHNSON**
	b) Place this text under the 6-sided shape.
	c) Size this text to fit the width of the 6-sided shape.
4c	**5** Save your artwork keeping the filename **Icorp**.
4d	**6** Print your artwork in colour.
	7 a) On the printout, write **your name**, **your centre number** and **today's date**.
	b) Check your printout for accuracy.
	c) Make sure that you have placed all items according to **Layout Sketch 1** and that you have carried out all the instructions for the completion of the tasks.

Assessment Objectives | **TASK 3**

Before you begin this task make sure that you have the file **research.gif**.

Continue working on your artwork saved in called **Task 2** called **lcorp**.

Refer to **Layout Sketch 2** and the Candidate Instructions for the Completion of all Tasks when carrying out this task.

1   Delete the image **corporation** on the right-hand side of the artwork.

2   a)   Change the text **CRANFORD SITE** to be:

   DARLASTON SITE

   b)   Size this text to fit the space between the **liqlogo** images.

3   a)   Insert the image **research**.

   b)   Crop this image to remove the word **Ltd**.

   c)   Position this image on the **right-hand** side of the artwork.

4   Save your artwork using the new filename **newcorp**.

5   Print your artwork in colour.

6   a)   On the printout, write **your name**, **your centre number** and **today's date**.

   b)   Check your printout for accuracy.

   c)   Make sure that you have placed all items according to **Layout Sketch 2** and that you have carried out all the instructions for the completion of the tasks.

7   Close all open files.

Assessment Objectives	TASK 4
	Before you begin this task make sure that you have the following images:
	• **a black and white image of a city in winter taken using a digital camera**
	• **cat.jpg.**
	1 Open a suitable software package to enable you to download a picture taken using a digital camera.
1a	2 a) Download a suitable picture of a city in winter.
	b) Make sure your picture is not offensive, inappropriate or unsuitable in any way.
2a	3 a) On the image, insert **your name** and **today's date**.
	b) You may position this text anywhere on the image. Make sure this text will be clearly readable on the printout.
4c	4 Save the image using a suitable filename.
4d	5 Print the picture in black and white.
4c	6 Close the picture.
	7 Open the image **cat**.
4b	8 Change the resolution of this image to be **30 pixels/inch** or **12 pixels/cm**.
4c	9 Save the changed image using the filename **newcat**.
4d	10 Print the image **newcat**.
	On the printout, write **your name**, **your centre number** and **today's date**.
4c	11 Close the file and exit the software
	12 Make sure you check your printouts for accuracy.
	You should have the following printouts in the following order:
	lcorp artwork
	newcorp artwork
	the digital picture of a city in winter
	newcat
	Make sure your name is clearly displayed on all printouts.

Practice assignment 3

Scenario

You are working as a Graphic Designer for a local Supermarket. Your have been asked to produce a poster to advertise a special offer.

Layout Sketch 1
Filename: offer

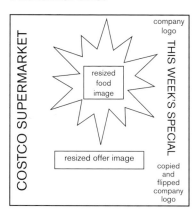

Layout Sketch 2
Filename: newoffer

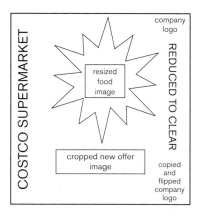

Assessment Objectives	TASK 1
	Before you begin this task make sure that you have the files **food.jpg** and **gourmet.gif**.
	Refer to **Layout Sketch 1** and the Candidate Instructions for the Completion of all Tasks when carrying out this task.
1b 3a 4a	**1** a) Create a new piece of artwork which is **13 cm** wide by **16 cm** tall. b) Fill the background with **light yellow**.
1g 3a	**2** a) Create an **explosion** shape in the top centre of your artwork. b) Fill this shape with **yellow**. c) Make sure that this shape remains inside the artwork. It should fill two thirds of the height of the artwork with one third of empty space below. It should fill half the width of the artwork with one quarter of empty space on each side.
1c 1d 1f	**3** a) Insert the image **food**. b) Resize this image so that it will fit inside the explosion shape. c) Position this image in the centre of the explosion shape.
4c	**4** Save your artwork using the filename **offer**.
1c 1d 1f	**5** a) Insert the image **gourmet**. b) Resize this image so that it is the same width as the explosion shape. c) Position this image below the explosion shape.
4c	**6** Save your artwork keeping the filename **offer**.

Assessment Objectives	TASK 2
	Before you begin this task make sure that you have the file **costco.gif**.
	Refer to **Layout Sketch 1** and the Candidate Instructions for the Completion of all Tasks when carrying out this task.
	Continue working on your artwork saved in called **Task 1** called **offer**.
1c	1 a) Insert the image **Costco**. b) Position this image in the top right corner of the artwork.
3d 3c	2 a) Copy the image **Costco**. b) Flip the copy of the image **vertically**. c) Position the copy in the bottom right corner of the artwork. d) Make sure the flipped image is the same size as the original image.
2a 3a 3b	3 a) Enter the following text in **red**: **COSTCO SUPERMARKET** b) Rotate this text **90° anticlockwise**. c) Place this text to the **left-hand** side of the artwork. d) Size this text to fit the full height of the artwork.
2a 3a 3b	4 a) Enter the following text in **red**: **THIS WEEK'S SPECIAL** b) Rotate this text **90° clockwise**. c) Place this text to the **right-hand** side of the artwork. d) Size this text to fit the space between the **costco** images.
4c	5 Save your artwork keeping the filename **offer**.
4d	6 Print your artwork in colour.
	7 a) On the printout, write **your name**, **your centre number** and **today's date**. b) Check your printout for accuracy. c) Make sure that you have placed all items according to the **Layout Sketch** and that you have carried out all the instructions for the completion of the tasks.

**Assessment
Objectives**

TASK 3

Before you begin this task make sure that you have the file **reduced.gif**.

Continue working on your artwork saved in called **Task 3** called **offer**.

Refer to **Layout Sketch 2** and the Candidate Instructions for the Completion of all Tasks when carrying out this task.

1   Delete the image **gourmet** under the explosion shape.

2   a)   Change the text **THIS WEEK'S SPECIAL** to be:
            REDUCED TO CLEAR

      b)   Resize this text to fit the space between the **costco** images.

3   a)   Insert the image **reduced**.

      b)   Crop this image to remove the words **per pack**.

      c)   Position this image below the explosion shape.

4   Save your artwork using the new filename **newoffer**.

5   Print your artwork in colour.

6   a)   On the printout, write **your name**, **your centre number** and **today's date**.

      b)   Check your printout for accuracy.

      c)   Make sure that you have placed all items according to **Layout Sketch 2** and that you have carried out all the instructions for the completion of the tasks.

7   Close all open files.

Assessment Objectives	TASK 4
	Before you begin this task make sure that you have the following images:
	• **a black and white image of some doughnuts taken using a digital camera**
	• **donkey.jpg.**
	1 Open a suitable software package to enable you to download a picture taken using a digital camera.
1a	2 a) Download a suitable picture of some doughnuts.
	b) Make sure your picture is not offensive, inappropriate or unsuitable in any way.
2a	3 a) On the image, insert **your name** and **today's date**.
	b) You may position this text anywhere on the image. Make sure this text will be clearly readable on the printout.
4c	4 Save the image using a suitable filename.
4d	5 Print the picture in black and white.
4c	6 Close the picture.
	7 Open the image **donkey**.
4b	8 Change the resolution of this image to be **40 pixels/inch** or **8 pixels/cm**.
4c	9 Save the changed image using the filename **newdonkey**.
4d	10 Print the image **newdonkey**.
	On the printout, write **your name**, **your centre number** and **today's date**.
4c	11 Close the file and exit the software.
	12 Make sure you check your printouts for accuracy.
	You should have the following printouts in the following order:
	offer artwork
	newoffer artwork
	the digital picture of some doughnuts
	newdonkey
	Make sure your name is clearly displayed on all printouts.

Seven Web Page Creation

To pass this unit you must be able to:

- ✓ identify and use web page creation software correctly
- ✓ import, format and place text and image files
- ✓ insert relative, external and email hyperlinks
- ✓ manage and print web pages

Before you start this chapter, you or your tutor should download a zipped file called **Resources for Chapter 7** from **www.payne-gallway.co.uk/newclait/student**. It will automatically unzip. Specify that the contents are to be saved in your **My Documents** folder.

The **World Wide Web,** or **WWW** for short, is the largest part of the Internet. It is a body of information that spans the entire Internet. Individuals and organisations provide pages of information on **websites**, which begin at their **home page**.

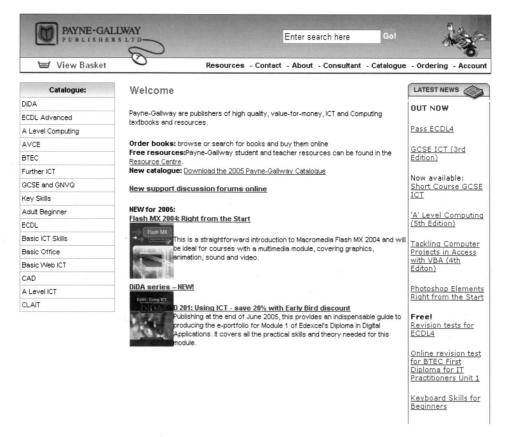

Figure 7.1

Web pages are created using **Hypertext Mark-up Language (HTML)** which is a fairly simple computer programming language. **Web browsing** software is used to view web pages. A commonly used web browser is **Microsoft® Internet Explorer**. HTML code tells **web browsers** how to display information on a web page.

```
<html>

<head>
<meta http-equiv="Content-Type"
content="text/html; charset=iso-8859-1">
<meta name="GENERATOR" content="Microsoft FrontPage 6.0">
<title>Crossways High School</title>
</head>

<body bgcolor="#C0C0C0">

<table border="0" cellpadding="2" width="100%">
  <tr>
    <td>
              <img src="images/LogoT.gif" align="left" hspace="0"
    width="212" height="184"></td>
    <td> </td>
    <td colspan="5"><p align="center"><font color="#000000"
    size="7" face="Arial"><strong>Crossways High School</strong></font></p>
    </td>
  </tr>
  <tr>
    <td colspan="6"> </td>
  </tr>
  <tr>
    <td valign="top">
    <h4><font size="4" face="Arial"><a href="parents.htm">Parents</a></font></h4>
    <h4><font size="4" face="Arial"><a href="pupils.htm">Pupils</a></font></h4>
    <h4><font size="4" face="Arial"><a href="teachers.htm">Teachers</a></font></h4>
    <h4><font size="4" face="Arial"><a href="visitors.htm">Visitors</a></font></h4>
    </td>
```

Figure 7.2

Computer users who have no knowledge of **HTML** can use **web design packages** to produce web pages in a **WYSIWYG** environment very similar to that offered by word-processing or DTP software to produce printed publications. **WYSIWYG** stands for **'What you see is what you get'**. This means that the way web pages look in the web design package will be almost the same as they'll actually appear when viewed with a web browser. There will be some differences because different web browsers or different versions of the same web browser all interpret and display **HTML** code in slightly different ways. The only guaranteed way to see what your web pages will actually look like is to view them using a web browser.

The practice tasks that follow cover all the techniques you need to learn in order to pass a New CLAiT Unit 7 WEB PAGE CREATION assignment.

Practice tasks

Task 1 Creating a new website

This task takes you through the steps needed to create a new website in Microsoft® FrontPage®.

Copying and renaming a resources folder

To get started you need to copy a subfolder called **unit 7 pt** containing some pre-prepared files into your **My Documents** folder or network home directory. Your tutor will tell you where to find the subfolder – in the example below it is in the **Shared Documents** folder.

My Computer

My Computer icon

▶ *Either* double-click the **My Computer** icon on your desktop,

▶ *or* click the **Start** button at the bottom left of the screen, then click **My Computer**.

▶ Click **Shared Documents** in the **Other Places** section of the **Task pane**.

Figure 7.3

▶ Click once on the subfolder called **unit 7 pt**.

▶ Click the **Copy this folder** icon in the **Task pane**. The **Copy Items** dialogue window will appear.

Figure 7.4

- Click **My Documents** or your network home directory icon in the **list** and then click **Copy**.

- Click **My Documents** in the **Other Places** section of the **Task pane**. A subfolder icon with the **unit 7 pt** name will be among the files and folders displayed.

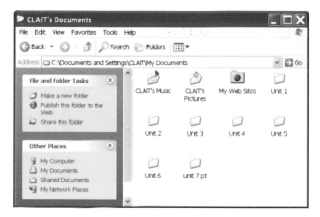

Figure 7.5

Next you need to rename this subfolder.

- Click once on the **unit 7 pt** icon.

- In the **File and folder tasks** section of the **Task pane**, click the **Rename this folder** icon, then type **your name (first name and last name)**, followed by **u7pt** (e.g. **Arthur Marshall u7pt**). Double-click the subfolder to view its contents – they should be exactly the same as the example below.

Rename Folder icon

Figure 7.6

- Close the folder window by clicking **X** in the top right-hand corner.

Creating a new website

Next you need to load **Microsoft FrontPage XP** (referred to as **FrontPage**) and use the resources folder to set up a new website. You can load **FrontPage** in one of two ways:

Microsoft Office
FrontPage
2003

Microsoft
FrontPage icon

▶ *Either* double-click the **FrontPage** icon on the Desktop in Windows,

▶ *or* click the **Start** button at the bottom left of the screen, then click **Programs, Microsoft Office FrontPage 2003**. The main **FrontPage** window will be displayed.

Figure 7.7

▶ Click **Create a new page or site...** at the bottom of the task pane.

> **TIP**
>
> If you can't see the task pane, click **View** and **Task pane** on the menu bar.

▶ Click **One page Web site....** The **Web Site Templates** dialogue window will appear.

▶ Click once on **One Page Web Site** if it isn't already selected.

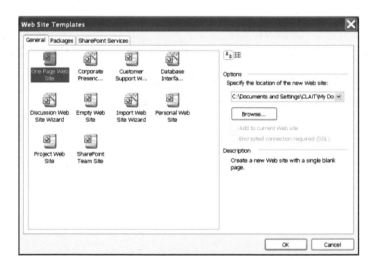

Figure 7.8

▶ Click the **Browse** button, then the small down arrow next to the **Look in:** box, then click on your **My Documents** or network home directory folder if it is not already selected.

▶ Click once on the folder called **your name (first name and last name) u7pt** (e.g. **Arthur Marshall u7pt**).

▶ Click **Open**, then **OK**. The website will be created and a list of available files will be displayed.

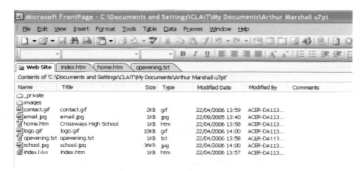

Figure 7.9

Creating a blank web page

Now you are ready to create a new blank web page.

TIP

In this New CLAiT unit you will work with a pre-prepared web page and create one basic page on your own. You will not be expected to create a completely new website from scratch.

If a new blank web page isn't displayed, click the **Create a new normal page** button on the **Standard** toolbar. Your screen should now look something like the one below.

New Page button

Figure 7.10

Inserting a text file

Now we need to insert the text for this page from a pre-prepared text file.

Click **Insert** on the menu bar, then click **File**…. The **Select File** dialogue window will appear.

Click the small down arrow next to the **Look in:** box and click on your **My Documents** or network home directory folder if it is not already selected.

⊙ Double-click the subfolder called **your name u7pt**.

⊙ Click the small down arrow next to the **Files of type:** box, click **Text Files (*.txt)** in the drop-down list of file types.

⊙ Click once on the file called **opevening,** then click **Open**. If you see the warning dialogue box shown below, click the radio button next to **Normal paragraphs with line breaks**.

Figure 7.11

The text in the file will be inserted on the web page – it should look like the example below.

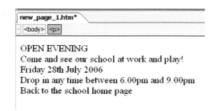

Figure 7.12

Inserting line spaces

Now we need to insert some blank lines to separate the different sections of the text.

⊙ Click at the end of the first line of text ending **...EVENING** and press **Enter**.

⊙ Click at the end of the second line of text ending **...and play!** and press **Enter**.

⊙ Click at the end of the fourth line of text ending **...and 9.00pm** and press **Enter**. Your web page should now look like the one below.

Figure 7.13

TIP

If you are asked to check that each paragraph is separated by one clear line space, make sure that single lines of text or paragraphs have a single blank line between them. You will probably need to insert these blank lines by hand using the technique described above.

Adding some more text

Next you need to add another line of text containing your name, at the bottom of the page.

▶ Click at the end of the last line of text ending **...home page** and press **Enter** twice.

▶ Type **Updated by your name (first name and last name)**, followed by **Centre** and **your centre number**, and **today's date** (e.g. **Updated by Arthur Marshall, Centre 30175, 14/05/06**). Your web page should now look like the one below.

Figure 7.14

Saving a new web page

Now we need to save the new web page.

▶ *Either* click **File** and then **Save** on the menu bar,

▶ *or* click the **Save** button on the **Standard** toolbar. The **Save As** dialogue window will appear. A folder called **My Web Sites** might be pre-selected.

You need to save this page in the folder containing the other resources for this website.

▶ Click the small down arrow next to the **Save in:** box and click on your **My Documents** or network home directory folder if it is not already selected.

▶ Double-click the folder called **your name (first name and last name) u7pt** (e.g. **Arthur Marshall u7pt**). The contents of the resources subfolder for this website will be displayed.

▶ Click in the **File name:** box, type **openeve.htm**, then click the **Change Title** button. The **Set Page Title** dialogue box will appear.

Figure 7.15

▶ Type **Crossways High School**, then click **OK**. This text will be displayed at the top of the window when the web page is viewed using a web browser.

> **TIP**
>
> You don't need to change the page title but it is good practice to have a meaningful title at the top of every web page in a site.

▶ Click **Save**. The name **openeve** will be displayed on the page tab at the top of the screen.

Figure 7.16

Closing FrontPage

Finally we need to close the website and shut down **FrontPage**.

▶ Click **File** on the menu bar, click **Close Site**, then…

▶ *Either* click **File** on the menu bar, and click **Exit**,

▶ *or* click **X** in the top right-hand corner of the screen.

Task 2 Formatting text and inserting images

Once you've created a web page you'll be asked to improve its appearance by formatting the text and adding some images. This task takes you through these techniques.

Opening a saved web page

To work through this task you need to load the web page called **openeve** that you have already created and saved.

▶ Load **FrontPage**, then…

▶ *Either* click **File** on the menu bar, and click **Open**,

Open button

▶ *or* click the **Open** button on the **Standard** toolbar. The **Open** dialogue box will appear.

▶ Click the small down arrow next to the **Look in:** box and click on your **My Documents** or network home directory folder if it is not already selected.

▶ Double-click the folder called **your name (first name and last name) u7pt** (e.g. **Arthur Marshall u7pt**). The contents of the subfolder for this website will be displayed.

▶ Click on **openeve** and **Open**. The website will be opened with the **openeve** page displayed.

Formatting text

You need to start by centre aligning all the text on the web page.

Center button

- Hold down the **Ctrl** key, then press the **A** key to select everything on the page. The page will turn black.

- Click the **Center** button on the **Formatting** toolbar, then click anywhere on the page away from the text, to remove the highlighting. The text on your web page should look like the example below.

OPEN EVENING

Come and see our school at work and play!

Friday 28th July 2006

Drop in any time between 6.00pm and 9.00pm

Back to the school home page

Updated by Arthur Marshall, Centre 30175, 14/05/06

Figure 7.17

Next you need to make the main page heading stand out more in the body text by changing the font to a **sans serif** type, increasing its size and using bold text.

- Position the mouse pointer just to the left of the heading **OPEN EVENING**.

OPEN EVENING

Figure 7.18

- Click once on the left mouse button to highlight just this line of text.

Figure 7.19

- Click the down arrow in the **Font name** box on the **Formatting** toolbar, then scroll down through the list of fonts and click on the font called **Arial.**

TIP

You should always use a **sans serif** font for text on a web page. Sans serif fonts are much easier to read on screen than **serif** fonts. They also help to make a site look modern and professional.

⊳ On the **Formatting** toolbar, click the **Font Size** box arrow, scroll through the list of sizes and click on **7 (36 pt)**.

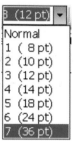

Figure 7.20

Bold button

⊳ Click the **Bold** button on the **Formatting** toolbar, then click anywhere on the page away from the text to remove the highlighting.

Your page heading should look like the one below.

OPEN EVENING

Figure 7.21

> **TIP**
>
> Unit 7 assignments will refer to **HTML size** when you are asked to change the font size of text. There are seven standard HTML sizes used for fonts on web pages. These range from **size 1** (8 pt) to **size 7** (36 pt). Always check to make sure you have used the specified HTML size.

Next we need to change the font type and size for the second line of text:

⊳ Highlight the second line of text **Come and see our school at work and play!**

⊳ Change the font type to **Arial** and set the font size to **5 (18 pt)**.

Now change the font type and size for the next three lines of text:

⊳ Click at the start of the third line beginning **Friday 28th...**

⊳ Click and hold down the left mouse button.

⊳ Drag down to the end of the fifth line ending **...home page**. If you go too far, keep your finger on the left mouse button and drag the mouse in the opposite direction. Three lines of text should now be highlighted.

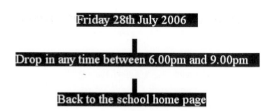

Figure 7.22

Change the font type to **Arial** and set the font size to **4 (14 pt)**.

Next we need to make just the third line of text bold.

Click anywhere on the page away from the text to remove the current highlighting.

Highlight the third line of text **Friday 28th July 2006**.

Click the **Bold** button on the **Formatting** toolbar, then click anywhere on the page away from the text to remove the highlighting.

Bold button

Next we'll change the font type and size for just the last line of text.

Highlight the last line of text, then change the font type to **Arial** and set the size to **2 (10 pt)**.

Click anywhere on the page away from the text to remove the highlighting.

Finally we need to format a specific part of the text rather than just a complete line or group of lines.

Click in the fourth line after the word **between**.

Click and hold down the left mouse button, then drag across to the end of this line. The text **6.00pm and 9.00pm** should now be highlighted.

Click the **Italic** button on the **Formatting** toolbar, and click anywhere on the page away from the text to remove the highlighting.

Italic button

The text on your web page should now look like the example below.

OPEN EVENING

Come and see our school at work and play!

Friday 28th July 2006

Drop in any time between *6.00pm and 9.00pm*

Back to the school home page

Updated by Arthur Marshall, Centre 30175, 14/05/06

Figure 7.23

Inserting an image

Next we need to add the school logo under the page heading.

▶ Click on the blank line underneath the page heading then…

▶ *Either* click **Insert** on the menu bar, then **Picture, From File,**

▶ *or* click the **Insert Picture From File** button on the **Standard** toolbar.

Insert Picture
From File
button

The **Picture** dialogue box will appear. The image file you need is called **logo** and is in the website subfolder called **your name (first name and last name) u7pt**.

▶ Click the small down arrow next to the **Look in:** box and click on your **My Documents** or network home directory folder if it is not already selected.

▶ Double-click the folder called **your name (first name and last name) u7pt** (e.g. **Arthur Marshall u7pt**). The contents of the subfolder will be displayed.

▶ Click on **logo**, then click the **Insert** button. The image will be inserted on the page but will be too close to the text just underneath it.

The easy way to deal with this is to insert another blank line:

▶ Click next to the start of the line underneath the text beginning **Come…**, to get the cursor flashing. If you highlight the text, click away and try again.

▶ Press **Enter** once to insert a blank line between this line of text and the image. Your web page should look like the one below.

OPEN EVENING

Come and see our school at work and play!

Friday 28th July 2006

Drop in any time between *6.00pm* and *9.00pm*

Back to the school home page

Updated by Arthur Marshall, Centre 30175, 14/05/06

Figure 7.24

After inserting an image you need to align it. This image needs to be aligned in the centre of the page. This should have been done automatically because centre alignment has already been used for the text on this page.

 If the image is not already aligned in the centre of the page, click once on it, then click the **Center** button on the **Formatting** toolbar.

Centre button

You could also be asked to align an image to the left or right of a web page. To do this just click once on the image and use the **Left align** or **Right align** button on the **Formatting** toolbar.

That's all the text formatting for this web page finished. Now we need to save it, keeping the same name **openeve**:

 Click the **Save** button on the **Standard** toolbar, then shut down **FrontPage**.

Save button

Task 3   Creating hyperlinks

Once you've formatted your new web page you'll be asked to link it to other web pages and websites by creating **hyperlinks**. A hyperlink is a piece of text or a graphic that contains the address of another location on the Web. When a user clicks on a hyperlink, they are taken to the location specified in its address. A text hyperlink is underlined and is normally identified by a distinctive colour, which changes once it has been clicked.

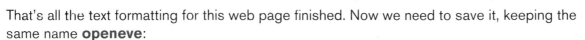

Figure 7.25

Creating a local hyperlink between web pages

Local hyperlinks are used to connect the pages in a website together; they do not link to external pages on other websites. You are going to create a local hyperlink from your new web page to the home page of the Crossways High School website which has already been created and saved.

- Load **FrontPage.**

- Open your saved web page called **openeve.**

- Click in the fifth line after the word **school.**

- Click and hold down the left mouse button, then drag across to the end of this line. The text **home page** should be highlighted.

Back to the school home page

Figure 7.26

Hyperlink
button

- Then, *either* click **Insert** on the menu bar, then click **Hyperlink,**

- *or* click the **Insert Hyperlink** button on the **Standard** toolbar. The **Insert Hyperlink** dialogue box will appear.

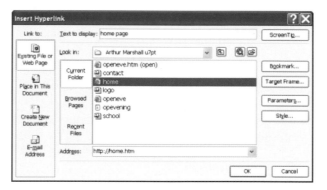

Figure 7.27

TIP

If the contents of the website subfolder are not listed, click the **Look in:** box down arrow, click on your **My Documents** or network home directory folder, then double-click the website subfolder called **your name (first name and last name) u7pt.**

- Click on **home**, then click **OK.**

- Click anywhere on a blank part of the web page. You will see that the text has turned blue and is now underlined to show that it is a hyperlink.

Back to the school home page

Figure 7.28

Save button

You will test this link later. For now, you just need to save the web page keeping the name **openeve.**

- Click the **Save** button on the **Standard** toolbar.

Creating a new hyperlink on an existing web page

Next you are going to create a new local hyperlink from the home page of the Crossways High School website to your new web page. This page can be opened in a slightly different way because the website is already open.

▶ Click the **Web Site** tab at the top of the screen. The contents of the website will be displayed with the page you've just been working on highlighted.

Figure 7.29

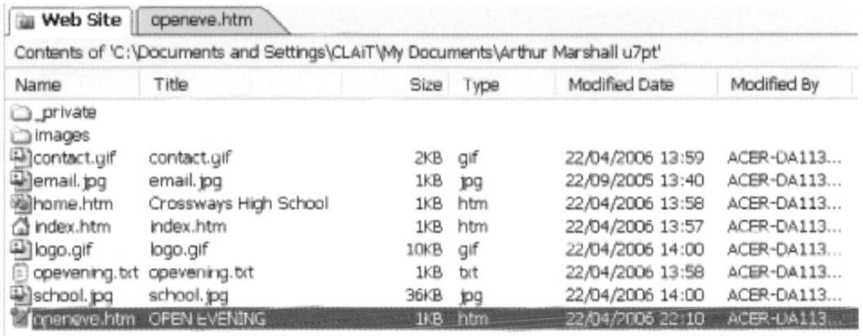

Web Site	openeve.htm					
Contents of 'C:\Documents and Settings\CLAiT\My Documents\Arthur Marshall u7pt'						
Name	Title	Size	Type	Modified Date	Modified By	
📁 _private						
📁 images						
contact.gif	contact.gif	2KB	gif	22/04/2006 13:59	ACER-DA113...	
email.jpg	email.jpg	1KB	jpg	22/09/2005 13:40	ACER-DA113...	
home.htm	Crossways High School	1KB	htm	22/04/2006 13:58	ACER-DA113...	
index.htm	index.htm	1KB	htm	22/04/2006 13:57	ACER-DA113...	
logo.gif	logo.gif	10KB	gif	22/04/2006 14:00	ACER-DA113...	
opevening.txt	opevening.txt	1KB	txt	22/04/2006 13:58	ACER-DA113...	
school.jpg	school.jpg	36KB	jpg	22/04/2006 14:00	ACER-DA113...	
openeve.htm	OPEN EVENING	1KB	htm	22/04/2006 22:10	ACER-DA113...	

Figure 7.30

▶ Double-click the page called **home.htm**, then click **OK.** The Crossways High School home page will be displayed – it should look like the one below.

CROSSWAYS HIGH SCHOOL

Click the links below for information and resources

Search the web

Click the button below to contact the school

Last updated by Webmaster on 31-03-06

Figure 7.31

▶ Click at the end of the second line after the word **resources**.

▶ Press **Enter** to insert a blank line, type **Open Evening**, then highlight this line of text.

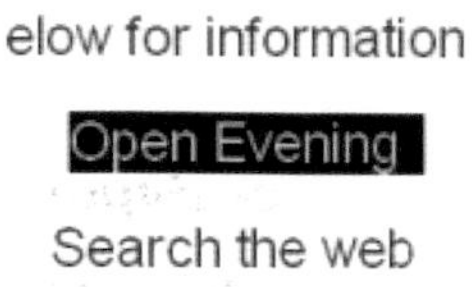

elow for information

Open Evening

Search the web

Figure 7.32

Hyperlink
button

▶ Then, *either* click **Insert** on the menu bar and click **Hyperlink**,

▶ *or* click the **Insert Hyperlink** button on the **Standard** toolbar. The **Insert Hyperlink** dialogue box will appear.

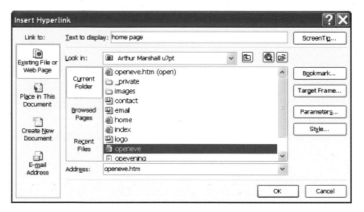

Figure 7.33

▶ Click on **openeve**, then **OK**.

▶ Click anywhere on a blank part of the web page. You will see that the text is now underlined to show that it is a hyperlink.

Open Evening

Figure 7.34

You will test this link later.

Editing text on an existing page

Next you are going to edit some of the text on the home page. On the last line, you need to replace the word **Webmaster** with your own name.

▶ Click in the last line just after the word **Webmaster** to get the cursor flashing.

▶ Press the **Backspace** key until the word **Webmaster** is completely deleted – do not delete any other text on this line.

▶ Type **your name (first name and last name) u7pt** (e.g. **Arthur Marshall u7pt**).

Creating a hyperlink to an external website

Next you are going to create an external hyperlink from the Crossways High School home page to the home page of another website on the Internet.

⊙ Highlight the line of text **Search the web**, then…

⊙ *Either* click **Insert** on the menu bar and click **Hyperlink**,

⊙ *or* click the **Insert Hyperlink** button on the **Standard** toolbar. The **Insert Hyperlink** dialogue box will appear with the cursor flashing in the **Address:** box.

Hyperlink button

⊙ Type the website address **www.google.co.uk**. The text **http://** will appear in front of the website address as you type – don't worry about this, just carry on typing.

Figure 7.35

⊙ Click **OK,** then click anywhere on a blank part of the web page. The text will be underlined to show that it is a hyperlink.

Search the web

Figure 7.36

You will test this link later.

Creating an email hyperlink

Next you are going to create a hyperlink from an image on the Crossways High School home page that will allow users to email the school.

⊙ Click once on the **Contact** button image at the bottom of the page, then…

⊙ *Either* click **Insert** on the menu bar, and click **Hyperlink**,

⊙ *or* click the **Insert Hyperlink** button on the **Standard** toolbar.

Hyperlink button

⊙ Click the **E-mail Address** icon in the **Link to:** column on the left.

 Type **office@crossways-school.org.uk** in the **E-mail address:** box. (The text **mailto:** will appear in front of the email address as you type – don't worry about this, just carry on typing.)

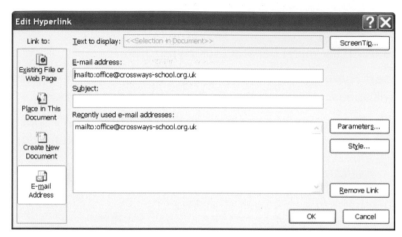

Figure 7.37

 Click **OK**.

You won't see anything happen this time because this hyperlink is associated with an image. You will test the link later, along with the others.

That's all the hyperlinks created for this web page. Now you need to save the web page, keeping the name **home**

Save button

Click the **Save** button on the **Standard** toolbar.

Close the website and shut down **FrontPage**.

Task 4   Page backgrounds, testing hyperlinks and printing

This task takes you through the steps needed to test hyperlinks and print web pages using a web browser. You will also learn how to change the appearance of a web page by changing the background colour.

Changing the page background colour

We're going to start by changing the background colour of the Crossways High School home page.

Load **FrontPage**.

Open the Crossways High School home page called **home**.

Click **Format** on the menu bar, then click **Background**. The **Page Properties** dialogue box will appear.

In the **Colors** section, click the menu arrow on the right of the **Background:** box. A choice of fill options will appear.

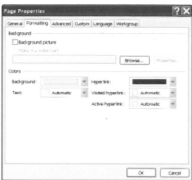

Figure 7.38

Click the yellow square on the **Standard Colors** palette, then click **OK**. Your web page should now look like the one below.

Figure 7.39

TIP

You can choose any background colour as long as the text and images remain clearly visible. Click **More Colors...** for more choices, if the colour you need isn't one of the standard colours.

Now you need to save this web page, keeping the name **home**.

Click the **Save** button on the **Standard** toolbar, then **Close** the website and shut down **FrontPage**.

Save button

Accessing a web page

Next we'll access the Crossways High School home page by viewing it in a **web browser**. The web browser we're going to use is **Microsoft Internet Explorer** (referred to as **Internet Explorer**).

Internet Explorer

Internet Explorer icon

You can load **Internet Explorer** in one of two ways:

▶ *Either* double-click the **Internet Explorer** icon on the Desktop in Windows,

▶ *or* click the **Start** button at the bottom left of the screen, then click

Internet
Internet Explorer

Figure 7.40

The **default web page** that Internet Explorer is set up to open when it is loaded will appear – in the example below the default page is Google™.

Figure 7.41

▶ Click **File** on the menu bar, then click **Open**. The **Open** dialogue box will appear.

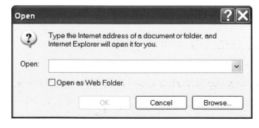

Figure 7.42

▶ Click the **Browse** button. The **Internet Explorer** dialogue box will appear.

▶ Click the small arrow next to the box labelled **Open:** then click on your **My Documents** or network home directory folder if it is not already selected.

▶ Double-click the website subfolder called **your name (first name and last name) u7pt** (e.g. **Arthur Marshall u7pt**).

▶ Click on **home**, then **Open**.

Figure 7.43

The **Internet Explorer** dialogue box will reappear with the name and location of the web page displayed in the **Open:** box.

▶ Click **OK** and the web page will be loaded.

Figure 7.44

Testing hyperlinks

Now you need to test the hyperlinks on this page.

▶ Click the hyperlink **Open Evening**. The page that you created at the end of Task 2 should be loaded and displayed.

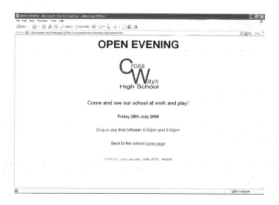

Figure 7.45

▶ Click the **home page** link at the bottom of this page. The Crossways High School home page should reappear.

▶ Click the hyperlink **Search the web**. The home page of the Google website should be loaded from the Internet and displayed.

Figure 7.46

> **TIP**
>
> If the correct page is not displayed from a hyperlink, open the page in **FrontPage**, highlight the hyperlink text and re-insert the hyperlink, following the procedure above.

Back button

▶ Click the **Back** button on the toolbar at the top of the screen. The Crossways High School home page should reappear.

Contact button

▶ Click the **Contact** button image at the bottom of the page. The default **email editor** for your computer should be loaded with a new blank message window already open. In the example below the email editor is **Outlook**® – your tutor will let you know if this is different on the computer that you're using.

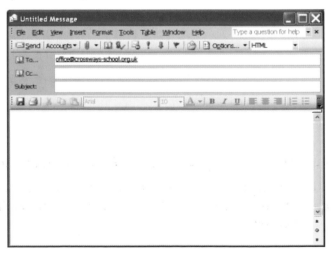

Figure 7.47

▶ Click **File** on the menu bar then, to close the program, then

▶ *Either* click **Exit**,

▶ *or* click **X** in the top right-hand corner of the email editor window. If you are prompted to save any changes to the message click **No**.

Printing web pages and HTML source code

First you need to print a copy of this web page exactly as it appears in your web browser window.

▶ Click **File** on the menu bar, then click **Page Setup…**. The **Page Setup** dialogue box will be displayed.

▶ In the **Orientation** section, click the radio button for **Landscape** if it isn't already selected.

> **TIP**
>
> Your printout must include the address (**URL**) of the web page in the format: **C:\Documents and Settings\My Documents\your name u7pt\home.htm**. To do this the text **&u** must appear in either the header or footer box of the Headers and Footers section to do this. Click in either the **Header** or **Footer** box and add **&u** if it isn't there.

The relevant part of your **Page Setup** dialogue box should look something like the screenshot below.

Figure 7.48

▶ Click **OK**.

▶ Click **File** on the menu bar, then click **Print**. The **Print** dialogue box will appear.

▶ In the **Select Printer** section, click once on the name of the printer you want to use. Your tutor will tell you which printer to choose if you're not sure. You don't need to print web pages in colour for this unit.

▶ Click **Print**.

Next you need to print a copy of the HTML code for this web page.

- Click **View** on the menu bar, then click **Source**. The HTML code for the web page will appear in a **Notepad** window.

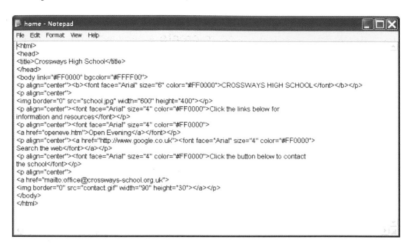

Figure 7.49

- Click **File** on the menu bar, then click **Print**. The **Print** dialogue box will appear.

- In the **Select Printer** section, click once on the name of the printer you want to use, then click **Print**.

- Click **File** on the menu bar, then click **Exit**, or click **X** in the top right-hand corner of the window to close **Notepad**.

Next you need to produce the same two types of printout for the Open Evening web page you created

Back button

- Click the **Back** button on the toolbar at the top of the screen until the **Open Evening** page appears – this was loaded when you tested the links on the **home page**.

- Print this page.

- Print the HTML code for this page.

- Close **Notepad**, then close **Internet Explorer**.

That's the end of the practice tasks. Now try the full New CLAiT assignments that follow.

Practice assignment 1

Scenario

You are working on developing a website for a local conservation group. You have been asked to update one partly completed web page and to create a new web page using images and text that have been provided for you.

Assessment Objectives	TASK 1
	Before you begin this task make sure that you have all the files below in one folder:
	• the unlinked HTML formatted page **cranford.htm**
	➤ this page requires the image files **shore.jpg** and **contact.gif**
	• the image **seafront.jpg**
	• the text file **meeting.txt**
	Make sure you save your updated web page, your new web page and all images in the same folder.
1b	1 Name/rename the folder the folder containing all the files with **your name**
1a	2 Open suitable software for editing and creating web pages.
	You have been asked to create and format a new web page.
1a	3 a) In your web page editing software, create a new document.
1b	b) Insert the text file **meeting**.
1c	c) Check that each paragraph is separated by one clear line space.
2a	d) After the text **where to put it** insert a clear line space and enter the following
2b	text on one line:
2c	**Updated by** (your **name**), your **centre number**, the **date**
2f	e) Save your document using the filename **action.htm**.

Assessment Objectives	TASK 2
	You will need to format your web page.
	Continue working on your file **action.htm**.
2i	1 Format all the text to be **centre-aligned**.
2g	2 a) Format the heading text:
	STOP THE DEVELOPMENT
	as **Arial** font, **HTML size 7 (36 point)**.
	b) Format the text beginning:
	ACTION GROUP... and ending **...Home Page**
	as **SansSerifType** font, **HTML size 4 (14 point)**.

c) Format the text you entered in Task 1 beginning:
Updated by... and ending with the **date**
as **Arial** font, **HTML size 2 (10 point)**.

2g   3   a) Format only the text **Wednesday 28th September 2006** to be **bold**.

b) Format only the text **7.30pm to 9.30pm** to be *italics*.

A picture will need to be inserted on this web page.

2d   4   a) Insert the image **seafront.jpg** under the heading

b) **Centre** align this image.

2e   Your web page layout should be similar to the image below:

STOP THE DEVELOPMENT

seafront.jpg

ACTION GROUP..

At the..

Wednesday

7.30pm

Home Page

Updated by Arthur Marshall, Centre 30175, 31/07/06

All the pages in the website need to be linked.

3a   5   Create a link in the **action.htm** page as follows:

> Text to be linked: **Home Page**
> Link to: **cranford.htm**

2c   6   Check your web page for accuracy.

1c   7   Save the web page keeping the name **action.htm**.

1c   8   Close the **action.htm** page.

Assessment Objectives	TASK 3
	The home page **cranford.htm** needs to be updated.
1c	1 a) Open the **cranford.htm** homepage. Do not change the font on this page.
2a	b) In the **cranford.htm** page, on a separate line below the text:
2f	**...the link below**.
2g	and above the text:
2i	**WEB SEARCHES**
3a	Insert the text:
	UPCOMING EVENTS
	c) **Centre** align this text.
	d) **Format** this text as **Arial** font, **HTML size 5 (18 point)**.
	e) Link this text to the **action.htm** page.
	f) Save the amended **cranford.htm** page.
2a	2 a) Replace the text **Webmaster** with your **name**.
2g	b) Make sure the size of your name is **Arial** font, **HTML size 2 (10 point)**.
	Some of the links on the home page have not been completed.
3b	3 Create an external link in the **cranford.htm** page as follows:
	Text to be linked: **WEB SEARCHES**
	Link to: **www.excite.co.uk**
3c	4 Create an email link in the **cranford.htm** page as follows:
	Image to be linked: **contact.gif**
	Link to: **office@cranford-cs.org.uk**
1c	5 Save the web page keeping the filename **cranford.htm**.

Assessment Objectives	TASK 4
	Continue working on your home page **cranford.htm**.
	A different background colour will improve the homepage.
2h	1 a) Change the background colour of the **cranford.htm** page.
	b) Make sure the background colour is different from the text colour and that the text and images are clearly visible against the background colour.
2c	2 Check your web page for accuracy.
1c	3 Save the web page keeping the name **cranford.htm**.
1c	4 Close all web pages and exit the web page editing software.

3a, 3b, 3c	5	Load the **cranford.htm** page into the browser and test the three links.
4a	6	From the browser print the **cranford.htm** page.
1c	7 a)	Display the **HTML source code** for the **cranford.htm** page.
4b	b)	Print the HTML source code for this page.
	c)	Close the **cranford.htm** page.
1c	8	Load the **action.htm** page into the browser and test the one link.
4a	9	From the browser print the **action.htm** page.
1c	10 a)	Display the **HTML source code** for the **action.htm** page.
4b	b)	Print the HTML source code for this page.
	c)	Close the **action.htm** page.
	11	Exit the browser.
2c	12	Make sure you check your printouts for accuracy.

You should have four printouts in the following order:

cranford.htm web page printed from the browser

HTML source code for the **cranford.htm** page

action.htm web page printed from the browser

HTML source code for the **action.htm** page

Practice assignment 2

Scenario

You are working on developing a website for a local dog breeder. You have been asked to update one partly completed web page and to create a new web page using images and text that have been provided for you.

Assessment Objectives	TASK 1

Before you begin this task make sure that you have all the files below in one folder:

- the unlinked HTML formatted page **welcome.htm**
  ➤ this page requires the image files **dog.jpg** and **mail.gif**
- the image **puppy.jpg**
- the text file **terriers.txt**

Make sure you save your updated web page, your new web page and all images in the same folder.

1b	1 Name/rename the folder the folder containing all the files with your **name**

1a	2	Open suitable software for editing and creating web pages.

You have been asked to create and format a new web page.

1a	3 a)	In your web page editing software, create a new document.
1b	b)	Insert the text file **terriers**.
1c	c)	Check that each paragraph is separated by one clear line space.
2a	d)	After the text **where to put it** insert a clear line space and enter the following
2d		text on one line:
2c		**Updated by** (your **name**), your **centre number**, the **date**
2f	e)	Save your document using the filename **breed.htm**.

Assessment Objectives

TASK 2

You will need to format your web page.

Continue working on your file **breed.htm**.

2i	1	Format all the text to be **centre-aligned**.
2g	2 a)	Format the heading text: **ABOUT THE BREED** as **Verdana** font, **HTML size 6 (24 point)**.
	b)	Format the text beginning: **English Toy...** and ending **...GO BACK** as **Verdana** font, **HTML size 3 (12 point)**.
	c)	Format the text you entered in Task 1 beginning: **Updated by...** and ending with the **date** as **Verdana** font, **HTML size 2 (10 point)**.
2g	a)	Format only the text **English Toy Terriers** to be **bold**.
3h	b)	Format only the text **very faithful** to be *italics*. A picture will need to be inserted on this web page.
2d	4 a)	Insert the image **puppy.jpg** under the heading.
	b)	**Centre** align this image.

Your web page layout should be similar to the diagram below:

All the pages in the website need to be linked.

3a	5	Create a link in the **breed.htm** page as follows:
		Text to be linked: **GO BACK**
		Link to: **welcome.htm**
2c	6	Check your web page for accuracy.
1c	7	Save the web page keeping the name **breed.htm**.
1c	8	Close the **breed.htm** page.

Assessment Objectives		TASK 3
		The home page **welcome.htm** needs to be updated.
1c	1 a)	Open the **welcome.htm** home page. Do not change the font on this page.
2a	b)	In the **welcome.htm** page, on a separate line below the text ending:
2f		**...contributed to the breed**.
2g		and above the text ending:
2i		**...SEARCH THE WEB**
3a		Insert the text:
		ABOUT THE BREED
	c)	**Centre** align this text.
	d)	Format this text as **Verdana** font, **HTML size 4 (14 point)**.
	e)	Link this text to the **breed.htm** page.
	f)	Save the amended **welcome.htm** page.
2a	2 a)	Replace the text **Webmaster** with **your name**.
2g	b)	Ensure the size of your name is **Verdana** font, **HTML size 2 (10 point)**.
		Some of the links on the homepage have not been completed.
3b	3	Create an external link in the **welcome.htm** page as follows:
		Text to be linked: **SEARCH THE WEB**
		Link to: **www.yahoo.co.uk**
3c	4	Create an email link in the **welcome.htm** page as follows:
		Image to be linked: **mail.gif**
		Link to: **info@woodford-breeders.org**
1c	5	Save the web page keeping the filename **welcome.htm**.

Assessment Objectives	**TASK 4**
	Continue working on your home page **welcome.htm**.
	A different background colour will improve the homepage.
2h	1 a) Change the background colour of the **welcome.htm** page.
	b) Make sure the background colour is different from the text colour and that the text and images are clearly visible against the background colour.
2c	2 Check your web page for accuracy.
1c	3 Save the web page keeping the name **welcome.htm**.
1c	4 Close all web pages and exit the web page editing software.
3a, 3b, 3c	5 Load the **welcome.htm** page into the browser and test the three links.
4a	6 From the browser print the **welcome.htm** page.
1c	7 a) Display the **HTML source code** for the **welcome.htm** page.
	b) Print the HTML source code for this page.
	c) Close the **welcome.htm** page.
1c	8 Load the **breed.htm** page into the browser and test the one link.
4a	9 From the browser print the **breed.htm** page.
1c	10 a) Display the **HTML source code** for the **breed.htm** page.
	b) Print the HTML source code for this page.
	c) Close the **breed.htm** page.
	11 Exit the browser.
2c	12 Make sure you check your printouts for accuracy.
	You should have four printouts in the following order:
	welcome.htm web page printed from the browser
	HTML source code for the **welcome.htm** page
	breed.htm web page printed from the browser
	HTML source code for the **breed.htm** page

Practice assignment 3

Scenario

You are working as a junior Website Designer for a large chain of luxury hotels. You have been asked to update one partly completed web page and to create a new web page using images and text that have been provided for you.

Assessment Objectives	TASK 1
	Before you begin this task make sure that you have all the files below in one folder:
	• the unlinked HTML formatted page **sunset.htm**
	➤ this page requires the image files **bay.jpg** and **enquiries.gif**
	• the image **health.jpg**
	• the text file **spa.txt**.
	Make sure you save your updated web page, your new web page and all images in the same folder.
1b	1 Name/rename the folder the folder containing all the files with your **name**.
1a	2 Open suitable software for editing and creating web pages.
	You have been asked to create and format a new web page.
1a	3 a) In your web page editing software, create a new document.
1b	b) Insert the text file **spa**.
1c	c) Check that each paragraph is separated by one clear line space.
2a	d) After the text where to put it insert a clear line space and enter the
2b	following text on one line:
2c	**Updated by** (your **name**), your **centre number**, the **date**.
2f	e) Save your document using the filename **starspa.htm**.

Assessment Objectives	
	TASK 2

You will need to format your web page.

Continue working on your file **starspa.htm**.

2i   1   Format all the text to be **centre-aligned**.

2g   2   a)   Format the heading text:
                   FIVE STAR HEALTH SPA
                   as **Tahoma** font, **HTML size 6 (24 point)**.

              b)   Format the text beginning:
                   NOW OPEN... and ending **...HOME PAGE**
                   as **Tahoma** font, **HTML size 4 (14 point)**.

              c)   Format the text you entered in Task 1 beginning:
                   Updated by... and ending with the **date**
                   as **Tahoma** font, **HTML size 2 (10 point)**.

2g   3   a)   Format only the text **NOW OPEN** to be **bold**.

              b)   Format only the text **PURE LUXURY** to be *italics*.

A picture will need to be inserted on this web page.

2d   4   a)   Insert the image **health.jpg** under text ending **...OPEN**.

2e   b)   **Centre** align this beach.

Your web page layout should be similar to the diagram below:

FIVE STAR HEALTH SPA
NOW OPEN

health.jpg

FOR ALL ....

PURE LUXURY ....

HOTEL HOME ....

Updated by Arthur Marshall, Centre 30175, 31/07/06

All the pages in the website need to be linked.

3a   5   Create a link in the **starspa.htm** page as follows:
                   Text to be linked: **CLICK HERE TO GO BACK**
                   Link to: **sunset.htm**.

2c   6   Check your web page for accuracy.

1c   7   Save the web page keeping the name **starspa.htm**.

1c   8   Close the **starspa.htm** page.

Assessment Objectives	TASK 3

The home page **sunset.htm** needs to be updated.

1c	1	a)	Open **sunset.htm**. Do not change the font on this page.
2a		b)	On a separate line below the text ending:
2f			**...quality and comfort**.
2g			and above the text ending:
2i			**...WEATHER INFORMATION**.
3a			Insert the text:
			LUXURY HEALTH SPA NOW OPEN
		c)	**Centre** align this text.
		d)	**Format** this text as **Tahoma** font, **HTML size 4 (14 point)**.
		e)	Link this text to the **starspa.htm** page.
		f)	Save the amended **sunset.htm** page.
2a	2	a)	Replace the text **Webmaster** with **your name**.
		b)	Make sure the size of your name is **Tahoma** font, **HTML size 2 (10 point)**.
			Some of the links on the sunset have not been completed.
3b	3		Create an external link in the **sunset.htm** page as follows:
			Text to be linked: **CURRENT WEATHER INFORMATION**
			Link to: **www.onlineweather.com**
3c	4		Create an email link in the **sunset.htm** page as follows:
			Beach to be linked: **enquiries.gif**
			Link to: **reservations@sunset-beach.com**
1c	5		Save the web page keeping the filename **sunset.htm**.

Assessment Objectives	TASK 4

Continue working on your home page **sunset.htm**.

A different background colour will improve the home page.

2h   1   a)   Change the background colour of the **sunset.htm** page.

           b)   Make sure the background colour is different from the text colour and that the text and images are clearly visible against the background colour.

2c   2   Check your web page for accuracy.

1c   3   Save the web page keeping the name **sunset.htm**.

1c   4   Close all web pages and exit the web page editing software.

3a, 3b, 3c   5   Load the **sunset.htm** page into the browser and test the three links.

4a   6   From the browser print the **sunset.htm** page.

1c   7   a)   Display the **HTML source code** for the **sunset.htm** page.

4b   b)   Print the HTML source code for this page.

           c)   Close the **sunset.htm** page.

1c   8   Load the **starspa.htm** page into the browser and test the one link.

4a   9   From the browser print the **starspa.htm** page

1c   10   a)   Display the **HTML source code** for the **starspa.htm** page.

4b   b)   Print the HTML source code for this page.

           c)   Close the **starspa.htm** page.

    11   Exit the browser.

2c   12   Make sure you check your printouts for accuracy.

       You should have four printouts in the following order:

       sunset.htm web page printed from the browser

       HTML source code for the **sunset.htm** page

       starspa.htm web page printed from the browser

       HTML source co de for the **starspa.htm** page.

To pass this unit you must be able to:

☑ identify and use email and browsing software

☑ navigate the World Wide Web and use search techniques to locate data on the Web

☑ transmit and receive email messages and attachments

Before you start this chapter, you or your tutor should download a zipped file called **Resources for Chapter 8** from **http://www.payne-gallway.co.uk/newclait/student**.

It will automatically unzip. Specify that the contents are to be saved in your **My Documents** folder.

The practice tasks that follow cover all the techniques you need to learn in order to pass a New CLAiT Unit 8 ON-LINE COMMUNICATION assignment.

Practice tasks

Task 1   Reading and sending email

Email, or **electronic mail**, is used to send messages from one computer to another. To use email you need both an **email address** and email software to use it. To use **email**, you type in your message along with the **email address** of the person that you are sending to. The message is then sent to its destination. Incoming **email** messages are often collected and stored by the recipient's **email service provider** on a central computer called a **mail server** until they open their **mailbox** and download them. Once a message has been downloaded it can be read, saved, deleted, printed out or forwarded to another user.

Reading an email message

Outlook
Express

Outlook
Express icon

The **email** software you will use in this chapter is **Microsoft Outlook Express** (referred to as **Outlook Express**). You can load Outlook Express in one of two ways:

▶ *Either* double-click the **Outlook Express** icon on the main screen in Windows,

▶ *or* click the **Start** button at the bottom left of the screen, then click **All Programs**, **Microsoft Office** and **Outlook Express**.

Figure 8.1

256

The main **Outlook Express** window will be displayed. You should see a window something like
the one below, with the contents of your **Inbox** already displayed.

 If the contents of your Inbox haven't been displayed automatically, click **Inbox** in the **Folder**
bar on the left of the screen.

📭 Inbox

Inbox icon

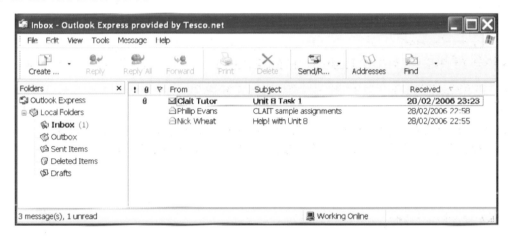

Figure 8.2

All received email messages in your **Inbox** will be listed on the right of the screen. The number
next to the **Inbox folder** tells you how many new messages have been received. Unread
messages are displayed in bold text in the list. The contents of the message currently selected
may well be shown in the **Preview pane** at the bottom of the window.

The message you need to read will already have been sent to you by your tutor and will have the subject heading **Unit 8 Task 1**.

▶ Double-click on this message to open it.

▶ Click the **Maximize** button in the top right corner of the message window.

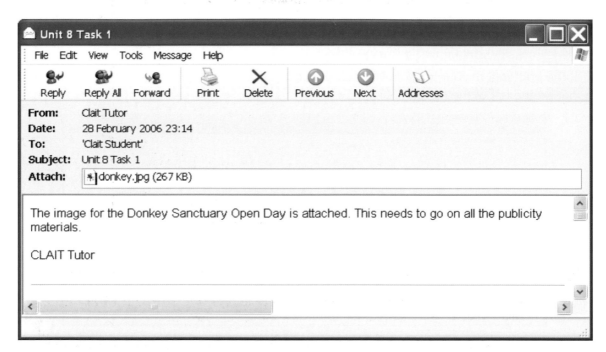

Figure 8.3

Saving an attached file

Before opening or saving an email attachment you should use **antivirus software** to scan it for viruses. Most antivirus software can be configured to scan email attachments automatically. You need to check with your tutor that automatic virus scanning has been set up on your computer and note the name of the virus checking software. If you don't scan an attachment before saving, this will count as one accuracy error. At the end of an **On-line communication** assignment, you will need to type or write the name of the virus checking software on a screenprint of your **My Documents** or network home directory.

Once you are sure that antivirus software will scan email attachments automatically, you can carry on and save the attachment to the email sent to you by your tutor.

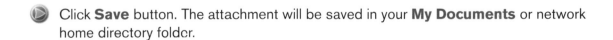 Click **File Save Attachments...** on the menu bar. The **Save Attachments** dialogue window will be displayed. The location of your **My Documents** or network home directory folder should be in the **Save To** box, like the example below.

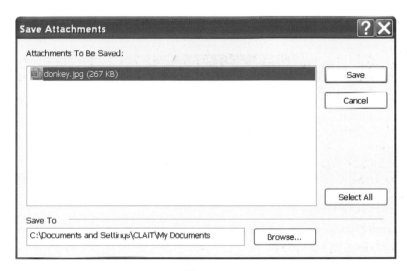

Figure 8.4

 TIP

If the location of your **My Documents** or network home directory folder is not in the **Save To** box, click the **Browse** button, click on your folder in the list, then click **OK**.

Click **Save** button. The attachment will be saved in your **My Documents** or network home directory folder.

Saving sent items

Before sending any messages you need to check that a copy of them will be saved in the **Sent Items** folder. Outlook Express should do this automatically but it is still worth knowing how to check this.

Click **Tools** on the menu bar, then click **Options...**. The **Options** dialogue window will appear.

Click the **Send** tab.

Click the check box next to **Save copy of sent messages in the 'Sent Items' folder** if it is not already ticked.

Click **OK**.

Replying to a message

Now you need to send an email replying to your tutor's original message.

Reply

Reply icon

Maximize
button

▷ Open the email from your tutor and maximize the message window.

▷ Click the **Reply** button on the toolbar at the top of the screen. A new message window will open.

▷ Click the **Maximize** button in the top right-hand corner of the new message window.

The email address or name of your tutor will already be displayed in the **To:** box. The **Subject:** box will contain the same subject as your tutor's original message with **Re:** inserted at the start. The contents of your tutor's message will be listed under a grey separator bar in the message area of the window.

▷ Type the reply: **Thank you for the picture. I will forward it to the design team**.

▷ Press **Enter** once to move down on to a new line.

▷ Type **your name (first name and last name)**, followed by your **centre number** (e.g. **Sajid Sumal 30175**).

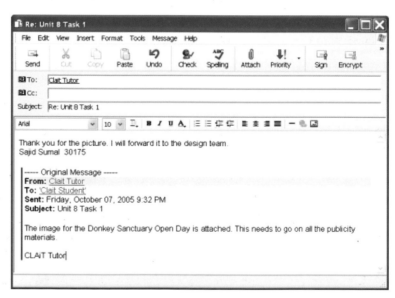

Figure 8.5

TIP

You can leave the original message out of a reply by clicking **Tools**, **Options** on the menu bar. Click the **Send** tab and uncheck the box next to **Include message in reply**. Leaving the original message is often useful because it can build up a 'message trail' that can be used to review what has already been said in a series of emails on the same topic.

We'll now check this message for errors using the **spellcheck** facility.

- Click the **Spelling** button on the toolbar at the top of the screen.

- Correct any errors, then click **OK** when the spellcheck is complete.

- Click the **Send** button on the toolbar at the top of the screen. The message will be sent to your tutor and the new message window will be closed.

Spelling button

Send button

TIP

You can quickly check if a message has been sent by clicking **Sent Items** in the **Folders** list. The messages you have just sent should be at the top of the list. Ask your tutor for help if your **Sent Items** list is empty.

Task 2 Forwarding and deleting email

This task takes you through the steps needed to send a copy of an email message in your **Inbox** to a new recipient using the mail forwarding facility in Outlook Express. You will also learn how to delete messages from your Inbox.

Forwarding a message

Next we'll send an email, forwarding your tutor's original message to a new recipient.

- Click on the email from your tutor in your **Inbox** message list if it isn't already shown in the **Preview pane**.

- Click the **Forward** button on the toolbar at the top of the screen. A new message window will open with the cursor flashing in the **To:** box.

Forward icon

- The **To:** box will be empty. The **Subject:** box will contain the same subject as your tutor's original message with **Fw:** inserted at the start. The contents of your tutor's original message will be listed under a grey separator bar at the bottom of the window.

- Click the **Maximize** button in the top right-hand corner of the new message window.

Maximize button

- Click in the **To:** box if the cursor isn't already flashing inside it, then type the email address: **xs-marketing.design@payne-gallway.co.uk**

- Click in the message area of the window and type the reply: **Please use this picture in all the Donkey Sanctuary Open Day publicity materials**.

- Press **Enter** once to move down to a new line.

- Type your **name (first name and last name)**, followed by your **centre number** (e.g. **Sajid Sumal 30175**).

- Press **Enter** once to move down, in order to leave a blank line before the start of the original message.

Check the file **donkey.gif** is still attached to the message by looking for the filename in the **Attach:** box.

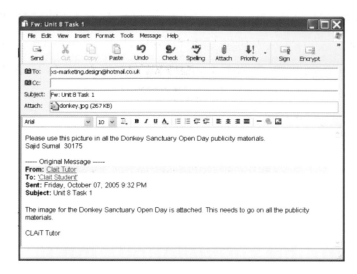

Figure 8.6

Spelling button

Click the **Spelling** button on the toolbar at the top of the screen and check the message for errors.

Send button

Click the **Send** button on the toolbar at the top of the screen. The message will be forwarded to the new recipient and the new message window will be closed.

Deleting a message

The next task is to delete your tutor's message from your **Inbox**.

In your **Inbox** message list, click on the message from your tutor with the subject heading **Unit 8 Task 1**.

Delete button

Click the **Delete** button on the toolbar at the top of the screen. The message will disappear.

Printing the contents of your Inbox

Now we'll produce a printout of your **Inbox**. The most straightforward way to do this is to take a screen print of the **Outlook Express** window, paste it into a new **Word** document and then print the new document.

TIP

Before proceeding, make sure that the **Inbox** folder is selected in the **Folder** bar on the left of the screen, and that any **Inbox** emails are displayed in the upper right-hand section of the screen.

▶ Take a screen print of the Outlook Express window by holding down the **Alt** key and then pressing the **Print Scr** key.

▶ Load **Word** and create a new blank document if there isn't one already displayed.

▶ Click **Edit** on the menu bar, then click **Paste**. The screen print will appear.

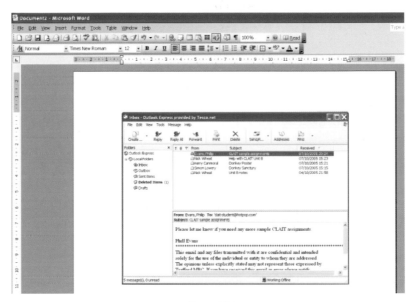

Figure 8.7

▶ Click the **Print** button on the **Standard** toolbar. You can now close the document and shut down **Word**.

▶ *Either* click **File** on the menu bar, then click **Exit,**

▶ *or* click **X** in the top right-hand corner of the screen. Click **No** when you are asked if you want to save changes to the document.

Task 3 Using the Address Book

This task takes you through the steps needed to add a new contact to your address book, then use the stored details to send the contact an email.

Adding a new contact to the Address Book

You are going to add these contact details to your address book:

Name/Title: **XS Marketing Manager**

Email address: **xs-marketing.manager@hotmail.co.uk**

▶ Click the **Addresses** button on the toolbar at the top of the screen. The **Address Book** dialogue box will appear.

Addresses

Addresses
button

263

New

New button

Click the **New** button, then click **New Contact...** in the drop-down list of options. The **Properties** window for the new contact will appear.

Normally you would enter a contact's names in the **First:**, **Middle:** and **Last:** boxes, but this contact only has a job title, so the best way to enter a title like this is by spreading it between these three boxes:

Click in the **First:** box and type **XS**. As you enter this information, the full contact name will start to build up automatically in the **Display:** box.

Click in the **Middle:** box and type **Marketing**.

Click in the **Last:** box and type **Manager**.

Click in the **E-Mail Addresses:** box and type **xs-marketing.manager@hotmail.co.uk**

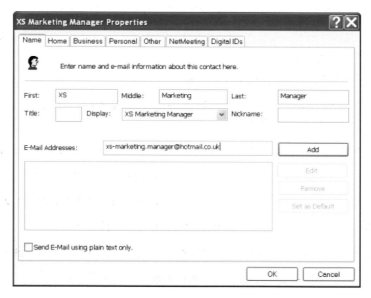

Figure 8.8

TIP

The **Title:** box should be used to enter titles like Mr, Mrs, or Miss, and not the full title of a contact like the one in this example.

Click **OK** – the name **XS Marketing Manager** will appear in the list of contacts, highlighted.

Figure 8.9

We now need to print this new **Address Book** entry.

Print button

▶ Click the **Print** button on the toolbar at the top of the screen. The **Print** dialogue window will appear.

▶ In the **Select Printer** section, click once on the name of the printer you want to use. Your tutor will tell you which printer to choose if you're not sure.

▶ In the **Print range** section, click the radio button next to **Selection** if it isn't already selected, then click the **Print** button.

▶ Close the **Address Book** window by clicking **X** in the top right-hand corner.

Attaching a file to a message

Now we'll create and send a message, with a file attached, to the new contact.

▶ Click the **Addresses** button on the toolbar at the top of the screen. The **Address Book** dialogue window will appear.

Addresses button

▶ Click on the name **XS Marketing Manager** in the list of contacts.

▶ Click the **Action** button, and then click **Send Mail**. A **New Message** window will appear with the contact's name in the **To:** box.

Action button

▶ Click the **Maximize** button in the top right-hand corner of the **New Message** window.

Maximize button

You need to send a copy of this message to the Printshop at XS Marketing:

▶ Click in the **Cc:** box and type the email address: **xs-marketing.printshop@hotmail.co.uk**

▶ Click in the **Subject:** box and type **Another donkey picture**.

▶ Click in the message text box and type **The other picture you need is attached**.

▶ Press **Enter** once to move down on to a new line.

▶ Type your **name (first name and last name)**, followed by your **centre number** (e.g. **Sajid Sumal 30175**).

Figure 8.10

Now we need to attach a file to this message. The file is called **fred.jpg** – your tutor will tell you where to find this. In the example below the file is in the user's **My Documents** folder.

▶ Click the **Attach File To Message** button on the toolbar at the top of the screen. The **Insert Attachment** dialogue window will appear.

Click on the file called **fred**, then click the **Attach** button...

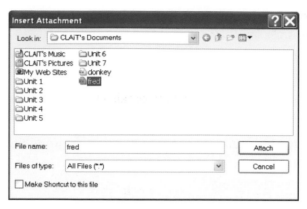

Figure 8.11

...the filename will appear in the **Attach:** box in the **New Message** window.

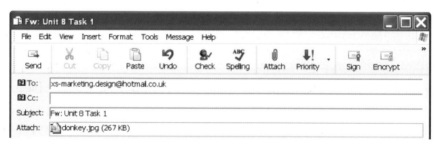

Figure 8.12

Next, the message needs checking for errors

Spelling

Spelling button

Send

Send button

Click the **Spelling** button on the toolbar, correct any errors, then click **OK** when the spellcheck is complete.

Click the **Send** button on the toolbar at the top of the screen. The message will be sent to your tutor and the **New Message** window will be closed.

Printing copies of sent messages

The next task is to print a copy of each email message you've sent

Sent Items

Sent Items
icon

Print

Print button

Click **Sent Items** in the **Folder** bar on the left of the screen. All the email messages you've sent will be listed.

Double-click the message sent to your tutor with the subject heading **Re: Unit 8 Task 1**.

Click the **Print** button on the toolbar at the top of the screen. The **Print** dialogue window will appear.

In the **Select Printer** section, click once on the name of the printer you want to use. Your tutor will tell you which printer to choose if you're not sure.

Click the **Print** button – a copy of the message will be printed.

Next, print a copy of the forwarded message with the subject heading **Fw: Unit 8 Task 1**.

Finally, print a copy of the message sent using the new address book entry, with the subject heading **Another Donkey picture**.

Closing Outlook Express

That's completed all the work you need to do with email. Now you just need to shut down **Outlook Express**:

Click **File** on the menu bar, then…

Either click **Exit**,

or click **X** in the top right-hand corner of the window.

Task 4   Using the Internet

The **Internet** links personal computers, public networks and business networks together using telephone lines to form one vast world-wide network. It allows computer users to share and exchange information with each other wherever they are in the world. The information on the **Internet** comes in many different formats. These range from simple email text files to music, video clips, computer software and even live television pictures.

The **World Wide Web**, or **WWW** for short, is the largest part of the Internet. It is a body of information that spans the entire **Internet**. Individuals and organisations provide pages of information on **websites**, which begin at their **home page**. **Search engines** allow users to **surf** the Internet for information by entering **keywords**. There is a huge number of search engines available on the Internet. Some common search engines are Google, Yahoo, AltaVista and Ask Jeeves.

Using a search engine

To complete this task you are going to use Google – perhaps the most popular search engine on the Internet   to find a UK web page with information about safe rules for the use of the Internet.

To get started you need to load a **web browsing program**. We are going to use **Microsoft® Internet Explorer**. You can load **Internet Explorer** in one of two ways:

Internet Explorer

Internet Explorer icon

Either double-click the icon on the **Desktop** in Windows,

or click the **Start** button at the bottom left of the screen, then click **Internet Explorer.**

Internet
Internet Explorer

Figure 8.13

The default web page that **Internet Explorer** is set up to open when it is loaded will appear.

⊙ Click in the address box and type the URL (see next page) **www.google.co.uk** and press **Enter**. The Google home page will be loaded and displayed.

⊙ Click in the search box and type the key search words: **rules safe use internet**

⊙ Click the radio button next to **pages from the UK** to search for UK sites only.

Figure 8.14

⊙ Click the **Google Search** button. Google will return a list of search results like the example below.

Figure 8.15

Once you have a set of search results like this you need to look through the list of links and decide which one looks the most relevant.

⊙ Click on the link for **Be Safe Online - Introduction** and scrolldown. The web page shown below will be displayed.

The contents of websites on the **Word Wide Web** is constantly changing. You might find that the search results listed by your Google search don't look like the example. If this happens you will need to look through the list of search results to see if the **Be Safe Online** site is still listed. If you can't find this site, try clicking on some of the other links until you find a different website with some relevant information on it.

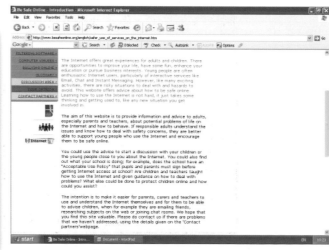

Figure 8.16

Click the link on this web page for **GOLDEN RULES** and scroll down. The page shown below will be displayed which contains the information that you need.

Figure 8.17

Printing a web page

Now you need to print a copy of this web page. Your printout must include the address (**URL**) of the web page in the format: **C:\Documents and Settings\My Documents\your name u7pt\ home.htm**. To do this the text **&u** must appear in either the header or footer box of the **Headers and Footers** section of the **Page Setup** dialogue box.

Click **File** on the menu bar and then click **Page Setup…**. The **Page Setup** dialogue box will be displayed.

Click in either the **Header** or **Footer** box and add **&u** if it isn't already there. Your **Page Setup** dialogue box should look like the one below.

Figure 8.18

- Click **OK**.

- Click **File** on the menu bar, then click **Print**. The **Print** dialogue box will appear.

- In the **Select Printer** section click once on the name of the printer you want to use. Your tutor will tell you which printer to choose if you're not sure. You don't need to print web pages in colour for this unit.

- Click **Print**.

Using the Favorites folder

You need to add the location of the current web page to your **Favorites** folder.

- Click the **Favorites** button on the toolbar. The **Favorites** bar will appear on the left of the screen.

- Click the **Add...** button. The **Add Favorite** dialogue window will appear with a suggested name for this favourite already displayed in the **Name:** box.

- You can either keep the suggested name or click in the **Name:** box and type a name that you'd prefer to use for this favourite.

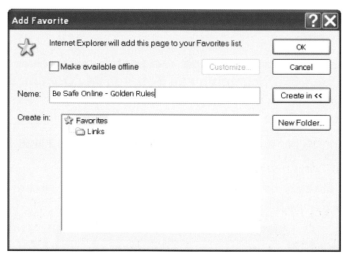

Figure 8.19

- Click **OK**. The name will appear in the list of favourites.

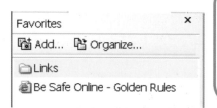

Figure 8.20

TIP

When you choose a name for a favourite try to make sure it reminds you about the type of information or service provided by the site.

Searching a website

Websites can be accessed directly using their **address** or **URL (Uniform Resource Locator)** rather than through a search engine. Most website addresses start with **http://www.** followed by the specific site address sub-divided with full stops and 'forward slashes' (/). Website addresses often reveal the country of origin such as **.uk** for the United Kingdom. They also indicate the type of organisation that the address belongs to: if the site is commercial, with either **.co** or **.com**; a government organisation with **.gov**, or an academic organisation with **.ac**.

Next you need to load a website using its **URL**, then use the local search facility on the website to find some information. **Local search** facilities are different from search engines because they search **only the website**, for pages matching certain keywords, and not the whole **World Wide Web**.

We're going to load the website for the publisher of this book/CD-ROM, and search for information about books on **Applied ICT for GCSE**.

- ▶ Click in the **Address** bar at the top of the screen. The URL of the current web page will be highlighted.

- ▶ Type **www.payne-gallway.co.uk** then press **Enter**. The Payne-Gallway home page will be loaded and displayed.

> **TIP**
>
> If the address of a website starts with **www** you don't need to type the **http://** before it.

- ▶ Click in the **Search** box in the top right-hand corner of the web page.

- ▶ Type **Applied ICT** then press **Enter** or click the '**Go!**' button.

Figure 8.21

You will see a list of search results similar to the example below.

Figure 8.22

⊘ Click on the link for **Applied ICT for GCSE (Double Award)**. The web page shown will be displayed.

Figure 8.23

⊘ Add the location of this web page to your **Favourites** folder.

⊘ **Print** a copy of this web page.

Saving an image

Now we'll save the image of the book cover shown on this web page to your **My Documents** folder or network home directory.

⊘ Position the mouse pointer over the image and click the right mouse button once.

⊘ Click **Save Picture As...** in the shortcut menu of options...

Figure 8.24

...the **Save Picture** dialogue window will appear.

⊘ Click the **Save in:** box arrow and from the drop-down menu, click on your **My Documents** or network home directory folder if it is not already selected.

⊘ Click in the **File name:** box and type **cover**.

⦿ Click the **Save as type**: box arrow and click on **GIF (*.gif)** in the list of file types if it is not already selected.

⦿ Click **Save**.

> **TIP**
>
> Image files come in many types; two main ones being **JPG** and **GIF**. **JPG** images can contain 16 million colours and are best for photography. **GIF** images can only contain 256 colours and are better for drawings and simple designs.

Closing Explorer

That's completed all the work you need to do with the Internet. Now you just need to shut **Explorer** down:

⦿ *Either* click **File** on the menu bar, then click **Exit**,

⦿ *or* click **X** in the top right-hand corner of the browser window.

Taking a screen print of your work area

The next task is to produce a printout of your **My Documents** folder or network home directory. The most straightforward way to do this is to take a screen print of the folder window, paste it into a new Microsoft **Word** document, then print the new document.

My Documents icon

⦿ To see the contents of your **My Documents** folder click the icon on your desktop.

> **TIP**
>
> If you don't have a **My Documents** icon on your desktop, click **Start**, then **My Documents** on the task bar.

The contents of your **My Documents** folder will be displayed in a new window.

⦿ Take a screen print of this window by holding down the **Alt** key and then pressing the **Print Scr** key.

⦿ Load Microsoft **Word** and create a new blank document if there isn't one already displayed.

⦿ Click **Edit** on the menu bar, then click **Paste**. The screen print will appear.

⦿ Click the **Print** button on the **Standard** toolbar.

Now you can close the document and shut down **Word**:

⦿ *Either* click **File** on the menu bar, then click **Exit**,

⦿ *or* click **X** in the top right-hand corner of the screen. Click **No** when you are asked if you want to save changes to the document.

That's the end of the practice tasks. Now try the full New CLAiT assignments that follow.

Practice assignment 1

Scenario

You are working for a local Cat Rescue Charity. You have been asked to help your line manager who is coordinating the production of a new publicity brochure for the charity.

Assessment Objectives	TASK 1		
1a	1	a)	Log on to your email system and open your Inbox.
1c		b)	Read the message from your tutor titled **Publicity Brochure.**
3a		c)	Make sure you scan the email attachment **catwalk.gif** for viruses.
3b		d)	Make a note of the name of the virus scanning software used.
3f			You will need this in Task 4.
		e)	Save the email attachment **catwalk.gif**.
1b	2	a)	Use the **reply facility** to reply to the sender of the message **Publicity Brochure**.
3g		b)	Enter the following message text:
			Thank you for the file. I will pass it on to the designers.
		c)	Add your **name** and your **centre number** under this sentence.
		d)	Displaying the original message from your tutor in this reply is optional.
		e)	Check your message for errors.
		f)	Check that your email system will save your **sent** message(s).
		g)	Send the reply.
		h)	Close the reply message.

Assessment Objectives	TASK 2		
1b	1	a)	Use the **forward facility** to forward the original message **Publicity Brochure** and its attachment to:
3c			**printdesigners.clait@payne-gallway.co.uk**
3h		b)	Do not change **anything** in the original message **Publicity Brochure**.
		c)	Add the following message text:
			This is the cover image.
		d)	Add your **name** and your **centre number** under this sentence.
		e)	Check that the attachment **catwalk.gif** is correctly attached to the message.
		f)	Check your message and correct any errors.
		g)	Check that your email system will save **sent** messages.
		h)	Send the message and its attachment.

3k	2	a)	Delete the message **Publicity Brochure** from your Inbox.
		b)	Produce a printout of your Inbox (This may be a screen print).
		c)	Make sure your **name** is clearly displayed on this printout.

Assessment Objectives

TASK 3

Before you begin this task make sure that you have the file **catplay.gif.**

3d	1	a)	Store the following details in your email address book:

Name/Title: **Design Manager**

Email address: **designmanager.clait@payne-gallway.co.uk**

		b)	Produce a printout of this entry from your address book.
		c)	Make sure your **name** is clearly displayed on this printout.

1b	2	a)	Create a new email message to the **Design Manager** using the stored address from your address book.
3c			
3e		b)	Use the **copy (cc:)** facility to make sure a copy of this message will be sent to:
3i, 3j			

printdesigners.clait@payne-gallway.co.uk

		c)	Enter the message subject **Replacement Brochure Image**
		d)	Enter the following message text:

Please use this image on Page 2

		e)	Add your name and your centre number under this sentence.
		f)	Attach the file **catplay.gif.**
		g)	Check your message and correct any errors.
		h)	Check that your email system will save sent messages.
		i)	Send the message and its attachment.

3l	3	a)	Locate the email messages you have sent and print a copy of each. There should be:

Your reply to the original message
Your forwarded message
The new message titled Replacement Brochure Image

		b)	On each of the 3 email prints, make sure that header details (To, From, Date and Subject) and all the message text is clearly printed.
		c)	On the prints of the forwarded message and the new message, make sure that there is clear evidence of the correct attachments.
	4		Log out of your mailbox and exit the software.

Assessment Objectives	**TASK 4**
2a	1 a) Use a web-based search engine to find a web page about **tips on web design**.
2b	b) Follow the links to find a specific web page about **layout**.
2d	c) Save this page in your **Favorites** folder.
2e	d) Print only the first page with information about **layout**.
2g	e) On the print of the web page, circle **layout**.
2h	f) Write your name and your centre number on this printout.

Another student has asked you to find some information on a book about ICT. Information about the book and a picture of the cover can be found on the publisher's website.

2 a) Access the website at:

www.payne-gallway.co.uk

b) Use the local search facility to find a page about:

Flash MX 2004

c) Save this page in your **Favorites** folder.

d) Print this entire web page.

e) From this web page, save only the image of the book as **flash.jpg** into your working area.

f) Make sure you save only the image in **.jpg** format, not the whole web page.

g) On your printout of the web page from the Payne Gallway site, write your name and your centre number.

3 Exit the web browser.

2f	4 a) Access your working area.
3f	b) Take a screen print of your working area, making sure that the image files **catwalk.gif** and **flash.jpg** are clearly visible.

c) On your screen print enter:

your **name**

your **centre number**

the **name of the virus scanning software** you used in Task 1.

d) Print the screen print.

5 Check all your printouts for accuracy.

You should have the following printouts in the following order:

A print of your Inbox.
Your address book.
The reply message.
The forwarded message.
The new message.
A single page from the website with information about web design tips for layout.
A single web page from the Payne Gallway website.
Your working area.

Practice assignment 2

Scenario

You are working as a Marketing Assistant for a Travel Company. You have been asked to help your line manager who is coordinating the production of a new set of Resort Information Sheets.

Assessment Objectives	TASK 1			
1a	1	a)	Log on to your email system and open your Inbox.	
1c		b)	Read the message from your tutor titled **Paphos Information Sheet**.	
3a		c)	Make sure you scan the email attachment **boats.gif** for viruses.	
3b		d)	Make a note of the name of the virus scanning software used. You will need this in Task 4.	
3f		e)	Save the email attachment **boats.gif**.	
1b	2	a)	Use the **reply facility** to reply to the sender of the message **Paphos Information Sheet**.	
3g		b)	Enter the following message text: **Thanks for this. I will forward it to the publications team.**	
		c)	Add your **name** and your **centre number** under this sentence.	
		d)	Displaying the original message from your tutor in this reply is optional.	
		e)	Check your message for errors.	
		f)	Check that your email system will save your **sent** messages.	
		g)	Send the reply.	
		h)	Close the reply message.	

Assessment Objectives	TASK 2			
1b	1	a)	Use the **forward facility** to forward the original message **Paphos Information Sheet** and its attachment to: **publications.clait@payne-gallway.co.uk**	
3c		b)	Do not change **anything** in the original message **Paphos Information Sheet**.	
3h		c)	Add the following message text: **Paphos Harbour boats image is attached.**	
		d)	Add your **name** and your **centre number** under this sentence.	
		e)	Check that the attachment **boats.gif** is correctly attached to the message.	
		f)	Check your message and correct any errors.	
		g)	Check that your email system will save **sent** messages.	
		h)	Send the message and its attachment.	
3k	2	a)	Delete the message **Paphos Information Sheet** from your Inbox.	
		b)	Produce a printout of your Inbox (This may be a screen print).	
		c)	Make sure your **name** is clearly displayed on this printout.	

Assessment Objectives	TASK 3
	Before you begin this task make sure that you have the file **fort.gif.**

3d	1 a) Store the following details in your email address book:
	
	      Name/Title: **Marketing Manager**
	
	      Email address: **marketing.clait@payne-gallway.co.uk**

	b) Produce a printout of this entry from your address book.
	c) Make sure your **name** is clearly displayed on this printout.
1b 1c	2 a) Create a new email message to the **Marketing Manager** using the stored address from your address book.
3e	b) Use the **copy (cc:)** facility to make sure a copy of this message will be sent to:
3i	**publications.clait@payne-gallway.co.uk**
3j	c) Enter the message subject **Paphos Sheet Update**
	d) Enter the following message text: **This is the new image for the section on history.**
	e) Add your name and your centre number under this sentence.
	f) Attach the file **fort.gif**.
	g) Check your message and correct any errors.
	h) Check that your email system will save sent messages.
	i) Send the message and its attachment.

3l	3 a) Locate the email messages you have sent and print a copy of each. There should be:
	
	      Your reply to the original message
	      Your forwarded message
	      The new message titled Paphos Sheet Update

	b) On each of the 3 email prints, make sure that header details (To, From, Date and Subject) and all the message text is clearly printed.
	c) On the prints of the forwarded message and the new message, make sure that there is clear evidence of the correct attachments.
	4 Log out of your mailbox and exit the software.

Assessment Objectives	TASK 4
2a 2b	1 a) Use a web-based search engine to find a web page about the **UK Sale of Goods Act**.
2d	b) Follow the links to find a specific web page about **key facts**.
2e	c) Save this page in your **Favorites** folder.
2g	d) Print only the first page with information about **key facts**.

2h

e)   On the print of the web page, circle **key facts**.

f)   Write your name and your centre number on this printout.

Another student has asked you to find some information on a book about ICT. Information about the book and a picture of the cover can be found on the publisher's website.

2   a)   Access the website at:

www.payne-gallway.co.uk

b)   Use the local search facility to find a page about:

Short Course GCSE

c)   Save this page in your **Favorites** folder.

d)   Print this entire web page.

e)   From this web page, save only the image of the book as **gcse.jpg** into your working area.

f)   Make sure you save only the image in **.jpg** format, not the whole web page.

g)   On your printout of the web page from the Payne Gallway site, write your name and your centre number.

3   Exit the web browser.

2f

3f

4   a)   Access your working area.

b)   Take a screen print of your working area, making sure that the image files **boats.gif** and **gcse.jpg** are clearly visible.

c)   On your screen print enter:

your **name**
your **centre number**
the **name of the virus scanning software** you used in Task 1.

d)   Print the screen print.

5   Check all your printouts for accuracy.

You should have the following printouts in the following order:

A print of your Inbox.
Your address book.
The reply message.
The forwarded message.
The new message.
A single page from the website with information about the UK Sale of Goods Act
A single web page from the Payne Gallway website.
Your working area.

Practice assignment 3

Scenario

You are working as an Administration Assistant for an association representing UK Dog Breeders. You have been asked to help your line manager who is coordinating the design of a new website.

Assessment Objectives	TASK 1
1a	1 a) Log on to your email system and open your Inbox.
1c	b) Read the message from your tutor titled **English Toy Terriers**.
3a	c) Make sure you scan the email attachment **chester.jpg** for viruses.
3b	d) Make a note of the name of the virus scanning software used. You will need
3f	this in Task 4.
	e) Save the email attachment **chester.jpg**.
1b	2 a) Use the **reply facility** to reply to the sender of the message **English Toy Terriers**.
3g	b) Enter the following message text:
	Thanks for the picture. I will forward it to the design team.
	c) Add your **name** and your **centre number** under this sentence.
	d) Displaying the original message from your tutor in this reply is optional.
	e) Check your message for errors.
	f) Check that your email system will save your **sent** message(s).
	g) Send the reply.
	h) Close the reply message.

Assessment Objectives	TASK 2
1b	1 a) Use the **forward facility** to forward the original message **English Toy Terriers**
3c	and its attachment to: **webdesigners.clait@payne-gallway.co.uk**
3h	b) Do not change **anything** in the original message **English Toy Terriers**.
	c) Add the following message text:
	This is an image for the home page of the website.
	d) Add your **name** and your **centre number** under this sentence.
	e) Check that the attachment **chester.jpg** is correctly attached to the message.
	f) Check your message and correct any errors.
	g) Check that your email system will save **sent** messages.
	h) Send the message and its attachment.
3k	2 a) Delete the message **English Toy Terriers** from your Inbox.
	b) Produce a printout of your Inbox (This may be a screen print).
	c) Make sure your **name** is clearly displayed on this printout.

Assessment Objectives	TASK 3
	Before you begin this task make sure that you have the file **barney.jpg**
3d	1 a) Store the following details in your email address book:
	Name/Title: **Web Design Manager**
	Email address: **webmanager@payne-gallway.co.uk**
	b) Produce a printout of this entry from your address book.
	c) Make sure your **name** is clearly displayed on this printout.
1b	2 a) Create a new email message to the **Web Design Manager** using the
3c	stored address from your address book.
3e	b) Use the **copy (cc:)** facility to make sure a copy of this message will be sent to:
3j	**webdesigners.clait@payne-gallway.co.uk**
3j	c) Enter the message subject **Puppy Page**
	d) Enter the following message text:
	This is an image for the page about puppies.
	e) Add your name and your centre number under this sentence.
	f) Attach the file **barney.jpg**.
	h) Check that your email system will save sent messages.
	i) Send the message and its attachment.
3l	3 a) Locate the email messages you have sent and print a copy of each. There should be:
	Your reply to the original message
	Your forwarded message
	The new message titled Puppy Page
	b) On each of the 3 email prints, make sure that header details (To, From, Date and Subject) and all the message text is clearly printed.
	c) On the prints of the forwarded message and the new message, make sure that there is clear evidence of the correct attachments.
	4 Log out of your mailbox and exit the software.

Assessment Objectives	TASK 4

TASK 4

2a
2b
2d
2e
2g
2h

1. a) Use a web-based search engine to find a web page about the **information rights included** in the **UK Data Protection Act**.
   b) Follow the links to find a specific web page about **information rights**.
   c) Save this page in your **Favorites** folder.
   d) Print only the first page with information about **information rights**.
   e) On the print of the web page, circle **information rights**.
   f) Write your name and your centre number on this printout.

Another student has asked you to find some information on a book about ICT. Information about the book and a picture of the cover can be found on the publisher's website.

2. a) Access the website at: **www.payne-gallway.co.uk**.
   b) Use the local search facility to find a page about: **A Level ICT**
   c) Save this page in your **Favorites** folder.
   d) Print this entire web page.
   e) From this web page, save only the image of the book as **alevel.jpg** into your working area.
   f) Make sure you save only the image in **.jpg** format, not the whole web page.
   g) On your printout of the web page from the Payne Gallway site, write your name and your centre number.

3. Exit the web browser.

2f

4. a) Access your working area.
   b) Take a screen print of your working area, making sure that the image files **chester.jpg** and **alevel.jpg** are clearly visible.
   c) On your screen print enter:
      your **name**
      your **centre number**
      the **name of the virus scanning software** you used in Task 1.
   d) Print the screen print.

5. Check all your printouts for accuracy.
   You should have the following printouts in the following order:
   A print of your Inbox.
   Your address book.
   The reply message.
   The forwarded message.
   The new message.
   A single page from the website with information about information rights in the UK Data Protection Act.
   A single web page from the Payne Gallway website.
   Your working area.

Index

Index

Index

Index